The Age of Nationalism and Reform
1850-1890

SECOND EDITION

THE NORTON HISTORY OF MODERN EUROPE

General Editor: FELIX GILBERT, Institute for Advanced Study

The Foundations of Early Modern Europe, 1460–1559

EUGENE F. RICE, JR.

The Age of Religious Wars, 1559–1689

RICHARD S. DUNN

Kings and Philosophers, 1689–1789

LEONARD KRIEGER

The Age of Revolution and Reaction, 1789–1850

CHARLES BREUNIG

The Age of Nationalism and Reform, 1850–1890

NORMAN RICH

The End of the European Era, 1890 to the Present

FELIX GILBERT

The Age of
Nationalism and Reform
1850-1890

SECOND EDITION

NORMAN RICH
Brown University

W · W · NORTON & COMPANY · INC · NEW YORK

Library of Congress Cataloging in Publication Data
Rich, Norman.
  The age of nationalism and reform, 1850–1890.
  Bibliography: p.
  Includes index.
  1. Europe—History—1848–1871. 2. Europe—History—1871–1918.
I. Title.
D359.R48   1977   940.2'8   76–21080
ISBN 0–393–05607–4
ISBN 0–393–09183–X pbk.

Cartography by Harold K. Faye
Picture research by Liesel Bennett

PRINTED IN THE UNITED STATES OF AMERICA

1 2 3 4 5 6 7 8 9 0

Contents

Introduction   xi

CHAPTER 1   *The Economic and Social Transformation*   1

THE REVOLUTION IN PRODUCTION
   *The New Agriculture • The Sweep of Industrialization •
   Construction, Transportation, Communication • The
   New Scale of Economic Enterprise*
SOCIAL CONSEQUENCES OF INDUSTRIALIZATION
   *The Demographic Revolution • The Changing Role of
   Women • Urbanization and the Transformation of So-
   ciety*

CHAPTER 2   *The Intellectual and Cultural Climate*   27

THE ENDURING INFLUENCE OF THE CHRISTIAN
CHURCHES
MATERIALISM AND REALISM; NEW PRINCIPLES OF
AUTHORITY
   *Faith in Science; Darwin and Darwinism • The Great
   Age of Classical Liberalism • Socialism; Marx and Marx-
   ism • Nationalism*
VOICES OF PROTEST: NIETZSCHE
THE ARTS
   *Popular and Official Art • Literature: Realism and
   Symbolism • Painting: Realism and Impressionism •
   Music: Romanticism and Nationalism*

CHAPTER 3 *The Growing Powers of the State* 66

THE NEW DEMANDS UPON THE STATE
*The Extension of Bureaucratic Government • The Army
and the New Arsenal • Compulsory Education*
IMPERIALISM

CHAPTER 4 *The Disruption of the Concert of Europe* 77

LOUIS NAPOLEON AND THE NEW ASCENDANCY OF
FRANCE
President and Parliament • The Coup d'État of 1851
THE CRIMEAN WAR, 1854–1856
The Conduct of the War • The Aftermath of the War
THE SECOND EMPIRE
*Economic Policy • The Liberal Empire • Imperial Foreign
Policy • The Fall of the Second Empire*

CHAPTER 5 *The National Revolutions, 1850–1870* 101

THE HABSBURG EMPIRE
*The Emancipation of the Peasants • Francis Joseph •
The Schwarzenberg Government and the Bach System*
THE UNIFICATION OF ITALY
*Cavour • Cavour's Diplomacy • The War of 1859 and Its
Aftermath • Garibaldi • Cavour and Garibaldi*
THE UNIFICATION OF GERMANY
*The Germanic Confederation and the Austro-Prussian
Rivalry • Prussia to 1862 • The Constitutional Conflict
in Prussia • Bismarck • Bismarck's Policies • The Polish
Revolt • The Schleswig-Holstein Question • The Austro-
Prussian War of 1866 • The End of the Constitutional
Conflict in Prussia*
THE FRANCO-PRUSSIAN WAR

CHAPTER   6   *The Course of Reform: Great Britain and Russia*   145

GREAT BRITAIN IN THE MID-NINETEENTH CENTURY
Palmerston • Domestic Reforms Before 1867 • The Reform Bill of 1867 • Gladstone's First Ministry • Disraeli's Second Ministry • Gladstone's Second Ministry • Gladstone vs. Salisbury
RUSSIA AFTER 1850
Alexander II and the Problem of Reform • The Industrial Revolution in Russia • Revolutionary Ferment • Alexander III • Territorial Expansion

CHAPTER   7   *The New Governments, 1870–1890*   184

FRANCE, 1870–1890
The Beginnings of the Third Republic • The Constitution of 1875 • The Triumph of Parliamentarianism • The Republic of the Republicans • The Boulanger Crisis
ITALY TO 1890
The Problems of Unification • The Politics of Trasformismo
THE HABSBURG EMPIRE TO 1890
The Creation of Austria-Hungary • Austria after the Ausgleich • Hungary after 1867
THE GERMAN EMPIRE, 1871–1890
The Kulturkampf *• New Conflicts with the Liberals • New Political Combinations • State Socialism • The Succession Crisis and the Fall of Bismarck*

CHAPTER   8   *The Search for a New International Stability, 1871–1890*   228

THE SEARCH FOR STABILITY IN EASTERN EUROPE
The First Three Emperors' League • The Balkan Crisis, 1875–1878 • The Congress of Berlin • The German-

*Austrian Alliance of 1879 • The Second Three Emperors'
League • Austria's Balkan Policy • The Problem of Bul-
garia*
THE SEARCH FOR STABILITY IN WESTERN EUROPE
*Germany and France • The Triple Alliance of 1882 • The
British Occupation of Egypt • Bismarck's Colonial Policy*
THE CLIMAX OF BISMARCK'S ALLIANCE SYSTEM
A GOLDEN AGE OF HOPE

Suggestions for Further Reading   251

Index   261

Maps

The Crimean War   89
The Unification of Italy   118
The Unification of Germany   141
The Expansion of Russia   182
The Dual Monarchy   204
The Treaty of Berlin   234
Bismarck's Alliance System   247

Illustrations

Liebig's chemical laboratory (German Information Center)   3
Drawing and photograph of the internal combustion engine developed by Otto
    and Langen (Klöckner-Humboldt-Deutz AG)   5
The Bessemer process (The Bettmann Archive)   6
Victoria Station (Country Life)   8
Brunel, photographed beside the *Great Eastern*'s anchor chain (Radio Times
    Hulton Picture Library)   9
The *Great Eastern* under construction (The Warder Collection)   10
The Paris-Bordeaux automobile run of 1895 (Daimler-Benz)   11
Birmingham in 1898 (British Industries)   14
Louis Pasteur (Roger-Viollet)   16
Petticoat Lane in 1890 (Radio Times Hulton Picture Library)   18
A German textile factory in the 1860's (Bildarchiv Preussischer Kulturbesitz)   20
Aux Champs-Élysées by Daumier (Liesel Bennett)   21
A tin mine in Cornwall (The Warder Collection)   24
A lodging house in London (The Mansell Collection)   26
Charles Darwin, photographed in 1854 (Down House)   35
Title page to *Das Kapital,* inscribed to Darwin (Down House and the Royal
    College of Surgeons of England)   39
Karl Marx and his wife Jenny von Westphalen (Karl Marx Haus, Trier)   42
The Bismarck monument in Hamburg (Inter Nationes)   45
The Goethe/Schiller monument in Weimar (Inter Nationes)   45
The ailing Nietzsche, photographed by Hans Olde (Nationale Forschungs- und
    Gedenkstätten der klassischen deutschen Literatur in Weimar—Goethe-
    und Schiller Archiv; Abk.: NFG/GSA)   48
"Abandoned," by Carl Carlsen (F. Bruckmann K.G. Verlag)   50
Clifton suspension bridge, Bristol (The Warder Collection)   53
Emile Zola, portrait by Manet (The Warder Collection)   55
Partial manuscript page from Dostoevsky's *The Possessed.* (The New York
    Public Library)   57
Courbet's *The Stonebreakers* (Roger-Viollet)   59
Manet's *Olympia* (Roger-Viollet)   60
Cézanne's *The Large Bathers* (Philadelphia Museum of Art. Purchased:
    The W. P. Wilstach Collection, Accession #: W'37–1–1)   62
Hector Berlioz in his mid-fifties (Alliance Française)   63
A German view of British imperialism (Simplicissimus)   72
A German view of their own imperialism (Simplicissimus)   73
Louis Napoleon taking the oath of office (Alliance Française)   78
Group of 8th Hussars preparing a meal (Imperial War Museum, London)   85

The harbor of Balaclava (Imperial War Museum, London) 86
Florence Nightingale tending the sick (The New York Public Library) 87
Napoleon III, Empress Eugénie, and their son (Roger-Viollet) 92
The grand staircase of the new Paris opera house (Propyläen-Verlag) 94
The new Paris sewers (The Warder Collection) 94
Letter from Napoleon III to King William I (Ullstein Bilderdienst) 100
Francis Joseph of Austria and his brothers (Historisches Bildarchiv Handke) 107
Count Camillo Benso di Cavour (Ambasciata d'Italia, Bonn) 111
Giuseppe Garibaldi (Roger-Viollet) 115
King Frederick William IV of Prussia (Historisches Bildarchiv Handke) 122
Bismarck, 1859 (German Information Center) 127
A Prussian coastal battery at Almor (Ullstein Bilderdienst) 131
Helmuth von Moltke in his office in Berlin (Bildarchiv Preussischer Kulturbesitz) 134
King William I of Prussia proclaimed German emperor (Bildarchiv
 Preussischer Kulturbesitz) 143
The Crystal Palace in London (The Mansell Collection) 146
Queen Victoria and the Prince Consort (The Mansell Collection)
 Photo by Roger Fenton 147
Lord Palmerston (The Warder Collection) 149
Benjamin Disraeli (The Warder Collection) 153
An illustration from Dickens's *Nicholas Nickleby* (The Mansell Collection) 157
The Disraeli Cabinet, 1876 (The Mansell Collection) 160
Gladstone during a whistle-stop campaign (Gernsheim Collection,
 University of Texas at Austin) 162
William E. Gladstone shortly before his retirement (Radio Times Hulton
 Picture Library) 166
Alexander II in his study (The Warder Collection) 169
Sleeping berths for Russian laborers in a municipal lodging house, 1890 (MYSL) 172
Tsar Alexander III, his wife, and three of their five children (The
 Warder Collection) 179
Gambetta's flight from Paris (Bibliothèque Nationale) 185
Adolphe Thiers and his Council of Ministers, 1872 (Bibliothèque Nationale) 189
General Georges Boulanger (Roger-Viollet) 196
Victor Emmanuel II (The Mansell Collection) 199
Count Taaffe at his desk (The Warder Collection) 209
A court ball in Vienna (Österreichische Nationalbibliothek) 211
Emperor Francis Joseph and Dr. Karl Lueger (The Warder Collection) 212
Kálmán Tisza (Historisches Bildarchiv Handke) 215
Emperor William I and his sister at the spa of Ems (The Warder Collection) 217
"Bismarck as Wild Animal Trainer" (Bildarchiv Preussischer Kulturbesitz) 219
"Blown Up, But Not Blown Out" (Ullstein Bilderdienst) 226
The second Three Emperors' League (Ullstein Bilderdienst) 235
Construction of the Suez Canal (Roger-Viollet) 241
Bismarck, photographed shortly before his dismissal (Bundesarchiv, Koblenz) 249

Introduction

ALMOST EVERY PERIOD in the history of modern Europe can be described as an age of revolution of some kind, and the last half of the nineteenth century is no exception. These years saw a continuation and acceleration of the scientific, technological, and social revolutions that were already well under way in many parts of Europe, and which within less than a century were to change the social and economic complexion of European society more rapidly and more dramatically than at any previous time in recorded history. These years also witnessed the eruption of national revolutions in every part of the continent: in Ireland and Poland, the Balkans and Hungary, Italy and Germany.

National revolution was no new phenomenon in European history. There had been a strong element of nationalism in the Protestant Reformation, in the struggle of the Dutch against the Spaniards, and in the French Revolution. In the later nineteenth century, however, the spirit of nationalism flared with new intensity, and it is not too much to say that the mystique of nationalism was the major ideological force making for change in European politics and society.

Between 1815 and 1848 national revolutionary movements had been held in check with considerable success by the European governments. Some historians categorically reject the term "Concert of Europe" to describe the cooperation among the powers in these years, and indeed their dissonances were frequently more in evidence than their harmony. The fact remains, however, that the statesmen of this period, whose political ideas had been shaped by the French Revolution and the Napoleonic wars, generally felt that it was safer to settle their differences by diplomacy than by war, for it seemed to them that even a successful war might unleash revolutionary forces they would be unable to control. Even the British, who are supposed to have seceded from the Concert when it became an instrument of oppression, pursued an independent course only when they could do so with impunity. Whenever British interests were seriously affected by events on the Continent, British statesmen took a prominent place in the councils of the major powers.

The international system established in 1815 survived the revolutions of 1848, but in the course of those revolutions some of the foremost champions of international conservatism, including Prince Klemens von Metternich, whose name had become synonymous with the old order, were swept away, and were succeeded by statesmen whose memories of 1789 were dim, or whose ambitions transcended the common interests of the European monarchies.

Foremost among the new leaders was Napoleon III, whose principal foreign-policy objective was to release France from the restrictions imposed by the 1815 treaties. His big opportunity came with the Crimean War, which temporarily put an end to effective co-operation among the great powers. He attempted to follow up this success by encouraging national revolutions in the spheres of interest of rival powers, hoping through the leadership of these national movements to re-establish French ascendancy on the Continent. He was to find, however, that he had conjured up forces he was unable to control, and that the breakdown of the Concert of Europe had cleared the way for political opportunists more ruthless and skillful than he. In the end he was destroyed by the forces he had done so much to release.

By 1871 the Italians and Germans had achieved political unification in independent national states, and the Hungarians had been granted quasi-independence within a new Austro-Hungarian empire. The successful example of these nations gave fresh impetus to others. The Irish became a major problem in Great Britain; Russia and Austria-Hungary were racked by national dissension; and the Ottoman empire in the Balkans began to fall asunder as Montenegrins and Serbs, Rumanians and Bulgars, followed the lead of the Greeks in overthrowing Turkish overlordship and gaining partial or complete independence. By far the most important of the new nation-states was the German empire, whose emergence on the political scene as the foremost military power in Europe invalidated all previous conceptions of the relations among the powers. After the establishment of the German empire, however, the governments of Europe began to cooperate anew, and developed the precarious international stability that endured until 1914.

Meanwhile, nationalism itself exploded into expansionism. Hardly had some of the new nations asserted their own identity than they aspired to conquest over others. Italians and Germans vied with British, French, and Russians for the spoils of empire, while on a smaller scale the new Balkan nations sought to expand at the expense of Turkey, Austria, and one another.

The national revolutions were not caused by nationalism alone. They took place in a period of unprecedented social and economic dislocation.

Industrialization, population increases, the mass migration of people from the country to the city, wrought a fundamental transformation in European life and society. To deal with these social and economic changes, all European governments were obliged to recognize the need for far-reaching revisions in their policies, laws, and institutions—in short, for reform.

Much of the strength of the reform movement derived from the belief that the improvement of society and mankind was actually possible. Many nineteenth-century Europeans were dazzled by the material progress of their era and looked upon scientific discoveries and improved living standards as evidence of an inevitable march of human progress toward a higher and more perfect civilization. There was a widespread conviction that in time, through further advances in science and technology and the use of human reason, all human problems could be solved and all abuses eliminated. Such optimism may seem naive in our own era, when so many illusions about mankind have been shattered, but faith in human progress, joined with a strong emphasis on good works in many of the political and religious movements of the period, did much to make the nineteenth century a humanitarian age. There was widespread agreement throughout Europe that the world should be rid of slavery and torture, of hunger and disease. Humanitarianism frequently lay behind government legislation to alleviate the social distress caused by the industrial revolution. Public opinion could be shocked by revelations of wretched conditions of child labor or by reports of the atrocities in the Turkish empire; and in no part of Europe could the demands of public opinion for reform be totally ignored.

In Great Britain, with its strong traditions of parliamentary government, most advocates of reform looked to Parliament to bring about the necessary changes through legislation; their most significant political agitation was for a further extension of the franchise, which would enable people to influence this legislation. The confidence of British reformers in parliamentary government was justified; their country passed through the social and economic crises of the nineteenth century without major upheavals. The British government served as a model for people of all states who wished to bring about political changes by peaceful means.

On the Continent, most of the parliamentary governments established in 1848 or earlier were discredited by their inability to satisfy the needs and aspirations of the people they represented. Instead, the requirements of a changing society were generally met by authoritarian governments, many of them operating behind a constitutional-parliamentary façade. The failure of genuine parliamentary government among the continental great powers was due not only to the weakness of parliamentary forces and traditions, but to the absence of the feature most necessary for its successful operation: broad agreement among the main power groups in a country about fundamental issues. Britain experienced the effect of this lack of agreement in dealing with the Irish, who by the end of the nineteenth century demanded national independence, which the English were not prepared to concede. Most continental governments were faced with many Irelands. The new German empire, for example, was forced to deal with a centuries-old heritage of political and religious cleavage—hostility between Bavarians and Prussians, Prussians and Poles, Protestants and Catholics—in addition to the social and class conflicts between landlords and peasants, factory owners and workers. These were differences so great that it seemed impossible to maintain the new empire, much less to govern it effectively, without a strong, centralized executive authority.

Whether the government of a state was parliamentary or authoritarian, however, its policies were carried out by the professional bureaucracy that staffed the various administrative departments. Although the bureaucracy was the indispensable tool of government leadership, it should not be confused with leadership itself. The professional bureaucrats ensured the continuous functioning of government processes; they might exercise enormous influence on government heads; but the crucial power to determine government policy remained in the hands of the executive leadership. Hence the quality of leadership in every country was at all times of paramount importance. In states where supreme power was vested in an authoritarian executive, no single aspect of life or society was more significant than the personality of this ruler because it was he who in the end determined the use—or misuse—of the immense new economic and military power which the industrial revolution had made available to the modern state.

As the nineteenth century progressed, the state assumed, or was obliged to assume, ever greater powers and responsibilities. It was the state that enacted—and enforced—laws for freeing the serfs, that supervised working conditions in mines and factories, that built sewers and water lines for the new cities, that provided facilities for free (and compulsory) elementary education. Finally, it was the state that protected its citizens from disorder at home and threats from abroad, that realized the aspirations of patriots for national unity, that responded to demands of people in all countries for glory and empire.

As the functions of the state expanded, so did the bureaucracy. The innovations of science and technology were bent to its needs. The telegraph and the printing press, the railroad and the steamship, the machine gun and the rifled steel cannon, became instruments of government departments, secret police, armies, navies, and tax collectors. Programs of compulsory military training by all continental great powers forced every able-bodied man into the service of the state; compulsory education provided the opportunity to indoctrinate each citizen with principles of patriotism and loyalty to the state.

By the end of the nineteenth century, the state had acquired unprecedented power to establish control over the minds and bodies of men, control actually welcomed by many nationalists and reformers who saw in the state the most effective instrument for the realization of their ideals. In countries where the government was traditionally associated with political oppression—for example, in Russia—anarchism and related political doctrines rejecting every kind of state authority claimed numerous adherents. But only a few isolated prophets like the German philosopher Friedrich Nietzsche and the Russian novelist Fëdor Dostoevsky envisaged clearly what the ultimate consequences of state control might be. For the most part the growth of state power went unheeded in the atmosphere of optimism and confidence in human progress that characterized the era.

CHAPTER 1

The Economic and Social Transformation

THE REVOLUTION IN PRODUCTION

BY 1850 AN ECONOMIC and social revolution had already been under way in Europe for well over a hundred years, most extensively in Great Britain. During the second half of the nineteenth century this revolution gathered momentum and spread to every part of the Europeanized world. Objections have been raised to the use of the term "revolution" to describe a transformation which took place over such a long period of time and which is still going on, but when the radical changes of the industrial era are viewed against the background of the entire span of human history, no other term seems appropriate.

The New Agriculture

The crucial factor in the entire process of economic and social change in the nineteenth century was the revolution in man's ability to produce, and fundamental to the revolution in production was the revolution in European agriculture. For the first time in history it became possible to support a significant growth of population on a fixed amount of land. The adoption of improved methods of agricultural production, and the timing of their adoption, varied widely according to local conditions, needs, and customs, and throughout much of Europe farming methods remained primitive and traditional. Far more surprising is the extent to which European landowners and peasants, usually so conservative, were willing to experiment with and make use of new production techniques.

In the early stages of the agricultural revolution in Europe, no innovation was more important than the popularization of various methods of crop rotation, a system of alternating traditional grain crops, which con-

1

sumed nitrogen, with root crops such as turnips or forage crops such as clover or alfalfa, which restored nitrogen to the soil. Crop rotation replaced the traditional three- or two-field system of agriculture under which one third to one half of the arable land lay fallow each year to regain its fertility. Besides almost doubling the amount of land that could be brought under cultivation, crop rotation contributed to a significant growth in animal husbandry. An abundance of root and forage crops enabled farmers to keep more livestock, both for dairying and stock raising. The animals in turn produced fertilizer, which further enriched the soil.

More efficient methods of land use were accompanied by the rapid development of improved strains of wheat and other traditional crops and the widespread cultivation of new ones such as American corn (called maize in Europe). Sugar beets began to be produced in large quantities when supplies of cane sugar from the West Indies were cut off during the Napoleonic wars, and became a mainstay of agriculture in central Europe, Russia, and France. Far and away the most important of the new crops, however, was the potato (also originally imported from America), which could be grown on poor soil, was comparatively insensitive to the vicissitudes of weather, and yielded from two to four times as much food as grain crops. Although cultivated throughout Europe, the potato became the staple diet of poorer peasants in the northern and central regions along a broad front from Ireland to Russia, a dependence which was to prove a disaster when the potato crop failed.

The agricultural revolution also owed much to improvements in traditional farming implements, and to developments in mining and manufacture which lowered the cost of iron and steel sufficiently to permit the use of these metals in the construction of farming equipment. The iron and later the steel plow, together with major changes in the design of the plow itself, permitted the digging of far deeper furrows and thereby opened up new and often rich levels of soil for cultivation. The harrow, a cultivating machine for breaking up clods of earth raised by the plow, was also made more effective through improvements in design which took advantage of the strength and malleability of iron and steel, as was the long-handled scythe with its long, broad, and perfectly balanced iron or steel blade, which replaced the short, narrow-bladed sickle as the principal instrument for mowing hay and grain crops. More complex and expensive farm machinery such as the reaper or the threshing machine came into general use in the United States after 1810. But only toward the end of the century did mechanization make an impact on European farming, and then only in the comparatively few areas where land and capital were plentiful and labor scarce.

On the lands of farmers with some capital, agricultural yields had been increased through the use of commercial fertilizers such as bone phosphates

Sketch of Liebig's chemistry laboratory. *He trained his students in the use of systematic research techniques which set new standards for the teaching and practice of chemistry in the later nineteenth century.*

or Peruvian guano (the excrement of sea fowl). The great breakthrough in the use of fertilizer, however, came with the discovery in the second half of the nineteenth century of chemical processes for producing relatively inexpensive artificial fertilizers. The scientist whose name is most closely associated with the application of chemistry to agriculture is Justus von Liebig (1803–1873), who observed that plants do not derive their principal nourishment from humus, as was commonly assumed at the time, but from a wide assortment of elements in the air and soil, and that plant growth could be stimulated by the use of artificial fertilizers containing nutrients which these plants required.

While carrying on his own research, Liebig made a major contribution to the study of chemistry in general. At the university of Giessen, and later at Munich, he established the first laboratories in which students were trained in systematic methods of research, which set a pattern for the teaching of chemistry that came to prevail in all German universities and technical schools. During the later nineteenth century, technical and agricultural schools were established throughout Europe and the United States, usually with state support, where scientific research methods were brought to bear on the problems of agriculture, leading to major improvements in methods of agricultural production: the development of medicines and insecticides to combat diseases of animals and plants; of better seed strains and better breeds of cattle; further improvements in methods of crop rotation; grafting techniques to improve the yield of vines and fruit trees.

The Sweep of Industrialization

At the core of the revolution in production, and a major reason for its continuing momentum, was the interaction between the various sectors of the economy. Innovations in one sector created conditions which stimulated or made possible innovations in others. By increasing the amount of food available, the agricultural revolution contributed to an unprecedented growth of the European population, which led to a similarly unprecedented growth in the demand for consumers goods. The creation of this vast new market encouraged the development of new methods of manufacture and led to that dramatic expansion of European manufacturing capacity known as the industrial revolution.

As in the case of agriculture, there had been many improvements in methods of manufacture over the centuries. The famous eighteenth-century inventions for the mass production of cloth, which are often described as marking the beginning of the industrial revolution in England, were actually part of a long tradition of technological innovation. The truly revolutionizing agent of the industrial revolution was the steam engine, much improved since the invention of a practicable engine by James Watt in the 1760's, which for the first time in history freed man from dependence on human or animal labor, or on such natural forces as wind and water.

The steam engine is a classic example of the interrelationship between the various processes of the revolution of production. It was originally developed in response to a need for power to pump water out of coal mines; coal was needed because it was cheaper and more efficient than wood (charcoal) for the smelting of iron; more iron was needed to meet the demands of agriculture for iron plows, iron harrows, iron horseshoes, and iron for the hubs and ribs of wagon wheels; smelting with coal led to improvements in metallurgy which made possible the construction of the steam engine in the first place; finally, to come full circle, the steam engine was harnessed to new mining machinery which facilitated the production of coal, the steam engine's principal fuel.

Coal and the steam engine were to retain a dominant position as the major sources of energy and power for many years to come, but well before the end of the nineteenth century they were to be supplemented and in some cases supplanted by new sources of energy and new engines. Natural gas, which had been used for street lighting and fuel since the beginning of the century, was used to power an internal combustion engine in 1862. The internal combustion engine possessed the advantage of greater lightness and mobility, but because natural gas was difficult to store and transport the new invention did not begin to come into its own until the 1880's, when liquid petroleum was successfully used as a fuel. The success of the petroleum-driven internal combustion engine quickly swelled

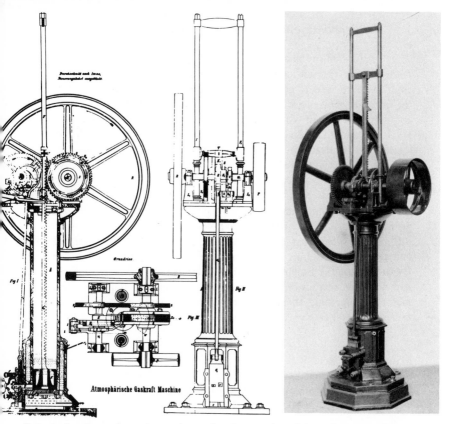

Patent drawing of an internal combustion engine driven by natural gas, designed by Nikolaus August Otto (1832–1891) and Eugen Langen (1833–1895). *Right, a photograph of the actual engine.*

the demand for oil, which was discovered in such diverse places as Pennsylvania, southern Russia, and Borneo, and was tapped with the aid of new drilling machinery. Not until well into the twentieth century, however, did petroleum become a major rival to coal as a source of power.

A more immediate rival was electricity. As early as 1831 Michael Faraday (1791–1867) had demonstrated that the movement of a coil of wire through a magnetic field produces a flow of electric current through the wire. Electricity did not become a practical source of power, however, until 1870, when the first efficient electric generator was developed. The importance of this invention was soon to be greatly enhanced by the discovery of the rotating magnetic field, which made possible the long-distance transmission of electric power. During the following decade, alternators and transformers for producing high-voltage alternating currents were developed, and central stations for the production of electric power were established in many parts of Europe. Electricity was a particular boon to countries without large supplies of coal, for water and even wind could be harnessed to generate electric current. The perfection in 1879 of the incandescent electric light by Thomas A. Edison (1847–1931) inaugurated the era in which electricity became the principal source of artificial light. In that same year Werner von Siemens (1816–1892) demonstrated the application of electric power to the railway. Besides serving as an increasingly important source of light and power, electricity made possible numerous scientific and industrial processes, such as electroplating, and entire new industries, such as the manufacture of aluminum.

New engines and new sources of power were harnessed to an ever-growing variety of new machines. The importance of coal-mining and oil-drilling machinery has already been mentioned. Equally vital was machinery for mining iron ore, the principal metal of industrial construction. By the end of the nineteenth century there was scarcely any industry that had not been revolutionized by machine technology, including the manufacture of machines themselves. The private household, too, began to experience the effects of this revolution with the invention in 1846 of the

Manufacturing steel by the Bessemer process. *This engraving shows molten pig iron (top, center) being poured into a metal mixer (left), while in the converter (right) a blast of oxygen causes the reactions that transform the mixture of low-grade ores into steel. Workers pour the molten steel by ladle into ingot molds (bottom, center).*

sewing machine, the first of the myriad of household gadgets that were to ease the labors of the housewife.

New mining machinery and refining techniques had meanwhile increased the availability of other metals, such as copper and lead. In 1886 came the revolutionary discovery of the Hall-Héroult electrolytic process for deriving aluminum from bauxite, which permitted the mass production of this light, malleable, noncorrosive, yet sturdy metal.

The development of techniques for the mass production of steel and aluminum were aspects of the revolution taking place in the field of chemistry, to which the research laboratories of universities and technical schools inspired by Liebig made a significant contribution. By the end of the nineteenth century the manufacture of chemicals had become a major industry in its own right as a result of the discovery of relatively economical methods for producing critical and heretofore scarce items, and the invention of an impressive array of new ones. Sulfuric and hydrochloric acid, ammonia, alkalis, soaps, bleaches, animal and vegetable oils, drugs, and photographic agents were all produced at prices that permitted their large-scale use in the industrial and domestic economy. Synthetic dyes were manufactured from coal tar, cheap paper and artificial silk (rayon) from wood pulp. In 1867 Alfred Nobel (1833–1896) invented a safe method for making dynamite from nitroglycerin, and twenty years later, combining nitroglycerin with guncotton, he developed a powerful and almost smokeless powder that was to revolutionize the armament industry. A more salutary contribution of the chemical revolution was the discovery of methods for producing cheap artificial fertilizers, which as we have seen played a major role in the agricultural revolution.

Construction, Transportation, Communication

The new mass-produced metals opened the way for an era of building on a scale never before realized. Scarcely less significant than the discoveries in the field of metallurgy was the development by the mid-nineteenth century of a high quality of Portland cement, another product of the science of chemistry. Its superior strength as a mortar facilitated construction with such traditional materials as stone and brick, but its greatest importance was in the production of concrete, an ancient building material consisting of cement, sand, and stone or gravel. With the new, high-grade Portland cement, concrete could be molded into manifold sizes and shapes, with varying degrees of hardness and resiliency. Unlike earlier concrete, it would harden under water and was thus especially valuable for installations such as dams and harbors. The practice of strengthening concrete with iron or steel bars (resulting in "reinforced concrete") further extended the possibilities of its use and permitted the construction of buildings and bridges of unprecedented dimensions.

Victoria station, London, in 1882.

In the field of transportation, too, revolutionary changes were taking place. Better road construction, the paving of a few highways, and the extension of Europe's canal network had already brought about some improvement by the early nineteenth century. The principal revolutionizing agent of transportation, however, was the railroad (the steam engine again), which became the backbone of Europe's inland transportation system. The first successful railway system (the Stockton-Darlington line, in England) went into operation as early as 1825, but the great boom in railroad building took place in the second half of the nineteenth century, when most of Europe's major railway lines were built.

The railway provided a new and powerful stimulus to the momentum of the entire industrial revolution. It created immense new demands for iron and steel, coal, concrete, and wood, and thus fostered the expansion of the metallurgical, mining, cement, and lumber industries, to name only a few; the demand for capital raised investment rates to new high levels and established a pattern for people with surplus capital to invest their money in business enterprises; while the demand for labor provided employment for a new body of construction, maintenance, and operational workers and created a new class of entrepreneurs among contractors, engineers, and bankers.

The railroads were crucial to the growth of great urban industrial centers, for they provided a means of transporting large supplies of coal and raw materials to the cities, and of distributing products manufactured in the cities to other areas. The railroads made possible for the first time the large-scale, economical, and rapid distribution of goods overland, they penetrated the remote interiors of countries and continents and opened up the markets of these regions to industry while giving agricultural regions access to urban markets. A refrigerator car, made by packing goods in ice and sawdust, was first used on railroads in 1851 and permitted the shipment of perishable goods over long distances. A mechanical system of refrigeration was invented in 1867 and soon became standard equipment on ocean-going ships, but until well into the next century railroads continued to use the ice and sawdust method because it was cheaper.

Overseas as well as overland, people and goods moved faster and farther. A practicable steamboat was developed early in the nineteenth century, but sailing vessels continued to dominate water transport throughout most of the century because of their greater economy and cruising range. They were not dependent on supplies of solid fuel, which took up a large part of the cargo space on early steamships and forced them to stay within

Isambard Kingdom Brunel (1806–1859), builder of the *Great Eastern,* photographed beside the ship's great anchor chain. *One of the most remarkable engineer-entrepreneurs of the nineteenth century, Brunel directed the construction of major railway lines, bridges, and tunnels, including the first tunnel under the Thames. He designed London's Paddington station, a landmark in functional architecture, and the lovely suspension bridge over the Avon at Clifton (see p. 53).*

The *Great Eastern* under construction at Millwall on Thames. *Launched in 1858, it was built of iron with a double hull (the prototype of future ocean liners) and equipped with a screw propeller as well as paddle wheels. This "Wonder of the Seas," 693 feet in length with a displacement of 32,000 tons, was four times larger than any ship built up to that time and in terms of displacement was the largest to be built until 1907. It was from this ship that the first transatlantic cable was laid in 1865–66.*

range of refueling stations. By the end of the century, however, steamships were rapidly supplanting sailing ships, thanks to the development of the compound engine and the screw propeller, which enormously increased their efficiency. Meanwhile iron, and by the 1880's steel, were replacing wood for ship construction.

Transportation over short distances was also improved and simplified. The first electric streetcar went into operation in 1879 and soon displaced horsedrawn vehicles as the chief means of urban public transport. The following decade saw the development of the automobile, driven by an internal combustion engine and using petroleum as its fuel. But for most Europeans the horseless carriage remained a curiosity piece, far too costly to own until the assembly line method of manufacture was introduced in the following century. It was the safety bicycle, driven by the rear wheel, which became the most popular means of private transportation soon after its invention in 1870. Both the bicycle and the automobile benefited from the development in 1889 of the pneumatic tire, which replaced iron or solid hard rubber for the rims of wheels and made the bicycle far more comfortable as well as easier to ride.

In communication as in transport, a host of inventions brought Europeans closer to each other and to the world beyond Europe. The electric telegraph was invented in 1844, and due in part to its importance for the railroads, a network of telegraph lines rapidly spread over much of Europe. In 1851 the first submarine cable was laid between Dover and Calais, the first transatlantic cable between Europe and the United States in 1866, cables from Europe to India in 1870, and from Europe to Hong Kong in 1872. In 1876 came the invention of the telephone, which by the end of the century had become a standard feature in most government and business offices and in some private homes. The typewriter came into general commercial use in the 1870's. In all European countries there were great improvements in the postal services. In 1875 the Universal Postal Union, with headquarters in Switzerland, was established to regulate and supervise international mail service.

The mass communication of news was facilitated by the perfection of high-speed printing presses and machines for the rapid setting of type—the rotary press in 1875, the linotype and monotype machines in 1885, and the straight-line press in 1889. These inventions, with the simultaneous develop-

The Paris to Bordeaux automobile run, 1895. *The snapshot shows a Benz five-horsepower Phaeton which is being closely followed by another recent development in transportation, the safety bicycle.*

ment of an inexpensive process for making paper, meant that newspapers could be produced cheaply, at least in countries where the taxes on them had been abolished. By the end of the century the newspaper was more influential in molding public opinion than ever before.

The New Scale of Economic Enterprise

The pace of industrial production was quickened by the formation of great corporations—joint-stock companies, trusts, and cartels, which made possible the large-scale and more efficient manufacture of goods. Although often more shoddy than articles fabricated by hand in small shops, mass-produced goods were far cheaper. Mass production thus made many items available to large numbers of people and was decisive in the creation of a mass market. The European economy continued to be dominated by small business establishments, but large companies provided the chief impetus for industrial expansion.

The construction of railways, the building of factories, and the purchase of machines and equipment to take advantage of new inventions and new manufacturing processes created an unprecedented demand for capital, which was met in part by a great influx of gold and silver resulting from the discovery of large deposits of these metals in western North America, Australia, and South Africa. Far more important, however, was the widespread adoption of new credit devices, the founding of a large number of investment banks, and above all the general recognition accorded the principle of limited liability, which meant that investors were not threatened with the loss of all their resources when a company failed. With the risk of investment lowered, individuals and institutions with surplus capital were tempted by the prospect of large profits to invest in business enterprises. Entrepreneurs thus found it easier to sell stocks and bonds to raise the money needed for expansion. Governments, too, began to sell bonds to the public, thus freeing themselves from dependence on loans from private banks. The stock exchange, where securities were bought and sold, became the center of the European business world. By the end of the nineteenth century the focus of European investment had changed from land to securities.

A major reason for the relaxation of official restrictions on business enterprises was that in the later nineteenth century most European governments became aware of the contribution such enterprises could make to their countries' strength and welfare. To an increasing extent governments not only eased economic restrictions, but actively aided the development of business and agriculture through state-sponsored banks, direct subsidies, tax concessions, and tariffs. For the same reason, continental European governments, especially France and Germany, sponsored the growth of science faculties and research facilities at state universities, technical, and agricultural schools, and encouraged a close association between their science and business communities.

Despite the marked rise in protective tariffs toward the end of the century, international trade flourished as never before. Linked by an international monetary system based on the gold standard, the economies of the various European countries became so interwoven that all of them went through similar cycles of prosperity and depression. The depression of the 1840's, so significant a part of the background of the revolutions of 1848, was followed by prosperity in the 1850's. Then in 1857 came a financial crash, and what has been called the first worldwide economic depression. The bank failures in Europe had been set off by overexpansion and unsound banking practices in the United States, where much European money was invested. The resulting financial chaos struck both industry and agriculture and affected the markets of South America and Asia. Economic revival in Europe came quickly after 1859, to be followed by another slump in 1866, another revival, and in 1873 another great financial crash.

The 1873 crash set off an economic depression which was to continue for another two decades in the form of a slower rate of growth, rising unemployment, and a general feeling of economic insecurity. This depression appears to have been caused primarily by overspeculation and overproduction. There was a decline in the rate of railway building, and a consequent drying up of this immense market for goods and materials. At the same time European agriculture was depressed by the competition of cheap agricultural products from the interior regions of Russia, America, and Australia, to which the railroad had given access.

During the depression years there was actually an increase in the real wages and a rise in the standard of living of many Europeans as a result of a steady fall in the prices of agricultural and manufactured products. The fall in prices, however, which brought hardship or outright ruin to many economic enterprises, together with the increase in unemployment and the overall sense of economic insecurity, aroused a widespread feeling of dissatisfaction with existing government economic policies and anger at the threat of foreign competition. The liberal doctrine of laissez-faire was discredited as industry, agriculture, and labor alike clamored for protective tariffs and state aid. And everywhere in Europe, with the notable exception of England, the state responded to these pressures. The 1873 depression thus inaugurated a new period of state intervention in economic affairs which was to increase steadily to the present day. It also contributed to the growth of an economic nationalism which was to strengthen the burgeoning forces of political and ideological nationalism.

Birmingham in 1898. *The new scale of industrial enterprise is strikingly illustrated in this photograph of one of England's greatest industrial centers, whose population rose from about 70,000 to well over half a million in the course of the nineteenth century.*

SOCIAL CONSEQUENCES OF INDUSTRIALIZATION

The Demographic Revolution

Less dramatic than the revolution in production, but in the long run perhaps even more significant, was the demographic revolution which accompanied it. There had been sharp rises and declines in the population of Europe in past centuries, but although statistics on the subject are scarce and many contemporary estimates may have been grossly inaccurate, it is safe to say that until about 1750 the population increased at a very slow rate. In the century between 1750 and 1850, however, the population of Europe (including European Russia) almost doubled—from an estimated 150 million to about 270 million. Between 1850 and 1900 the population grew to 420 million, an increase in fifty years as great as the entire population in 1750. Moreover, with the exception of France, where the growth rate had already slowed markedly by the beginning of the nineteenth century, this sharp rise in population was a general European phenomenon, although there were wide regional and local variations as a result of different geographical, economic, or cultural circumstances.

The reasons for this unprecedented population growth are far from clear. Existing statistics indicate that from about 1750 there was a steady decline in the death rate, which automatically made for an increase in the birth rate as more people survived for a longer time to produce children. Demographers are now skeptical that the decline in the death rate was the result of improved standards of public health and advances in medicine, because there is little evidence of progress in either field until after 1850, and then only in some sections of western and northern Europe. (A vaccine for smallpox had been discovered as early as 1798, but mass inoculations did not become a standard practice until many years later.) A more likely explanation is the theory that the particularly virulent outbreaks of plague and other mass-killing epidemics that had swept over Europe in the seventeenth century had given the European population a certain immunity to these diseases. After 1820 the plague disappeared almost completely from Europe, and there was a decline in the incidence of other epidemic diseases. But the evidence is not conclusive, and this theory provides at best only a partial explanation.

Most plausible of all is the theory that there was a connection between the population increase and the greater availability of food in Europe, for the beginning of the sharp rise in population coincided with the beginning of the agricultural revolution. With a better diet, Europeans may have become more healthy generally and thus more resistant to disease. The greater overall prosperity may also help explain the fairly general drop in the age of marriage after 1750. Earlier marriages meant a lengthening of the child-bearing period, while better nutrition made conception and fetal survival more certain.

Already by the end of the eighteenth century, many Europeans were becoming alarmed about the perils of overpopulation (the most famous treatise on the subject, Thomas Malthus's *Essay on Population*, was published in 1798), and at about this time there began a long-range trend toward the limitation of families in France, which can only have been the result of deliberate and rational planning. How birth control on a large scale was practiced at this time cannot be known for certain, but as mechanical and chemical contraceptives were not generally available until the twentieth century, it is probable that the most common method was coitus interruptus—or abstinence. The trend toward a limitation of births spread to other parts of Europe by midcentury as growing numbers of people, especially members of the middle classes, began to restrict the size of their families to allow themselves greater freedom and a higher standard of living.

It was just at this time, however, that the ecological balance of the human species was radically altered by the discovery of methods for destroying the microorganisms which had previously kept the human population in check. The effect of this medical revolution was a sharp decline in the death rate, a corresponding rise in the birth rate, and an increase in the average age of the population that was to alter the entire composition of human society. In the words of Arthur Koestler, it was "a change more drastic and far-reaching than all the technical inventions . . . put together."

The revolution in medicine of the mid-nineteenth century may be said to have begun with the discoveries of Louis Pasteur (1822–1895) and Robert Koch (1843–1910), who after years of research proved conclusively that microorganisms (germs) were not spontaneously generated, as was commonly assumed at the time, but reproduced themselves through breeding and were a major cause of disease. The son of a tanner, Pasteur received a doctorate in science in 1847, and when only thirty years of age he was appointed professor of chemistry at the University of Strasbourg. Here he began to study the problem of fermentation in connection with the production of beer and wine, and in the course of his research made his discoveries about the nature of microorganisms.

Koch, working independently of Pasteur, reached many of the same conclusions. After taking a degree in medicine at Göttingen, he went as district physician to a small town in eastern Germany in 1872 and in his spare time began researches on the etiology of infectious diseases. By 1876 he had found conclusive evidence that anthrax, a disease of sheep and cattle (and occasionally of men) was caused by a specific bacterium.

Louis Pasteur in his laboratory.

In making this discovery he devised technical means of handling bacteria and growing them in a pure culture which are still used and which were to prove of great value in identifying the bacteria responsible for other diseases. Appointed to the imperial health office and faculty of the University of Berlin in 1880, Koch assembled a brilliant group of assistants who were to make significant contributions of their own in the field of bacteriology.

During the last part of the century, Pasteur, Koch, and their followers identified the microorganisms responsible for malaria, tuberculosis, diphtheria, cholera, bubonic plague, and typhoid. The evidence about the germ theory of disease also created a new public attitude toward sanitation and resulted in the passage of public health laws by most central and local governments.

Pasteur went beyond the identification of bacteria. Building on Edward Jenner's discovery in 1798 of a means of immunization against smallpox, he began experimenting with methods of inoculation against other diseases. He found a vaccine for anthrax in 1881 and one for rabies in 1885, and established principles of research methodology that led to a succession of similar discoveries. By the end of the nineteenth century, the major endemic diseases had been brought under control in western Europe.

Unlike many regions that have experienced great and sudden increases in population, western Europe was able to absorb most of its new members. Men were displaced by machines in many old industries, but the industrial revolution created far more jobs than it eliminated. The industrial revolution did not spread uniformly over Europe, however. In Ireland, southern Italy, and other areas relatively unaffected by industrialization, the surplus population starved or was forced to leave the country. The total population of Ireland declined by as much as 50 per cent when the failure of the potato crop led to famine and large-scale emigration.

Human migration, in fact, was one of the most significant concomitants of the industrial revolution and the population explosion. During the last half of the nineteenth century, approximately 85 per cent of the entire population of Europe was on the move. This was by far the greatest and perhaps the most important migration in history, dwarfing, in numbers at least, the vast folk migrations of the late Roman empire. Contrary to popular conception, however, by far the greatest part of this migration took place within Europe itself and consisted of a movement from the country to the cities. Seventy per cent of the population took part in this urbanization movement, causing so great an increase in the size and number of European cities that by the end of the century western Europe was transformed from a predominantly rural into a predominantly urban society.

Sunday morning on Petticoat Lane, the center of the Jewish quarter in London, 1890. *The overcrowded and squalid conditions prevailing in London were typical of most European cities in the later nineteenth century.*

Emigration, too, occurred on a massive scale. Well over 50 million people, about 15 per cent of the population, left Europe altogether. Approximately 45 million settled in the Americas, Australia, New Zealand, and South Africa. Another 6 million moved from Europe to the sparsely populated areas of Asiatic Russia in a migration that rivaled the European settlement of the western part of North America. These migrations Europeanized some parts of Russia, and they reinforced the European quality of other areas.

This movement of the peoples of Europe was due in part to the abolition of serfdom in all European countries except Russia by 1848 (even after the freeing of the serfs in Russia in 1861, the Russian peasant was not entirely free to leave his land) and to improvements in transportation, which opened the interiors of continents to large-scale settlement. While the migrations were vast in scale, they followed no plan or pattern, and were almost completely lacking in organization. They resulted from personal decisions by individuals and small groups, decisions occasionally made under threat of political or religious persecution or because of economic necessity, but for the most part voluntary. Most people seem to have moved to the cities when times were good, when jobs were plentiful and the pay (by the standards of rural labor) high. They emigrated abroad when they could save money to pay for their passage and accumulate enough capital to make a start in a new land. In periods of prosperity big business and industry in the United States—the railroads, steel companies, and later, petroleum companies—offered attractive inducements to immigrants in order to obtain fresh supplies of cheap, and unorganized, labor.

Economic reasons alone, however, do not explain why the traditional inertia and conservatism of the European peasant were overcome to such a remarkable degree in the last part of the nineteenth century. Political and social ideas stirred up by revolution and the Napoleonic wars may have played their part, and the freeing of the serfs removed the legal obstacles to migration. But most important was probably the self-generating quality of the migration movement. As adventurous young men went to the cities and found jobs and a more exciting life, their example stimulated others, until movement to the cities became a natural and accepted pattern of behavior —as it has remained ever since. In the same way, emigration abroad was fostered by the example of pioneers who found land and opportunity in other countries and then encouraged friends and relatives to follow their lead.

The Changing Role of Women

Until the later nineteenth century, the great majority of European women had been peasants, who not only performed most of the household chores but who labored in the fields side by side with men, often as long as fourteen hours or more a day during the long European summers. During the winter months, and in the case of landless peasants throughout the entire year, women as well as men were employed in cottage industries, principally spinning and weaving, which were organized by local entrepreneurs who paid minimal piece-work prices for the goods produced by these isolated and unorganized workers.

Industrialization and mass production ruined many of the cottage industries and compelled peasants in search of employment to migrate to industrial towns, where work in factories and mines replaced work in fields and cottages. Here too women worked side by side with men; indeed, in some light industries women were employed in preference to men because they tended to be more docile, they worked just as effectively, and they consistently received lower rates of pay. Hard as work was in the factories, many women regarded the shift from rural to urban life as a change for the better. Although the hours of work in industry were long, they were at least fixed and a relief from the endless drudgery of rural labor. Factory wages were generally better than what could be earned in cottage industries, and in years of prosperity they enabled women to save enough for a dowry or even a small shop which might lift their families into the ranks of the lower middle class.

A German textile factory in the 1860's showing the machinery of mass production. *Note that all the workers in the factory are women, who were as skillful as men at such work and normally received lower wages. The only man in the picture may be a foreman, but is more likely a mechanic employed to keep the machines in operating order.*

Apart from agriculture the greatest single source of employment for women in the nineteenth century, far greater than any industry, was in domestic service. The households of the wealthy employed literally dozens of servants, and the most humble middle class family generally employed at least one maid. The conditions of work for all domestic servants were difficult, the hours long, the pay poor. The situation was usually best in large establishments, where servants had their own quarters and formed a society of their own; worst in poorer households, where the maid of all work might be obliged to sleep in the kitchen or on a pallet under the staircase, deprived of all privacy, and where she was forced to labor from before dawn until long into the night polishing boots, laying fires, cleaning, washing, and at the call of her employers until the last of them had retired to bed. Even then she might be disturbed in order to satisfy the desires of male members of the household, a situation reflected in the particularly high illegitimacy rate among maidservants. Yet women (and men also) generally preferred domestic service to industrial labor because working conditions, miserable as they might be, were nevertheless preferable to conditions in factories and mines, and because service in the more affluent households brought them into contact with a more genteel way of life and elevated them (in their own estimation at least) to a superior status within the working class community.

The demand for servants increased greatly in the course of the nineteenth century as a result of the rapid growth of the middle classes in industrial societies. The aspiration of members of the rising middle classes was to free their women from the need to do physical labor or at least from the most onerous household chores, and in the days before the widespread availability of household gadgets such freedom could only be provided by servants. The employment of servants was in fact the most obvious feature that distinguished middle from lower class families, and the fashions of the time reflected this distinction. The tight corsets, hoop skirts, and crinolines in which middle and upper class women were clothed showed clearly that the women who wore them did not need to do physical labor and were a sign of affluence and status comparable to the bound feet of women in China.

A stroll on the Champs-Élysées. *The great French artist and cartoonist Honoré Daumier (1808–1879) found ample material for satire in the ostentatious and impractical fashions worn by Parisian ladies of leisure in the mid-nineteenth century.*

Virtually all European women, however, no matter what their class, were still in a position of legal, economic, and social subservience to men in 1850. With few exceptions, their persons and their property were subject by law to the authority of fathers, husbands, or brothers. All channels of direct political influence were closed to them. Although there was an extension of male suffrage in many European countries, women everywhere continued to be denied the vote. Apart from the hereditary rulers of a few royal houses, women could hold no political office. Women were barred from all professions except teaching until Florence Nightingale made nursing a respectable profession for women in the course of the Crimean War, but even then the·opportunity for middle class women to gain a certain degree of economic independence remained extremely limited. In this respect working class women enjoyed greater equality with men, an advantage which most of them would no doubt have been happy to forego.

The feminist movement, a drive to achieve greater legal, political, and social equality or at least greater independence vis-à-vis men, first assumed permanent and significant form in the mid-nineteenth century and was largely confined to politically conscious women of the upper and middle classes. It was a joint product of the social changes wrought by industrialization and the idea of the equality of all human beings inherent in European liberalism. Stimulated by the emancipation movements on behalf of slaves and serfs, in which women had played a prominent part, educated women became acutely conscious of their own condition of relative servitude in a male-dominated society and sought to remove the fetters with which they themselves were burdened. The case for women's equality was argued most persuasively by the eminent British political philosopher John Stuart Mill (1806–1873). In his essay "On the Subjection of Women" (1869) he maintained that "the principle which regulates the existing social relations between the two sexes—the legal subordination of one sex to the other—is wrong in itself, and now one of the chief hindrances to human improvement; . . . it ought to be replaced by a principle of perfect equality, admitting no power or privilege on the one side, nor disability on the other."

After some unsuccessful efforts to win suffrage rights equal to those of men—in France in 1848, in England in the 1860's—most feminists settled into the long struggle for educational reform, admission to the professions, and the removal of juridical disabilities; only in the 1890's did women resume their campaign to win the vote.

In Europe, the feminist movement was most powerful and successful in England, where by 1890 it had gained a few important victories. The Married Woman's Property Act of 1870 (amended in 1882 and 1887) allowed married women to possess property in their own name and opened the way for legislation which eventually gave women complete equality with respect to property rights. In 1869 women were permitted to vote in municipal elections and to hold offices in municipal and local governments without restriction, but despite the efforts of feminists and their supporters in parliament, women continued to be denied the vote in national elections until after the First World War. Although the teaching profession was open to women throughout the nineteenth century, their formal educational opportunities were extremely limited, with the result that most women teachers and governesses in private families were poorly educated and untrained. The first formal system of training for women teachers in England was provided with the establishment of Queen's College, London, in 1848, and after that educational opportunities for women were gradually extended. The women's struggle to enter professions other than teaching, however, remained difficult and frustrating, and did not achieve any large-scale success until well into the twentieth century.

On the Continent, the feminists were fewer in number and their successes were even more limited. The introduction of compulsory education for girls as well as boys in many European countries created a new demand for women teachers and led to improvements in women's education on a broad scale, but on the whole European women had to wait until after the First World War for significant improvements in their status. A serious problem on the Continent, which may help explain why the women's movement on the Continent was less successful than in England, was the growing strength of radical political movements, most of which championed the rights of women but which at the same time harnessed this and every other part of their program to their demand for a complete change in the existing political and economic system. Thus the feminist movement, which demanded no more than equality for women, came into conflict with or became associated with political radicalism, with the result in either case that the cause of feminism as such was weakened.

Urbanization and the Transformation of Society

The dislocation of European society brought about by the industrial revolution inevitably caused much human misery. The movement of peasants from the soil to alien environments, the crowding of people into squalid and unsanitary tenements, the wretched working conditions in mines and factories, the long hours and low wages, the exploitation of child and female labor, the absence of safety precautions, the lack of accident and sickness insurance—all these abuses of the industrial revolution were exposed and angrily denounced, and with reason. This was an era when men and women worked fourteen to sixteen hours a day in unheated factories; when little children were used to draw coal carts in the mines because they were a cheap source of labor and were small enough to crawl

A tin mine in Cornwall, 1893. *Dangerous working conditions prevailed in most mines and factories until well into the twentieth century.*

through the narrow shafts; when a single drowsy moment at a machine might result in the loss of an arm or a leg for which there was no insurance or compensation, even though it might put an end to a man's ability to work. The system of unrestricted free enterprise brought great wealth and power to nations and to a number of individuals, but for the common man it meant freedom to be ill paid, ill housed, and ill fed, and when times were bad, freedom to be unemployed and to go hungry.

Economic misery was nothing new in Europe, however, and if work in factories and mines was oppressive, so also had been work in the cottage industries. It is easy to romanticize rural life, but the existence of the average farm laborer in the nineteenth century was generally even more wretched than that of the city worker. The dwellings of the rural poor were often little more than mud huts, as cramped, dark, and unsanitary as any city tenement. Wages were even lower than in the city, and work was more seasonal. Few farm laborers could afford to eat meat or cheese regularly; their diet often consisted of little more than bread, potatoes, turnips, and such fruits or vegetables as might be in season. They were seldom allowed to hunt or fish in local woods or streams, and poaching was severely punished. One of the reasons for the drift to the cities was the desire for a better standard of living, and toward the end of the century the cities began to provide it.

By this time the flagrant abuses of the industrial revolution in big cities had forced many governments to recognize the need to remedy them. The concentration of people in the cities had made it possible for the workers themselves to agitate more effectively for reforms, and trade unions and labor parties had been organized to give common voice to their grievances. During the second half of the nineteenth century a long series of government regulations gradually improved working conditions in the larger industries of western Europe. As a result of legislation requiring higher standards in housing and sanitation, and of the introduction of amenities such as gas and electric lights, the cities became more bearable places in which to live.

Industrial workers formed the chief market as well as the labor force of the new industrial society. For the first time a large number of laborers could afford to eat meat regularly. Sugar, citrus fruits, cocoa, were made available to a mass market. Tea and coffee, once luxury items, became standard drinks for every class. Shoes, clothing, furniture, toys, all were produced in increasing quantities at prices most people could afford. On balance it can be said that the industrial revolution, with all its evils, brought a great increase in material prosperity to a majority of the members of the societies which it transformed. It is only necessary to compare the living conditions of laborers in nonindustrial areas with those of industrial workers, miserable as these may be in some cases, to be aware of the material benefits of the conversion to machine technology.

The revolution in the economy of Europe produced important changes in European society. Land, for centuries the economic base of the aristocracy, was no longer the chief source of wealth. New industries, finance capitalism, and commerce brought ever-increasing wealth to the middle classes. With mounting importunity these classes demanded political power to match their economic power, and through the greater part of the nineteenth century they challenged the political authority of the landed aristocracy.

A growing segment of the population of the new industrial society consisted of the urban proletariat, the great reservoir of industrial labor, but also a great reservoir of potential political strength. In the early part of the century most industrial workers were content to accept middle-class political leadership. After the collapse of the revolutions of 1848, however, workers became increasingly aware of the divergence between their interests and those of the middle classes, and they began to turn to economic and political organizations—trade unions and socialist parties—designed to promote their interests.

The change in western Europe from a predominantly rural to a predominantly urban society had other important effects. A population concentrated in cities was more accessible to the influence of new ideological trends than a population scattered through the countryside. The man who had severed his traditional local ties to live in the impersonal and anonymous city searched for something he could identify with, for new loyalties and attachments. The city became the great center of the mass movements of the industrial age, the breeding ground of nationalist and socialist doctrines, of new religious sects, temperance societies, reform movements, and revolutionary associations, and of new movements in science and the arts.

A lodging house and soup kitchen for men recently discharged from prison, a photograph taken in 1877. *This establishment was run by a Mr. Baylis, the figure on the left, a former policeman who is credited with providing Dickens and other English writers with much of their information about London's underworld.*

CHAPTER 2

The Intellectual and Cultural Climate

THE ENDURING INFLUENCE OF THE CHRISTIAN CHURCHES

IT IS COMMONLY assumed that the economic and social upheavals of the nineteenth century, the impact of scientific thought, and an ever-growing emphasis on materialist values produced a sharp decline in religious faith. There is ample evidence to support this view. In every European country a substantial percentage of the working class, especially migrants to the big cities, lost contact with the church, and for many people the authority of the Bible was irretrievably undermined by scientific refutations of the literal truth of the Book of Genesis and by textual criticisms showing apparent inconsistencies in both the Old and the New Testaments. Yet in view of the political power wielded by the churches after 1850, their ability to resist pressure and persecution, and the vitality and scope of their missionary activity in Europe and overseas, the conclusion is inescapable that the Christian churches were still a vigorous force in European society and retained a powerful hold over the minds and spirits of men.

The Roman Catholic Church remained the strongest and most important church in Europe. Pius IX, hailed as the Pope of Progress soon after his accession in 1846 because of the reforms he introduced in the Roman government, was denounced by Italian patriots as a traitor two years later for his refusal to support the Italian national cause in the war against Austria. Forced into exile by a republican revolution in his territories, he returned to Rome in 1850 as an uncompromising defender of traditional institutions and values. In the period of political reaction following the 1848 revolutions, he was able to conclude advantageous treaties with a number of secular governments, which now looked to the Roman Catholic Church as an ally against revolution.

In the encyclical *Quanta cura* issued in 1864, and the appended *Syllabus of Errors,* Pius IX launched an attack on the major intellectual tendencies of his day: nationalism, socialism, communism, Freemasonry, natural science, religious indifference, religious tolerance, secular education, and the separation of church and state. It was an error to believe "that the Roman Pontiff can and ought to reconcile himself to and agree with progress, liberalism and contemporary civilization."

While defending the *status quo* in all other spheres, Pius IX carried out a revolution within the Church itself. In 1869 he convened an ecumenical council at the Vatican, the first since the Council of Trent in the sixteenth century. The Council proclaimed that a pope cannot err, when speaking officially *(ex cathedra)* on matters of faith and morals, because at such times he is endowed with divine authority. Acceptance of the dogma of papal infallibility by the council marked the triumph of the pope over movements within the Church· to limit papal authority by transferring substantial powers to the councils or the bishops, and represented the victory of centralized authoritarian government in the Church.

The assertion of papal supremacy in spiritual affairs was made even as the Church was losing the last vestiges of its temporal power. The greater part of the Papal States had been lost in 1860 during the wars of Italian unification. French troops protected Rome itself from Italian nationalists, but in 1870 these soldiers were withdrawn to fight against Prussia. While the Vatican Council was in session, troops of the Italian national government occupied Rome and made it the capital of the newly united Italy. The pope was left only the territory containing the Vatican and St. Peter's. Pius IX and his successors refused to recognize the loss of Rome, and until 1929 the popes followed a policy of self-imprisonment in the Vatican.

The loss of Rome and the Papal States, although at the time regarded as a disaster by the papacy, actually gave it new opportunity to assert its spiritual authority. The papacy could now become what Pope Gregory the Great, more than a thousand years before, had thought it should be, the conscience of the world, without the need to consider the effect of its actions on its earthly holdings.

Pius IX's assertion of papal authority and his violent denunciations of all contemporary political and intellectual trends alarmed and alienated many secular governments and liberal Catholics. Leo XIII, pope from 1878 to 1903, adhered to his predecessor's views on papal authority, but was diplomatic in his presentation of papal claims and more willing to recognize the problems of his age. He promoted a revival of the study of St. Thomas Aquinas (c. 1225–1274), whose writings dealt with many moral questions still alive in the nineteenth century; Aquinas had taught, for example, that there is no conflict between true science and true religion. On his authority, Leo relaxed the Church's opposition to science and encouraged the work of Catholic scientists.

Leo XIII realized that the Church was discrediting itself in many countries by its support of extremist conservatives and lost monarchist causes. He argued that democracy was as compatible with Catholicism as more authoritarian types of government, and that genuine personal liberty had its firmest basis in Catholic Christianity. He believed that the Church could accomplish its purposes far more effectively by forming political parties, and working through representative governments instead of opposing them, and that the Church should take a deeper interest in social problems. In his encyclical *Rerum novarum* (1891), the pope urged the application of Christian principles to the great social issues of the age. He deplored the abuses of unrestricted free enterprise and the consequent degradation of the worker. Although he defended the institution of private property, he acknowledged that there was much in socialism that was Christian in principle. State, Church, and employer had the duty of improving the condition of the worker, but the worker should also be encouraged to help himself, through the formation of Catholic political parties and Catholic labor unions.

The Roman Catholic Church could not be dismissed as an elaborate superstructure maintained on dead or decaying foundations. In its frequent and bitter conflicts with secular authorities in the nineteenth century it revealed a capacity to draw on popular support rivaled only by that of the new ideology of nationalism. In Italy, where the Church clashed directly with the nationalist movement, it succeeded in holding its own against the attacks of the secular government, and in Ireland and Poland, where the Church's interests often coincided with national interests, it played a leading role in efforts to shake off foreign rule. Napoleon III, a weather vane of public opinion, granted extensive powers to the Church in order to gain support for his regime, and made some of his most critical decisions in both domestic and foreign policy in response to the pressure of Roman Catholic opinion. During the first years of the Third Republic in France, the Church lost a number of valuable privileges, but by 1890 it had made a strong comeback through its newly founded political and labor organizations. In Austria the government sought Church support of its efforts to impose a centralized administration on the Habsburg empire. During the period of anticlerical liberal government in Austria after 1867, the Church retained its hold on the country's national minorities by cooperating with regional national movements; after 1879 it was one of the bulwarks of the Taaffe regime, which attempted to conciliate these minorities. In Germany the Roman Catholic Church proved to be the only organization capable of thwarting Bismarck. His campaign to break the power of the Church, one of his few political failures, resulted in the consolidation of the Catholic Center party, which was to become the most powerful and stable political party in the German Reichstag. In resisting Bismarck and the new German national state, Roman Catholic leaders exhibited a courage and adherence to principle that put liberal and radical intellectuals to shame, and in doing so they received firm and ungrudging support from the majority of Germany's Roman Catholic population.

The Protestant churches were more seriously affected than the Catholic by scientific and textual criticisms of the Bible because Protestant faith had always depended more heavily on biblical authority. Scholarly criticism of the Bible was nothing new, however, and Protestant as well as Catholic theologians had long dealt with seemingly inconsistent or irrational passages by interpreting them in a symbolic sense. Biblical criticism does not seem to have shaken the faith of the majority of Protestants, and church membership grew at least at the same rate as the overall population. In the major Protestant countries the role of religion in everyday life did not change appreciably except among town laborers and a minority of intellectuals. In Russia the Orthodox Church, controlled by the tsar, continued to play a major role in politics and society.

The loyalty of Protestant congregations was less demonstrable than that of members of the Catholic Church. Since the largest Protestant churches were state churches, their adherents were not subject to persecution. But in areas where they did suffer official harassment, Protestants, too, exhibited courage and tenacity in standing by their beliefs. In Great Britain the Protestant dissenters—Methodists, Baptists, and members of other sects that rejected the authority of the Church of England—were a strong force in the Liberal party, especially in Wales and Scotland. Failure of Liberal leadership to pay sufficient regard to the religious feelings of this group was an important cause of the liberal election defeat in 1874.

Further evidence of the continued strength of the Christian churches can be found in the remarkable upsurge of Christian missionary movements in the last decades of the nineteenth century. Overseas missionary activity was facilitated by improvements in transportation and by the new accessibility of territories once closed to all but the most intrepid traveler. The very fact that missionaries went out in large numbers and risked their lives in unknown, unhealthy, and often hostile lands indicates that in addition to the prevailing optimism regarding the human capacity for improvement, a spirit of faith and sacrifice persisted in Europe.

The most important missionary work of the age was done by the French, who supplied more missionaries and more money to support them than all the other peoples of Europe put together. Largely through the activity of French missionaries, the Roman Catholic Church established full-fledged Church hierarchies for China in 1875, for North Africa in 1884, for India in 1886, and for Japan in 1891.

By the end of the nineteenth century approximately forty thousand Roman Catholics, eighteen thousand Protestants (of all denominations) and two thousand of the Russian Orthodox faith were missionaries in

Africa, Asia, and the Pacific area. The Christian churches estimated that they had converted some forty million people in these territories. This figure in itself means little, for the statistics of most churches tended to be inflated and the quality of the conversions varied widely. Yet there can be no doubt of the vigor of the European missionary movement and of the strong support it received from congregations at home.

Nor should the activity of missionaries within Europe itself be overlooked. The Roman Catholics claimed large-scale conversions in Protestant countries, but the Protestant churches also claimed sizable gains in membership. Statistics on conversions in Europe, like those on conversions overseas, tended to be exaggerated, but the fact that conversions did take place in large numbers is another indication of the continued appeal of Christianity.

Strong as was the continued hold of Christianity on men's loyalties, however, the Christian churches, and indeed all forms of traditional authority, were being thrown increasingly on the defensive in the course of the nineteenth century. The cultural shocks produced by the economic and social upheavals of the era were intensified by the promulgation of scientific theories which challenged commonly accepted concepts about man's place in time and the universe, and by political theories which challenged traditional concepts about his place in society.

MATERIALISM AND REALISM; NEW PRINCIPLES OF AUTHORITY

So great was the material progress in the latter part of the nineteenth century and so profoundly did men appear to be dominated by material considerations that this period in history has been called an age of materialism. In all classes of society people seemed obsessed with the desire to amass goods, and judged themselves and their neighbors by standards of material wealth. Many intellectual leaders embraced the philosophy of positivism, which held that everything, including mental and spiritual qualities, was the product of natural forces. In 1864 Pius IX, pope from 1846 to 1878, thought it necessary to condemn the view "that no other forces are recognized than those which reside in matter and which . . . are summed up in the accumulation and increase of riches by every possible means and the satisfaction of every pleasure."

The pope had reason for concern. Yet the nineteenth century was an extremely moralistic, if not always a moral, age. Rarely has pleasure been more generally condemned by the classes most capable of pursuing it. The accumulation of riches was regarded not as a means of enjoying life, but as a sign that a man had not spent his time in idleness or frivolous pursuits. In this respect the attitudes of the middle class in the nineteenth century resembled those of the Calvinist world in the sixteenth and seventeenth centuries.

Closely associated with the materialistic outlook was a belief in the necessity of viewing the world and its problems "realistically." Impressed by the triumphs of science, which were regarded, at least in the popular mind, as the result of objective analyses of factual evidence, many people turned away from abstract ideals and took pride in their ability to face facts, to see the world as it actually was. This point of view was widely adopted by politicians in the period of disillusionment following the failure of the revolutions of 1848, which was generally ascribed to the excessively visionary idealism of revolutionary leaders. So great was the emphasis on realism by articulate members of late-nineteenth-century society that subsequent historians have tended to accept contemporary estimates of this attitude at face value. They find a new realistic understanding of politics in the statecraft of Bismarck and Cavour—a recognition of the preeminence of force in achieving political success, and a willingness to brush aside morality and idealism as unrealistic and hence irrelevant. This political realism has been seen to correspond with realism in the sciences and with a new realism in the arts.

But did a new realism in fact prevail in the later nineteenth century? Were Bismarck and Cavour more realistic in their appraisal of the interests of their governments than diplomats of earlier decades, such as Metternich or Castlereagh? Did they have a more acute sense of the importance of power than Napoleon? Were they more willing to disregard conventional standards of morality than Talleyrand?

There is even more reason to wonder whether any of the distinctive ideological forces of the period—liberalism, nationalism, social Darwinism, Marxian socialism—can be called realistic, despite their scientific pretensions. Belief in representative government, in national uniqueness or superiority, in the triumph of the proletariat and the withering away of the state—all depended on faith quite as much as did religious convictions; indeed more so, because these secular beliefs could so readily be challenged by facts.

In the arts, too, the realism of the period was neither so realistic, so original, nor so generally accepted as many contemporary and later interpreters have assumed. The novelist Émile Zola and the painter Gustave Courbet, who made realism something of a cult, formed part of a long tradition of European genre art. Moreover, there was a strong element of romanticism in their celebration of the sordid and the commonplace.

The genuinely popular art of the era, far from being realistic, was frankly sentimental and escapist, and popular taste was profoundly shocked (or pretended to be) by the realistic writers and painters. Gustave Flaubert, who wrote a novel about adultery without overtly moralizing on the subject, was sent into exile by Napoleon III, himself hardly a model of sexual morality, while another Frenchman, the painter Édouard Manet, who dared to depict naked women without disguising them as nymphs or allegorical figures, was branded a moral pervert and vilified by critics and public alike.

In short, the men and women of the nineteenth century, with all their emphasis on material values and realism, were as hypocritical and as much influenced by emotional and ideological forces as those of any other period in history.

Faith in Science; Darwin and Darwinism

The crucial role of science in Europe's economic and social revolutions was paralleled by its influence on European intellectual life. Europeans were surrounded to an ever-increasing extent by products of scientific discovery, and science was steadily providing explanations for natural phenomena that had once been considered miraculous. Science, in fact, offered a comprehensive view of life and the universe to rival the cosmology of revealed religion, and for many it became something of a religion in its own right.

Faith in science was not confined to a minority of intellectuals, but became part of the popular culture of the era. People of widely different educational and social backgrounds trooped to public lectures on new discoveries and theories, and the lecturers themselves were often imbued with missionary zeal. The efforts of the popularizers of science, together with the remarkable scientific achievements of the age, produced a popular belief that science could ultimately explain everything and in time eradicate poverty, disease, even death itself.

Scientists themselves were rarely so optimistic. Some of the most eminent, fully aware of their own limitations, recognized that science would probably never be able to explain such mysteries as the origins of the universe or of life, and they still looked to revealed religion for the ultimate explanation of existence. A substantial number, however, including some of the most vociferous popularizers of science, categorically rejected all supernatural theories and took the view that whatever could not be ascertained rationally and scientifically was forever unknowable.

Revolutionary as were many of the discoveries of science in the nineteenth century, the methodology and goals of scientific endeavor had not changed significantly since the days of Isaac Newton. Scientific research was based on experimentation, observation, and the systematic accumulation of factual evidence. Scientists looked upon nature as an objective reality, they believed in the possibility of finding fundamental principles governing the operations of natural phenomena, and the discovery of many such principles in the course of the nineteenth century seemed to confirm these assumptions. The formulation as early as 1791 of the principle of the indestructibility or conservation of matter by Antoine Lavoisier was followed by the discovery of principles on the atomic structure of the universe, the cellular structure of living organisms, and the nature of bacterial and plant growth. Perhaps the most significant single scientific generalization of the nineteenth century in the field of the natural sciences was the formulation in 1847 of the law of the conservation of energy by Hermann von Helmholtz (1821–1894) which held that the total amount of energy in the universe, like matter, remained the same. The law of the conservation of energy provided the basis for the discovery that such apparently different phenomena as heat, light, electricity, and magnetism were in fact only different forms of the interaction of matter and energy (the laws of thermodynamics and the electromagnetic theory of light).

Scientific methodology was also applied to the study of human society in the belief that general principles could be discovered for human conduct as well as for natural phenomena. The founder of the study of sociology, Auguste Comte (1798–1857), who coined the term *positivism* to describe his outlook, believed that man was, in fact, nothing more than a natural phenomenon and therefore governed by natural laws. According to Comte, all human qualities, including reason, spirit, imagination, and creativity, were the product of natural forces and measurable by scientific methods. This was the line of reasoning followed by Karl Marx, the most famous prototype of a new breed of social scientist.

Toward the end of the nineteenth century a revolution took place within the field of science itself which was to shatter previously held assumptions about the natural world. As a result of discoveries that began to be made at this time, physical scientists found themselves compelled to recognize that the basic structure of the universe, far from being fixed or permanent, was everywhere in flux, and that their universal laws and principles had to give way to theories of probability and relativity. As one historian of science summed up the situation: "Until 1890 systems were being founded; after 1890 they were being confounded."

In the mid-nineteenth century, however, faith in science was not yet clouded by such doubts. On the contrary, everywhere in Europe admiration for the achievements of science was rapidly increasing, and as the prestige of science grew so did the popular belief in its revelations. It was in this intellectual atmosphere that a great storm broke over the principles advanced by the naturalist Charles Darwin (1809–1882), whose theory of biological evolution supplied a scientific explanation for the development of life on earth. The idea of evolution did not originate with Darwin. Philosophers had long thought in evolutionary terms, and geologists and naturalists had already accumulated a great deal of evidence on the subject. It was Darwin, however, who compiled—in his *On*

Charles Darwin photographed in 1854 at the age of forty-five.

the Origin of Species by Means of Natural Selection, published in 1859 —the first large-scale body of information to support the hypothesis that living organisms evolve. He was also the first to link evolution to the theory of natural selection (another theory that did not originate with him) to explain how evolutionary changes take place. In Darwin's view the world is far from well ordered or harmonious. On the contrary; all living things are engaged in a constant struggle for existence, and in this struggle the organisms with the best-developed qualities for obtaining food, for reproduction, or for self-defense are "naturally selected" to survive. From this theory came the formula "survival of the fittest," which Darwin's popularizers put forward as a scientific law governing all aspects of life.

In considering the impact of Darwin's ideas on nineteenth-century thought, one must distinguish between Darwin and Darwinism. Darwin himself advanced his theories with caution and surrounded his main propositions with reservations and qualifications. In poor health during the later part of his life, he shunned scientific meetings and rarely became involved in the bitter controversies his views aroused. Darwinism was created by Darwin's popularizers, who reduced his theories to oversimplified and easily comprehensible slogans. "Your boldness sometimes makes me tremble," Darwin told one of his followers. It was Darwinism, not Darwin the man, that had the greatest influence on the intellectual climate of the period.

To many of Darwin's contemporaries the chief significance of Darwinism lay in its threat to the Christian religion and public morality. By denying the account of the creation in the Book of Genesis and by equating man with other animals, Darwinism seemed to strike at the root of Christianity and to undercut the concept of Christian morality based on belief in man's uniqueness in a divine world order. In reality, Darwinism was not so great a threat to Christianity as many feared. Students of theology had long interpreted parts of the Bible in a symbolic or allegorical sense, and most Christians had little difficulty in reconciling the theory of evolution with their religious beliefs after the first shock had worn off.

The influence of Darwinism on popular social attitudes was far more profound. The theory of the survival of the fittest gained tremendous vogue and in the form of "social Darwinism" was used to explain every kind of social phenomenon, including the existence of various classes. According to convinced Darwinists, the poor were poor because they lacked the intelligence, the initiative, and the energy of the more favored members of society; the rich were rich because of their natural endowments. In an era when consciences were disturbed by the problem of poverty and social distress, this was a comforting assumption—unless one happened to be poor.

Darwin's theories were used to explain not only inequalities within a society but inequalities among societies. His ideas were eagerly seized by nationalists, racists, and imperialists to prove the superiority of entire nations or social groups over others. The concept of the survival of the fittest led many Frenchmen, Englishmen, and Germans to believe that their present positions of international power were proof of their respective nations' fitness to survive and to rule. Perhaps most important was the fact that this view engendered a moral compulsion in these nations to provide further proof of their fitness, which many nationalists believed could be demonstrated conclusively only on the field of battle. As a result of their victory in the Franco-Prussian War of 1870–1871, many Germans smugly assumed that they were intellectually, morally, and physically superior to the French; the French, in turn, harbored a desire to regain their self-respect through a successful war of revenge. Theories of racial fitness asserted the superiority of whites over blacks, of Anglo-Saxons over Gauls, of Teutons over Slavs. These nationalist-racist ideas were not necessary consequences of Darwinism, but this viewpoint did seem to provide a rational and scientific justification for one of the oldest and most cherished of human beliefs, the conviction that one's own group is a chosen people. The popular acceptance of social Darwinism does much to explain the force of European imperialism and the strident nationalism in the years before 1914.

The Great Age of Classical Liberalism

Scientific theories and assumptions penetrated into political thought and left an indelible mark on the political philosophy of liberalism, which reached the crest of its influence during this era. Most liberal theories, like those of science, were based on faith in human reason and belief in the existence of a natural order which could be understood and utilized for the benefit of mankind through the use of reason.

Liberalism, as the name implies, is a philosophy of freedom, a belief that man could be trusted to govern himself and deal with his affairs with a minimum of interference from outside authority, whether church, state, guild, or labor union. Left to his own devices, each man would pursue his own best interests, and the sum of these individual efforts would make for the greater welfare of all. Liberal theories reflected this individualism, for there were almost as many varieties of liberalism as there were liberals. One of the great weaknesses of liberalism as a political movement was the lack of unity or agreement among its adherents.

With all its emphasis on freedom of the individual, liberalism was not anarchistic. Liberal theorists recognized that man lived in society, and that in his search for freedom he might impinge on the freedom of others. They therefore stressed the need for laws, for written constitutions and bills of rights, which would guarantee the rights, liberties, and property of every individual, protect him from arbitrary governmental interference, and from the rapacity of his fellow man.

In theory, and even more so in practice, liberals tended to be pragmatic. Most liberals professed to believe in self-government through representative institutions, but only a minority of them advocated complete democracy and universal suffrage. Moderate liberals generally thought that political representation should be extended just to educated property owners, who could be trusted to use their political power wisely and responsibly—in other words, to men like themselves. There was widespread fear that if those without education or property were given the vote they would be easily swayed by demagogues. Many liberals had a strong faith in education, however, and were willing to consider the extension of voting privileges as literacy increased.

Liberalism has been called the political ideology of the middle class, for most of the active liberals belonged to this class and their political doctrines reflected middle-class interests. After the failure of the revolutions of 1848, liberals tended to renounce the use of tactics of violence to achieve their political aims. These revolutions had demonstrated the ineffectiveness of violence, and they had also exposed the dangers of revolution by the propertyless masses. Radical revolutionary programs demanding the abolition of private property and an equitable distribution of economic and political power had alarmed the members of the middle class, who had too much at stake in the existing order of society to desire a social as well as a political revolution. After 1848 they therefore emphasized the need to create or strengthen institutions of representative government as a means of gaining a greater share of political power, still largely monopolized by the landed aristocracy in most European countries. With the acquisition of political power, they intended to carry out the political and social reforms they considered desirable by orderly, legal, and peaceful means.

Most liberals believed in free enterprise in economic affairs (*laissez-faire*). They wanted to remove government constraints at home to permit maximum scope for their economic activities, and they wanted free trade among nations to create the largest possible market for their products. But at the same time liberals expected government protection of private property. Moreover, despite their objections to government interference, liberal businessmen seldom hesitated to ask the government for subsidies and loans, and they were quick to agitate for tariff protection when international competition became too intense, and to demand government military intervention when their investments abroad were threatened.

Whether for religious, humanitarian, or practical reasons, many liberals were among the foremost advocates of social as well as political reform in the nineteenth century. Liberals worked for the abolition of slavery and serfdom; they sought to alleviate the miseries of the working class; they recognized the need for broader popular education and improved sanitation facilities. The introduction of social reforms necessarily meant added government interference in the affairs of the individual, and liberals wrestled with their consciences over the problem. By the end of the century, however, many of them were willing to advocate increased government controls in the interest of human betterment. Indeed, their association with social reform grew so strong that today liberals are often confused with socialists or communists, whose doctrines are the antithesis of liberalism.

Socialism; Marx and Marxism

Although liberalism was the reigning philosophy among advocates of political change and reform in the later nineteenth century, it did not have the field to itself. The most serious challenge came from socialist theories, which were also permeated with scientific assumptions and which gained rapidly in influence after the revolutions of 1848. Socialism was essentially a denial of the liberal view that, given maximum freedom, man could work out his problems to the greatest benefit of society. Although there were as many shades of opinion among socialists as among liberals, socialists generally believed in a greater regulation of society. They viewed the free-enterprise system as chaotic and unjust, and favored some kind of control over the means of production and distribution to give the workers a fairer share of the fruits of their labor. Many socialist political thinkers, like many liberals, believed that there were certain natural laws at work in society, but unlike the liberals they did not consider government regulation the chief obstacle to the ideal operation of these laws. Instead, they regarded it as man's duty to discover the laws and, by means of government action, to organize society in conformity with them.

The outstanding figure in the history of socialism was Karl Marx (1818–1883), who formulated a theory of history that provided a key—*the* key, Marx was convinced—to understanding the past, present, and future of human society. Marx viewed history in evolutionary terms, and in describing the evolutionary process in human society he claimed to have done for human history what Darwin had done for natural history. Marx's friend and frequent collaborator, Friedrich Engels (1820–1895), echoed this belief in his funeral speech at Marx's grave: "Just as Darwin discovered the law of development of organic nature, so Marx discovered the law of development of human history." Marx wanted to dedicate the English translation of the first volume of his major work, *Das Kapital*, published in German in 1867, to Darwin, an honor which Darwin, with characteristic caution, declined.

"Mr. Charles Darwin on the part of his sincere admirer Karl Marx." *Marx's inscription of the first volume of* Das Kapital *to Darwin. His subsequent offer to dedicate the English translation of this work to Darwin was courteously refused.*

Marx's ideas, like those of Darwin, were not entirely original, nor were his theories altogether clear or systematic. His writings contain many puzzling ambiguities and paradoxes. It has therefore been possible for Marx's followers and popularizers frequently to tailor his ideas to their own needs and prejudices. As in the case of Darwin, it is necessary to distinguish carefully between the master and his interpreters, between Marx and Marxism—or anti-Marxism.

Some recent interpretations of Marx, for example, have leaned heavily on manuscripts he wrote in Paris in 1844 and on formulations of his economic theories written in 1857–58. The Paris manuscripts in particular have appealed to contemporary scholars because they reveal a strong humanitarian impulse and concern with the problem of human alienation in a capitalist society. Marx himself, however, never attempted to publish these manuscripts (they were not published until almost a century later), and soon moved away from a humanitarian emphasis toward what he regarded as a more rigorous and scientific analysis of the human condition. The central theme of his published works—the principal source of Marxist theory until the second half of the twentieth century—was the replacement of a utopian or "idealistic" point of view with a realistic and "materialistic" interpretation of the historical process. On taking the first volume of *Das Kapital* to the printer, Marx acknowledged to his friend Engels that a work such as his must have many shortcomings, but he was convinced that the overall theoretical structure was sound and "a triumph of German science." Marx's awareness of the shortcomings of his work and his ceaseless search for further confirmation of his laws may explain his failure to complete *Das Kapital*, but to the end of his life he remained convinced of the soundness of his basic principles.

Marx's first principle, and the assumption underlying all his other theories, was that the economy was the mainspring of all human activity, and that the economic structure of society was the basis of its legal and political institutions, its morality, and its culture. In all societies, he said, "the mode of production in material life determines the general character of the social, political and spiritual processes of life." Through his economic interpretation of society, Marx believed, he had discovered a fundamental pattern in history: the class struggle. The truly significant conflicts in history, he maintained, were not political or national rivalries but conflicts between slaves and slaveholders, plebeians and patricians, serfs and landlords, workers and bourgeois-capitalists.

Although Marx regarded the class struggle as the key to all historical conflicts, he did not expect it to continue indefinitely or regard it as a permanent historical phenomenon. On the contrary, he believed that the final cataclysmic struggle between the classes, the economic Armageddon, was at hand; the capitalist system was creating conditions for the ultimate clash between workers and capitalists. The total amount of the world's wealth was being concentrated in ever fewer hands, with the result that an ever smaller number of capitalists were growing richer, while more and more people were being pressed into the ranks of the wretched proletariat. The consequent social tensions would inevitably produce a revolution. This, however, would be the final revolution, for the new society would be organized according to the scientific economic laws Marx had discovered and hence the fundamental causes of conflict and revolution would be eliminated.

One of the most important of Marx's economic formulations was the theory of surplus value. This theory held that the real value of any commodity could only be measured by the labor used to produce it. Under capitalism, labor was not given just compensation, and the surplus went into the pockets of the capitalists. After the revolution the worker, the actual producer of wealth, would control the means of production and distribution and would receive full value for his work.

Marx saw that to organize society according to scientific economic laws, some sort of supervisory control would be necessary, and he assigned a definite place to the state in the period immediately following the revolution. Once this organization had been carried out, economic classes would no longer exist and the class struggle would come to an end. The state would then become unnecessary and would gradually wither away. This new society, completely freed from state controls, was described by Marx as an association "in which the free development of each is the condition for the free development of all." His vision of the social order was remarkably similar to the ideal conception of the free-enterprise system, although not even the most optimistic liberal believed that a society operating freely according to natural laws would be so perfect that there would no longer be any need for the state. Marx did not think that human controversy would cease after the social conflict had been resolved, but he suggested that future disagreements would involve intellectual or cultural issues instead of wealth and power.

Besides supplying the socialist movement with a theoretical foundation, Marx imbued it with a revolutionary dynamism. He urged the working class to prepare constantly and systematically for the revolution and the overthrow of the bourgeois-capitalist system. Conditioned by centuries of subjugation and ignorance, the workers would need help in recognizing their true interests. Providing this help was to be the task of the socialist parties, which would educate the masses and take the lead in preparing for the revolution. The people had to be taught that government, law, religion, and traditional standards of morality were all bourgeois creations meant to deceive and subjugate them. The workers had to learn to see through such artifices, to identify themselves with their class and realize that efforts to

Karl Marx and his wife Jenny von Westphalen, the daughter of a Prussian government official, photographed about 1860. *The advocate of violent revolution, a brutal and vicious polemicist, overbearing and offensive in dealing with opponents or persons who presumed to disagree with him, Marx was at the same time a devoted husband and father, and, despite all his contempt and loathing for the bourgeoisie, appears to have lived the life of a model bourgeois family man. His daughter Eleanor described him as "the cheeriest, gayest soul that ever breathed . . . the kindliest, gentlest, most sympathetic of companions."*

improve their status within the capitalist system were a betrayal of class interests, that petty gains in wages or working conditions achieved through trade unions or government legislation were actually harmful. Such minor benefits only delayed the revolution, which alone could give them their just share of worldly goods. The workers had to be welded into a disciplined fighting force to wage continuous class war until the final revolution had been won.

Marx's basic error was his failure to appreciate the importance of noneconomic forces in society: religion, emotion, prestige, genius, stupidity, and such factors as climate and geography. His economic theories themselves were based on antiquated conceptions of a static economy. The theory of surplus value did not take sufficient account of the importance of capitalist equipment, administrative ability, initiative, and the willingness to take risks. The capitalist-industrial revolution, far from pressing more and more people into proletarian poverty, increased production to such an extent that it improved the general standard of living of all men; indeed, in the most highly industrialized countries the proletarian class is rapidly disappearing. The great revolutions inspired by Marxist doctrines have taken place not in industrial societies, where Marx expected them to occur, but in societies still overwhelmingly agricultural, beset by very real economic hardships. In all the revolutions inspired by Marxism, the state has played a dominant role in the reorganization of society, but nowhere is there any sign of its withering away.

Like many intellectuals, Marx misjudged the responses of the working class. Socialist parties were to find it difficult to keep workers in a constant state of belligerent excitement. Moreover, there was a fundamental contradiction between Marx's theory of the inevitability of revolution and his appeal to the workers to get ready for it. If revolution was inevitable, why was there so much need for preparation?

The fallacies and contradictions in Marx's theories, the obvious incorrectness of his prophecies, the perversion of Marxist doctrine in modern Russia and China, should not blind us to the fact that his ideas are among the most significant ever produced by the human mind. His economic interpretation of history, although by no means original, was presented with such cogency and such a wealth of supporting evidence that it has compelled a recognition of the role of the economy in every aspect of human affairs. The economy may not be generally accepted as the basic motivating force in society, but its importance can no longer be ignored even by the most violent anti-Marxist. His theory of the class struggle, too, has provided valuable new insights for the study of history and society, and has led to important reinterpretations of past events and present problems. His call to revolution and his definition of the role of socialist parties has supplied a rationale and a dynamism for insurgent parties in every part of the world.

Marx was more than a political or economic theorist. He was a prophet, and in a very real sense, the founder of a faith. His prediction of the coming revolutionary holocaust from which a new and perfect society would emerge was not political theory; it was political theology, with the allure of a religion. But Marxism did not depend on faith alone. With its scientific apparatus it appealed to would-be rationalists; with its promise of social justice it appealed to humanitarians; with its call to revolution it appealed to that important segment of society formed by the discontented and the maladjusted, who looked to revolution to provide scope for their energies. Marxism, with all its fallacies and inconsistencies, has qualities that have gripped the hearts and minds of men of every race and nationality; like nationalism, it remains one of the most potent revolutionary forces in the modern world.

Nationalism

Great as was the enduring strength of traditional values, the new appeal of science and the various forms of liberalism and socialism, there can be no doubt that the most pervasive and dynamic ideological force in nine-teenth-century Europe was nationalism. On the basis of the national principle Germany and Italy were unified; the independence of Hungary was recognized within a new Austro-Hungarian empire; Serbia, Monte-negro, and Rumania were conceded complete independence from Turkish rule. In areas where the national principle did not win recognition, it became one of the most disruptive forces in domestic and international politics.

There was nothing inevitable about the triumph of the new nation-states. Germany, for instance, might have remained divided as a result of the effective operation of the international balance of power—that is, France and Russia might have joined forces to prevent the establishment of a new great power directly on their borders. Or Germany might have been united under Austria, in which case the entire Austrian empire, with all its national minorities, might have survived. Today Germany is again divided, and there is little prospect of its reunification. Russia has extended its imperial dominion over most of the national minorities once governed by Austria, and has ruthlessly suppressed national uprisings in the areas under its control.

Nor is there anything inevitable about nationalism itself. People are not born with feelings of national self-consciousness. The desire to be part of a community, and a sense of loyalty to that community, appear to be natural human characteristics; but the object of that loyalty has varied widely from age to age and from country to country, and has taken the form of tribes and clans, of city-states, kingdoms, and empires. The nation, far from being the fundamental and unique component of human society according to a system of divine or natural law, as it was represented by propagandists of nationalism in the nineteenth century, is simply one of many forms of social organization.

During the early development of national feeling in a particular society, national self-consciousness is generally restricted to a minority of the educated and the politically aware. This was the situation in Germany and Italy in the early nineteenth century, and a similar situation has existed in the developing countries of Asia and Africa in more recent times. The majority is only gradually imbued with a spirit of nationalism.

In countries where nationalities lived under foreign rule, national senti-ment was nourished by resentment of foreign political repression or economic exploitation. It is more difficult to explain how nationalism became a mass movement in every other part of Europe by the end of the nineteenth century. Clearly the convulsive economic and social up-heavals of the era had something to do with it. The mass migration of Europeans from the countryside to the cities meant a severance of ancient ties with parish and manor, with familiar modes of thought and

The changing nationalist style in public monuments. *The transition from the cultural nationalism which prevailed in the first part of the nineteenth century to a political and militant nationalism can be seen in the contrast between the monument erected in honor of Goethe and Schiller in Weimar in 1857, when the majority of public monuments in Germany still celebrated Germany's cultural heroes, and the grotesque monument to Bismarck in Hamburg of 1891.*

conduct, and a corresponding loss of emotional and psychological security. These displaced persons were searching for new ties and loyalties, a new sense of identity and community, and many appear to have found their needs fulfilled in nationalism.

Old loyalties died hard, however, as the continuing vitality of the Christian churches demonstrated, and throughout Europe many members of the population adhered with stubborn tenacity to traditional forms of government and society, to local or regional authorities and customs. In addition there was the competition of other intellectual and ideological forces such as science and socialism. To overcome resistance to the nationalist ethic and instill a proper sense of loyalty in their citizens, national governments, especially those of new national states where old loyalties remained particularly strong, resorted to deliberate and intensive programs of indoctrination through state-controlled systems of education, compulsory military service, manipulation of the press, and all other powers at the disposal of the modern state. In countries where a nationality did not control the government, as in Ireland and many parts of Austria-

Hungary, nationalist indoctrination was carried out by national revolutionary associations or cultural societies. In either case, indoctrination appears to have played a major role in conveying the spirit of nationalism to the masses.

An important part of the process of nationalist indoctrination was the formulation of theories proving that members of a nation sprang from the same racial background and shared the same cultural and historical traditions, the same national tragedies but also the same national triumphs. It was no accident that the nineteenth century witnessed a great increase in the study of history, with emphasis on the national origins and development of the European peoples, together with a new and intensive interest in national folklore, myths, and music. In Germany, for example, the brothers Jacob and Wilhelm Grimm (1785–1863; 1786–1859) collected old and almost forgotten folk tales, and Richard Wagner (1813–1883) based his music dramas on Teutonic legends. "In eastern and central Europe," Hans Kohn, a distinguished student of nationalism, has written, "it was the poet, the philologist, and the historian who created the nationalities."

In the course of the nineteenth century, the cultural nationalism represented by Johann Gottfried von Herder (1744–1803) and his followers, which held that each people has a unique folk spirit worthy of preservation, gave way to political nationalism, the belief that to maintain national values effectively each nation must establish itself as a sovereign state. At the same time the liberal nationalism of political idealists, who saw in the nation-state a means of achieving constitutional representative government that would ensure liberty and justice for all citizens, gave way to a more arrogant and bigoted nationalism, a belief in the superiority of one nation over another in which racism played a prominent part. Advocates of this view were increasingly willing to sacrifice the rule of law and the protection of individual rights to the greater power and glory of the national state.

The extraordinary feeling of satisfaction that some people seem to derive from the belief that they are members of a superior nation or race is undoubtedly one of the great appeals of modern nationalism. Another and perhaps even greater appeal is the concomitant belief that this superior nation was chosen by God or fate to fulfill a unique and particularly exalted mission in the world. This conception of a national mission meets a human requirement which may be even more basic than a sense of identity and belonging: the need to feel part of a cause greater and more noble than self, a cause worthy of sacrifice, dedication, and commitment. This messianic quality of nationalism was eloquently expressed by the great Italian nationalist prophet Giuseppe Mazzini (1805–1872). "Nationality," he said, "is the role assigned by God to each people in the work of humanity, the mission and task which it ought to fulfill on earth so that the divine purpose may be realized in this world."

VOICES OF PROTEST: NIETZSCHE

In every age there are independent spirits who react against the dominant political or intellectual currents of their time. Since the late eighteenth century, many artists and writers, imbued with the spirit of romanticism, had considered it almost obligatory to assume a pose of protest against society. By the last decades of the nineteenth century, however, the belief in the necessity of protest had become deadly serious. Mass production, mass education, and mass ideologies all seemed designed to crush human individuality and the creative spirit, to reduce European culture to the lowest common denominator of mass taste. In various ways anarchists and artists, philosophers and poets, expressed their hatred for the contemporary world, but none did so more passionately or eloquently than the German philosopher Friedrich Nietzsche.

Nietzsche (1844–1900) was actually no more representative of his age than are rebels at any time, but in his case the society he loathed committed the ultimate crime against a thinker, the perversion and distortion of his ideas. This was largely the work of his sister, who gained custody of his papers after his insanity and death, and falsified his unpublished manuscripts to make him appear as a spokesman for German nationalism and racism. Not until after the death in 1935 of Elisabeth Förster-Nietzsche did reliable scholars gain access to these papers, and since then a new and very different picture of Nietzsche has emerged.

Far from being an apostle of Nordic superiority and racism, Nietzsche denounced German nationalism and race hatred as "a scabies of the heart and blood poisoning." He refused to share "the utterly false racial self-admiration and perversion which today displays itself in Germany," an attitude he deemed doubly worthy of scorn in a people with a sense of history. The new German national state, he predicted, would annihilate the German spirit. Obsessed with a sense of power, the Germans would soon surrender what was left of their culture to prophets of national greatness, a contemptible and self-destructive ideal.

At the same time, Nietzsche was not in sympathy with the prevailing intellectual climate in Europe: the mediocrity, hypocrisy, complacent smugness, and superficiality that seemed to permeate society. The scholars involved in myopic literary criticism or in investigating the minutiae of the past, the scientists with their sensational discoveries about the natural world—none seemed to be concerned with universal, timeless questions. What did their discoveries amount to? What were they trying to achieve?

Nietzsche, photographed by Hans Olde in 1899, one year before his death. *Nietzsche had suffered from ill health throughout his life and, in 1889, suffered a mental breakdown. He never recovered.*

What, above all, were their values?

The search for values—this, in Nietzsche's opinion, should be the fundamental and permanent concern of thoughtful men; for values cannot be defined once and for all, but must be submitted to constant reexamination. Not to those who have the courage of their convictions should honor be paid, but to those who have the courage to question their own convictions.

Nietzsche's own supreme value was culture and the creation of culture. His famous Superman was no crude German racist or conqueror, but the creative spirit: the artist, philosopher, or statesman whose genius lifted him above the common level of mankind, and whose thoughts and works infused life with new beauty and meaning. Michelangelo, Goethe, Beethoven, Caesar—these were Nietzsche's Supermen.

Nietzsche made his own contribution to culture by propounding a theory of human behavior in many ways more profound than the ideas of either Marx or Freud. Not economics or sex is the basic drive in man, Nietzsche said, but the Will to Power, an urge to which all other human instincts are subordinate. This Will to Power is also the basic ingredient in human creativity, and it is the strength of that quality in the Superman that distinguishes him from other human beings. The person without strong will, without passionate feelings and impulses, can no more create the beautiful than a castrated man can beget children. Nietzsche did not eulogize power for its own sake. The supreme evidence of man's possession of power is his ability to control it, to direct his impulses into creative channels, to "sublimate" his energies. "It is the weak characters without power over themselves who hate the constraint of style . . . and who find it necessary to interpret themselves and their environment as *free* nature— wild, arbitrary, fantastic, disorderly, astonishing." The truly creative spirit will override old traditions, he will break laws of style and composition, as Beethoven and Michelangelo broke laws, but he will feel compelled to create and submit to new laws, new forms. "It will be the strong and domineering natures who find their greatest satisfaction in such compulsion, in such restraint and perfection under laws of their own."

Nietzsche felt nothing but contempt for contemporary optimists who regarded evolution as progress and believed in the ultimate perfectibility of mankind. Had the worth of man increased? Had beauty progressed? Had aesthetic values advanced to a higher plane? What could another ten or twenty centuries bring that could be interpreted as progress over the life and works of Socrates and Jesus, Shakespeare and Goethe? In them and through them the events of history had been "intensified into symbols." History itself was not a progression but a timeless allegory, with the great problems of history its unchanging themes.

THE ARTS

Subsequent events have shown that Nietzsche's pessimism about progress and human perfectibility was justified, but as he demonstrated through his own example, the political and intellectual climate of the later nineteenth century did not halt the flow of human creativity. Artists might be alienated from society, or subjected to censorship and ridicule, but both the quantity and the quality of the cultural production of the period were impressive.

Not to be forgotten are the revolutionary discoveries in science and technology, themselves significant products of the human spirit, which made the greatest contribution in history toward raising the standard of living of the European masses. If a civilization is judged by the number of people sharing its benefits, that of nineteenth-century Europe may well have been the greatest the world had so far produced, for never before had so large a proportion of the population been able to enjoy the material and cultural advantages of their age. This was the unique contribution of the civilization of industrialism.

Popular and Official Art

The industrial civilization had other effects, however. In the later nineteenth century a distinct cleavage took place between popular art and what can only be called art-for-art's-sake. Mass production for the first time created a mass market, and, perhaps inevitably, it catered to the mass taste. Mass taste itself, however, certainly in the urban centers of industrial society, was formed to a large extent by the mass producers, by the merchandise they popularized through advertising and offered for sale in the marketplace. The producers for their part, most of them without strongly developed aesthetic judgments of their own, took their lead from the styles endorsed by government schools and academies of art, and from the shops patronized by the wealthy aristocracy, which still set the tone for fashion in most European countries. It is therefore hardly surprising that popular taste corresponded far more closely to what might be called official taste than to any other standard, and that mass-produced articles, household decorations, furniture, and Sunday apparel, should have been cheap, perhaps vulgarized, but nevertheless easily recognizable imitations of similar articles available in shops of highest fashion. This popularization of official art was facilitated by the fact that official taste in the later nineteenth century, although it had rarely been more eclectic, was by and large traditional and safe. The governments which sponsored and the wealthy patrons who purchased works of art demanded art that could be immediately recognized as such, that showed skill in execution

"Abandoned," by the Danish artist Carl Carlsen, a painting which tells a story with moral overtones. *Executed with the craftsmanship and technical skill demanded of painters who aspired to popular success, this picture also illustrates the popular taste in interior decorations of the mid-nineteenth century.*

and polish in technique. They, and the general public with them, generally ignored, ridiculed, or actually persecuted artists whose work did not correspond with accepted standards and expectations, which disturbed or shocked sensibilities by its style or subject matter.

Among the affluent of all classes (not only the despised *nouveaux riches* and the bourgeoisie) there was an unabashed desire for opulence and ostentation. Architecture, perhaps the best mirror of the taste of a period, produced elaborate imitations of Gothic castles and Chinese pagodas, Swiss chalets and Greek temples. Interior decoration matched the flourishes of architecture. Bright mosaics and stained-glass windows, copies of ancient masterpieces of sculpture and painting, graced the walls and vestibules of public and private buildings. Furniture, of wood or iron, was elaborately decorated and well upholstered; frills and flounces dangled from beds and sofas, lamps and chandeliers. Stuffed birds and animals, pastorals in porcelain, and potted palms and ostrich plumes filled corners and covered tables, against a background of intricately patterned shawls and oriental rugs.

Taste in painting was modified by critical theories that art should be not only decorative but morally uplifting, a criterion given considerable authority by the influential critic John Ruskin (1819–1900), who maintained that the more a work of art elevated the spirit the greater was its artistic merit. So it was that traditional academic or salon pictures of the birth of Venus or Diana surprised in her bath were challenged for critical favor by scenes of Christian martyrs in the arena or classical heroines defending their virtue, which permitted equally generous displays of female nudity while contributing to spiritual edification. Moral uplift was also supplied by a large school of nationalist painters, who provided patriots with pictures of stirring scenes from their country's history and portraits of national leaders in heroic poses. The most popular pictures of the era were those that told a story—"The Gambler's Wife," "The Soldier's Farewell," or "Waiting for the Doctor." Reproduced by the thousands in formats ranging widely in price, pictures such as these as well as copies of old masters could be found on the walls of the homes of people of every class.

In the creation of popular taste, no influence was greater than newspapers and magazines, which achieved a mass circulation with the invention of mass-printing techniques, the elimination of taxes on paper and published materials in most European countries, and the introduction of systems of compulsory education which created a mass reading public. The cheap morning and evening newspapers specialized in crime, gossip, and sports. Easy to read and increasingly sensational in style and make-up, they added a sense of drama and excitement to the drab daily lives of their readers, but they also catered to and exploited popular passions and prejudices. More than any single force, the popular press stirred up and kept alive the spirit of strident nationalism that characterized the later nineteenth century and aroused the interest of the masses in imperialism.

Almost all of the greatest novels of the age were first published in serialized form in popular journals—there were occasions when large crowds assembled on the docks of New York waiting for the latest installment of the newest novel by Dickens—but popular literature on the whole was far below Dickensian standards. Most of it was frankly escapist and featured tales of romance and adventure in which the typical heroine was chaste and weak, the typical hero strong and virile. Virile though he might be, the hero and all other "good" characters in these popular tales were expected to behave in accordance with the highest moral principles, for literature too was supposed to be morally uplifting. Victorian readers as well as viewers liked to have their imaginations titillated, however, and books with titles such as *The Loves of a Harem* and *The Seamstress, or the White Slave of England* made G. W. M. Reynolds (1814–1879) the best-selling author of his day.

It has long been customary to ridicule the popular art of the Victorian era for its vulgar ostentation, its sentimentality and moralizing. A distinguished critic has called it a "nadir in taste"—a bold judgment in view of the amount of competition for that distinction and the marked shifts in aesthetic standards that have taken place over the centuries. Much of this popular art was executed with great technical skill, and almost all of it is imbued with a lively gusto and unselfconscious exuberance which reflects the general optimism of the age. Aesthetic judgments aside, however, this popular art represents for the historian invaluable material for establishing contact with another age. The best-selling novel, the widely circulated journal or art reproduction, may provide a far more accurate reflection of contemporary attitudes and opinions than works of art that appeal to later or more educated tastes.

Often overlooked when considering the aesthetic contributions of late nineteenth-century Europe are products of human creativity whose primary purpose was functional rather than artistic. Many of the technological innovations of the era—steam and turbine engines, machine tools, optical equipment—reveal such creative imagination and were built with such craftsmanship and sense of design that they cannot be denied consideration as works of art. The outstanding architectural achievements of the age were not the pseudo-classic or Gothic productions of professional architects, but railway bridges and viaducts. Although these structures too were often overloaded with ornamentation, many of them were miracles of engineering and in their use of concrete and iron indicated the architectural possibilities available with these materials. Considering the physical obstacles that had to be overcome and the sheer size of many of these

Brunel, Clifton Suspension Bridge, Bristol.

structures, they are in many ways even more impressive than the much admired aqueducts of the ancient Romans.

The strength of iron and concrete made possible an entirely new type of construction without the massive struts and supports which had been needed heretofore. The Clifton suspension bridge at Bristol in England, completed in 1864 but designed many years earlier by an extraordinary engineer-entrepreneur named Isambard Kingdom Brunel (1806–1859), lies across the Avon valley in a single span of 705 feet. It is an unprecedented achievement, an architecture without weight, and in its simplicity of design and the graceful nobility of its lines deserves to be ranked among the most beautiful structures in the world. The Crystal Palace, built in London in 1851 to house the first great international exhibition of art and industry, was also not designed by a professional architect but by a builder of greenhouses, Joseph Paxton (1801–1865). An immense vaulted building, longer than the royal palace at Versailles, it was constructed entirely of prefabricated sections of iron and glass and in its method of construction was a landmark in the history of architecture. Equally innovative was the famous Eiffel tower, designed by the engineer Gustave Eiffel (1832–1923) for the Paris international exhibition of 1889; it was built entirely of iron and remained the tallest building in the world until after the First World War.

Even in the case of works more generally recognized as "art," however, much of the art that was popular in the later nineteenth century—for example, the novels of Charles Dickens (1812–1870) and the music of

Giuseppe Verdi (1813–1901)—possessed from the beginning, and still retains, a universal appeal. Dickens and Verdi are representative of the large number of outstanding novelists, poets, and other artists whose work did not mark a sharp break with the past but carried on and developed some of the best traditions of an earlier age.

Nevertheless, many nineteenth-century artists whose works have stood the test of time remained outside the mainstream of popular culture—not necessarily because they were in revolt against society, although this was often the case, but because they followed their own artistic bent without regard to popular taste. The production of this group of nineteenth-century artists was distinguished by the desire of its creators to experiment, to discover new techniques and forms of expression, to explore new dimensions of human experience. In this respect the innovative artists of this era were akin to the scientists and inventors, who must after all be regarded as artists in their own right.

The innovative artists were in fact profoundly influenced by science, and attempted to apply what they believed to be the methods and theories of science in their own fields of endeavor. The impact of science was most obvious on those artists who looked upon themselves as realists, and who believed that the essential quality of scientific method was the accumulation, examination, and analysis of facts without preconceptions or illusions. The aim of art, according to a defender of the realist point of view writing in 1863, should be "to examine with scientific precision the quality of life and nature in all its phases and at all levels."

Literature: Realism and Symbolism

The principal vehicle for realism in literature was the novel, which surpassed drama and poetry as the favorite form of literary expression in the course of the nineteenth century. As mentioned earlier, there was nothing particularly original about literary realism, which was part of a long European tradition going back to the age of Chaucer and beyond. Few novelists have been more realistic than the incomparable Jane Austen (1775–1817) or the great French writers Stendhal (1783–1842) or Honoré de Balzac (1799–1850), who wrote during the heyday of romanticism. Indeed, the only novelty in the work of the latter-day realists was their scientific emphasis. The novel, according to contemporary literary theorists, had now assumed "the methods and duties of science," and was therefore entitled to "the liberties and frankness of science."

The writer who took these claims and duties most seriously was the French novelist Émile Zola (1840–1902), who attempted a scientific analysis of society in a multivolume chronicle which he subtitled *A Natural and Social History of a Family under the Second Empire*. A firm believer in the positivist theory that human mental as well as physical qualities

The novelist Émile Zola, painted by his friend Édouard Manet in 1868. *Note in the background a reproduction of Manet's notorious "Olympia" (see p. 60); a copy of a painting by the great Spanish realist Velázquez; and a Japanese screen and print. Japanese prints, with their vivid colors and novel approaches to realism, exerted a profound influence on European artists of this time.*

were governed by natural laws, Zola sought to demonstrate through remorselessly detailed observations how human conduct was determined by physiological and biological principles. The writer, he said, was like a surgeon or chemist, able impartially to dissect or establish laws of cause and effect in the human organism. Fortunately for his art, Zola was unable to maintain a consistent attitude of scientific detachment. He was in fact a moralist with a highly developed social consciousness, and when his thoroughly unscientific passions were aroused he revealed the greatness of his talents in searing descriptions of the miseries of the human condition. But Zola was not a confirmed pessimist. Believing as he did that human nature was a purely physiological phenomenon, he also believed that its ills could be cured by physiological means and that when science discovered how this could be done, human nature might be perfected.

A far more disciplined writer than Zola was his compatriot Gustave Flaubert (1821–1880), whose reputation as a novelist of realism rests largely on one book, *Madame Bovary* (1857). It is the story of an adulterous wife of a provincial doctor whose romantic imagination leads her into dreary love affairs and eventual suicide. The book caused a scandal when it was first published, not so much because of its subject matter, which had been dealt with often enough in French literature, but because the author refused to pass moral judgments on his characters. "The author in his work must be like God in the universe," Flaubert said, "present everywhere and visible nowhere." In fact there are few authors more visible than Flaubert, who believed that the obligations of a writer were not fulfilled merely by compiling a record of his observations, no matter how accurate or detailed. These observations had to be analyzed and distilled through the genius of the writer if they were to emerge as a work of art—or even as meaningful realism. Less concerned with scientific theories of human behavior than Zola, Flaubert aspired to achieve a style "as precise as the language of science."

The nineteenth-century obsession with science inevitably provoked a reaction, which was nowhere expressed more forcefully than in the works of the great Russian novelist Fëdor Dostoevsky (1821–1881). In his youth a revolutionary, Dostoevsky developed into an extreme conservative and national chauvinist. He believed it was Russia's destiny "to reconcile the European contradictions" by uniting the nations of Europe under Russian dominion, and the duty of the Orthodox church to lead the peoples of the world into the paths of righteousness. Like Nietzsche, Dostoevsky had nothing but contempt for the mindless optimism of his age, the general confidence in human reason, and the naive faith of reformers in the essential goodness and ultimate perfectibility of man. The central theme of his greatest novels—*Crime and Punishment, The Brothers Karamazov, The Possessed*—is that man is neither good nor reasonable but evil, and that his sinful nature is only kept in check by belief in the principles of Christianity and fear of retribution in an afterlife; whenever he abandons these principles and allows himself to be guided by his reason, man turns into a monster. "It is clear," he said, "that evil is buried more deeply in humanity than the cure-all socialists think, . . . that the laws that govern man's spirit are still so unknown, so uncertain, and so mysterious that there are not and cannot be any physicians or even judges to give us a definitive cure or decision, but that there is only He who says: 'Vengeance is mine, I will repay.' "

In his novels Dostoevsky employed all the resources of realism, and so prodigious were his talents that he must be ranked among the greatest masters of the realistic novel. But in exploring the inner motivations of man he rejected what he regarded as the facile explanations of scientific determinism and human reasonableness. Instead, Dostoevsky emphasized the subconscious and the irrational, including that supreme irrationality which springs from an arrogant confidence in human reason. With his relentless probing into the lower depths of human nature, he led the way to new psychological insights in literature and, ironically, established himself as a pioneer in what was soon to become another science for the study of human behavior.

A fragment of a manuscript page from Dostoevsky's novel *The Possessed*, with a cartoon-sketch self-portrait at the center. *The handwriting and doodles are in many ways as revealing of the intensity and self-doubts of the author as are his published texts.*

Some of the most innovative literature of the later nineteenth century was produced by a group of writers who rejected not only science but realism as well. They employed a wide variety of new techniques and forms of literary expression, and created a literary movement which came to be known as symbolism.

The symbolist movement drew its immediate inspiration from the poet Charles Baudelaire (1821–1867). Like Dostoevsky, Baudelaire attempted to delve into the inmost nature of man, where he too found evil and depravity. In Baudelaire's case, however, it was not his psychological insights which proved most influential, but his poetic craftsmanship and use of imagery. Man is surrounded by a forest of familiar symbols, he said, whose perfumes, colors, and sounds correspond with and are reflected in each other, and could therefore be regarded as multiple symbols of a single reality. The symbolic relationships suggested by Baudelaire, and the possibilities they offered of representing not only colors and sounds but sensations, emotions, and ideas through symbols provided the theoretical basis of the symbolist movement. The symbolists were also strongly influenced by the theories of the composer Richard Wagner (1813–1883), in particular his concept of the *Gesamtkunstwerk*—the universal or all-embracing work of art, which should combine music, poetry, drama, the visual arts, and visible action in a single supreme art form.

The principal figure of the symbolist movement, its greatest poet and major theoretician, was Stéphane Mallarmé (1842–1898), who in his youth had suffered a crisis of faith "before the terrible light of science," but who had discovered a new and enduring faith in "Beauty . . . and its one perfect expression, Poetry." Mallarmé distinguished among the various functions of language, and rejected narration, description, and instruction as suitable tasks for poetry. "It is not description which can unveil the purpose and beauty of monuments, seas, or the human visage in all their depth and quality," he said, "but rather evocation, allusion, suggestion."

The concept of literary expression through images and symbols found adherents in every part of Europe. In their search for methods of conveying thought and emotions, the symbolist poets began to find radically different ways of using not only words but rhythms, rhymes, punctuation, the position of the words on the page, and the very material on which the poems were reproduced. New techniques in poetry passed almost simultaneously into prose, with the result that the self-conscious use of imagery and symbols became part of the equipment of every creative writer.

Painting: Realism and Impressionism

Similar experimentation and innovation took place in the field of painting, which was also strongly influenced by scientific theories and methods. As in literature, many of the most gifted and original artists of the era took the route of realism in their search for truth.

The greatest and certainly the most flamboyant realist painter in the mid-nineteenth century was Gustave Courbet (1819–1877), who combined a powerful artistic intelligence and a superb sense of color and form with passion and energy. His work was very uneven, but at his best he was capable of producing masterpieces in almost any form of pictorial representation—portraits, nude figures, landscapes, and monumental compositions. In 1861 he opened a studio which attracted a large group of students and sympathizers and made him the center of a realist school of painting.

Courbet's realism has been called a revolution in art, "a decisive break with all established standards, in theory and practice," but such claims correspond rather better with Courbet's own far from modest evaluation of his contribution to art than to his true position in art history. In many ways Courbet was a very traditional painter; he drew heavily on the example and methodology of the great masters of the past, and his realism was not so much a revolution as a part of the great tradition of European genre painting. His realism itself was far from objective, but, like that of Zola, was fired by social consciousness and concern for the poor and

Courbet's painting "The Stonebreakers" (1849). *A notable example of this artist's realism, the painting was at the same time a monument and tribute to the wretched of the earth and something of a landmark in changing the popular conception of laboring men and women from "people" to "The People."*

oppressed. A picture such as "The Stonebreakers" (1849), although certainly realistic, is at the same time a poetic celebration of the working man and evokes a sympathy for the wretchedness of his condition which the artist, an ardent socialist, obviously intended.

More detached and original in his conception of pictorial realism was Courbet's compatriot Édouard Manet (1832–1882). Manet, too, was much influenced by the old masters, and his notorious picture "Olympia" (1863) seems at first sight a parody of the innumerable reclining goddesses to be found in the Louvre. It shows a female nude sitting up in bed in a pose that recalls Titian's Venus of Urbino, but instead of an idealized Olympian deity, Manet has portrayed a commonplace and somewhat vulgar young woman who might be anyone's wife or mistress and who looks at the viewer with a totally unconcerned and matter-of-fact air; beside her is a black servant bringing flowers, presumably from an admirer; a black cat sits at the foot of the bed, its dirty paw marks clearly visible on the sheet. Manet, however, did not mean his picture to be a parody, nor did he intend it to shock, as Courbet so delighted in doing. The "Olympia" was simply a study in contrast in the use of blacks and whites, an

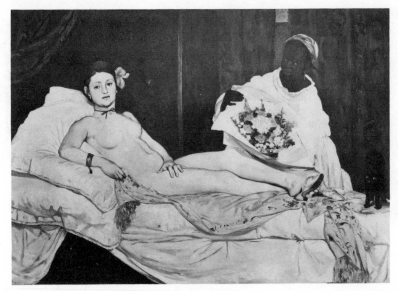

Manet's "Olympia" (1863). *Contemporary viewers were profoundly shocked, or pretended to be, by this realistic representation of a naked woman who was not disguised in the conventional manner as a classical goddess or allegorical figure.*

exercise in new painting techniques with which Manet was experimenting, and the female figure was no more than that: a figure, a scenic rather than a humanistic fact. Manet, a well-to-do and somewhat conservative bourgeois, was astonished by the storm of outrage his picture provoked among the moral citizens of the Second Empire—"a deliberate manifestation of inconceivable vulgarity," one critic called it. By the standards of the time, the outrage is understandable. Manet's picture was not decorative drawing room art; it conveyed no lesson in morality, much less a sense of moral uplift; it did not even reveal a social consciousness. It was simply realistic, and the shock of recognition was obviously a very great shock indeed.

Toward the end of the 1860's, Manet became the center of a circle of painters who were later labeled "impressionists," although their aims were so diverse as to render any general stylistic category meaningless. Influenced by scientific theories of color and light (which they misunderstood), the impressionists developed what they believed to be a "scientific" palette. They used primary colors without mixing their pigments, and they created the effect of blending by the juxtaposition of complementary colors on the canvas itself. To capture the fleeting "impression," the mood of the moment, they painted with great speed, using short choppy strokes to reproduce texture and the vibrating quality of light. Claude Monet (1840–1926), one of the few great impressionists who continued to paint in this style all his life, insisted that in order to record the true quality of light it was necessary to abandon the studio and paint out of doors, a procedure facilitated by the technical innovation of packaging colors in tubes. He persuaded a skeptical Manet to follow his example, and by the 1870's painting in the open air had become an article of faith for most members of the impressionist circle.

The impressionist painters were reviled by academicians as unskilled botchers, indeed as enemies of society, but a few perceptive critics understood what they were attempting to do (that they were, in fact, in pursuit of a different and perhaps truer form of reality), and appreciated the extraordinary beauty of their work. Over the years this appreciation has gradually been communicated to the majority of art lovers.

The greatest of the impressionists did not remain content with the results achieved through the rapid application of pigments and a relative disregard of line and contour. Auguste Renoir (1841–1919), while retaining the luminosity achieved through new color techniques, developed a purity of line and an emphasis on form that amounted to a return to classical ideas. Paul Cézanne (1839–1906), who had always paid great attention to form as well as color, began to see these as the essential qualities in all painting and to eliminate detail that distracted attention from architectonic and coloristic effects. His aim was not to record superficial pictorial truth, but to portray the fundamental structure behind the fleeting scenes the eye took in, and he resorted to deliberate distortion to achieve the effects he was seeking. Some of his followers, pressing his ideas further, concentrated on form and color alone and abandoned all pretense of objective representation. It was Cézanne, not Courbet, who was the true revolutionary in the history of modern painting, for it was he who demonstrated the immense range of artistic possibilities that lay beyond realism.

Georges Seurat (1859–1891), following another line of development, applied scientific theories of light and color in a far more doctrinaire and systematic way than the impressionists had done. Instead of working rapidly, he painstakingly placed his colors on the canvas in tiny dots which were supposed to blend in the eye of the viewer when seen from a distance. This method is generally known as pointillism, although Seurat himself did not call it that, and it represented another serious misunderstanding of scientific theories. The effects Seurat produced were nevertheless extraordinarily impressive; his austere and severely disciplined paintings convey an atmosphere of quiet and stability, and his simplification of form was even more radical than Cézanne's. "They see poetry in what

"The Large Bathers" (1898–1905). *This painting by Cézanne illustrates the artist's abandonment of literal pictorial realism in order to concentrate on what he considered fundamental shapes, forms, and colors. Philadelphia Museum of Art.*

I have done," he said, referring to the comments of one of the few contemporary critics who praised his works. "No. I apply my method, and that is all there is to it."

A complete contrast to Seurat was the brilliant and tragic Vincent van Gogh (1853–1900). There was nothing scientific about him. He used painting to express his inmost feelings, and like Cézanne he departed from "correct" drawing to obtain the effects he desired. "Instead of trying to reproduce exactly what I have before my eyes," he wrote, "I use color more arbitrarily so as to express myself more forcibly." Although almost totally ignored in his lifetime, van Gogh became a major influence on painters who shared his views about art as an expression of emotion, and his theories have been a principal source of inspiration for a school of painting known as expressionism.

Music: Romanticism and Nationalism

In contrast to the other arts, music did not break out of the romantic mold during the later nineteenth century. In music too, however, there was experimentation and innovation, most notably in the employment of new harmonic structures and rhythmic techniques to give music greater color and intensity, especially in compositions for the orchestra. New instruments were added to the orchestra, older instruments were redesigned to make them more sonorous and flexible, and different combinations of instruments were used to create new orchestral sonorities. Symptomatic of the interest in new color and tonal effects was the appearance in 1844 of a textbook on the subject, *Treatise on Instrumentation and Orchestration* by Hector Berlioz (1803–1869), himself one of the most original and imaginative composers of the era and one of the greatest masters of orchestration in the history of music.

Music is frequently described as the most ethereal, unworldly, and "pure" of all the arts, but it is only necessary to recall a rousing military march or a love song to realize that this concept is absurd. None of the arts, in fact, can match the power of music to stir the emotions, and throughout the ages it has been used for this purpose, often in a very mundane cause. In the nineteenth century music was harnessed to the cause of nationalism, and played a role whose importance can probably never be accurately assessed in stirring up nationalist feeling and creating a national self-consciousness. Patriotic songs and anthems, most of them written in the nineteenth century, were given a prominent place in national collections of "folk" songs of the era, and singing them became a ritual at most public gatherings (rising to sing the national anthem, for example) and in state schools, where they often replaced Christian hymns.

Hector Berlioz in his mid-fifties when he was writing his great opera *The Trojans*.

Among nationalities living under foreign rule, national songs were used as vehicles to keep alive (or awaken) national sentiment and were important instruments in all national revolutionary movements.

Nationalism also had a profound effect on more formal types of musical composition. Everywhere in Europe there were serious composers who consciously set out to write "national" music which should be free from foreign influences and express the unique genius of their people. Surprisingly, in view of the banality of most of the painting or literature produced in the national cause, nationalism inspired some of the finest music of the nineteenth century.

The greatest Italian composer of the century, Giuseppe Verdi, was an ardent nationalist, whose early operas, written while Italy was still divided and partly under Austrian rule, are filled with moving expressions of love of country and longing for freedom from foreign oppression. Throughout his life Verdi maintained a resolute independence in his musical style and deplored the influence of foreign, especially German, ideas on the work of his compatriots. In Germany, Richard Wagner deliberately turned away from classical and foreign themes and based the majority of his operas on Germanic legends. His delightful opera *Die Meistersinger von Nürnberg* is a eulogy to medieval Germany when it was still free from foreign influences, and closes with a paean of praise to German art.

Verdi and Wagner, for all their nationalism, were both working within a powerful national musical tradition and did not have to look elsewhere for national musical forms. In countries where the national musical tradition seemed to be overwhelmed by foreign influences, national composers sought musical inspiration in the harmonies and rhythms of their national folk or religious music, and in their national language. These composers, however, were for the most part trained in traditional methods of composition and they generally transformed folk melodies to accord with formal rules of composition. As a result their works were rarely so original in a "national" sense as they might have wished, but remained part of the mainstream of European music.

Some of the most distinctive national music of the nineteenth century was written by Russian composers, and among these the outstanding figure was Modest Mussorgsky (1839–1881). A clerk in the Russian civil service and without a formal musical education, Mussorgsky laboriously worked out his themes and harmonies on the piano. He found inspiration in the modalities, the nonmetrical chants, of Russian liturgical music and in the many-voiced harmonies of Russian folk songs, which differed markedly from the contemporary music of western Europe; in his own compositions for voice he tried to fit his music to the quality of the Russian language. Instead of developing his themes to reach a musical climax, as was the custom in western Europe, he created his effects through repetition and the gradual accumulation of impressions. The result was some of the boldest and most original music of the century, so original in fact that Mussorgsky's compatriot Nikolai Rimsky-Korsakov (1844–1908) thought it necessary to rework his music and eliminate many of its "crudities" in order to make it acceptable to European audiences. It was not until many years after his death that his greatest works, including his operatic masterpiece *Boris Godunov*, were performed as he had written them and the true nature of his genius and originality could be appreciated.

Although the greatest composers of the nineteenth century (with the notable exception of Mussorgsky) adhered to the traditional forms of European music, the various techniques they employed to achieve more sensational tonal and coloristic effects shocked and baffled many listeners. The dynamics and dissonances of Berlioz and Wagner and the complicated harmonies of Johannes Brahms (1813–1897) gave the impression that these late romantic composers represented a revolutionary departure in music, which was not strictly speaking the case. Nevertheless, these composers may be said to have pushed to the limits of what was possible in the romantic style, and virtually compelled musicians with any pretensions to originality to seek new styles, to abandon familiar concepts of melody, tonality, and form. As artists in other fields had already been experimenting with new forms for some time, it was only natural that composers would do the same and that music, too, would soon undergo revolutionary changes.

The innovations in the arts broke new ground for artistic expression and understanding in every field. But in one important way their effect was unfortunate. The new poetry, art, and music, with their unfamiliar techniques, their obscure and frequently incomprehensible terminology, not only failed to appeal to the general public but awakened feelings of hostility and fear. The consequence was a marked separation of the artist from society, and a decline in appreciation of the importance of art and aesthetics in daily life that is one of the most unfortunate aspects of the modern world.

CHAPTER 3

The Growing Powers of the State

THE NEW DEMANDS UPON THE STATE

One of the most conspicuous features of the age of nationalism and reform was the growth in the prestige and power of the state. Nationalists looked upon the state as an extension of themselves, as a guardian against foreign foes and a vehicle to fulfill national aspirations. Among national minorities living under foreign rule, the chief goal of nationalist leaders was a national state of their own. And in multinational states threatened by nationalist revolutionary movements, government leaders felt obliged to assign new powers to the state to combat nationalist subversion.

Reformers for their part generally came to realize that the state alone possessed the power and the administrative machinery to carry out reforms on a state-wide basis, to push them through against the opposition of vested interests, and to overcome popular indifference and inertia, which are often the greatest obstacles to change. State authority and a network of state officials were required to implement such major reforms as the abolition of serfdom, the regulation of child and female labor, or the introduction of safety measures in mines and factories.

Even doctrinaire opponents of state controls and state interference in the private affairs of its citizens found it increasingly necessary to admit an extension of state authority in many sectors, and looked to the state to safeguard and further their private interests. In a rapidly changing society undergoing the process of industrialization and urbanization, many problems had become too general, too complex—and too expensive—to be dealt with by local county or city governments, or by private enterprise. The state was called upon to protect private property at home and abroad, to provide a stable currency, to facilitate economic enterprise, and in times of economic slump to stimulate the economy by direct or indirect subsidies and by erecting tariff barriers against foreign competition. State authority and state aid were needed to build railroads and highways, construct dams and harbor installations, open mines, provide adequate sewer systems and water supplies, operate the post and telegraph offices. The state generally had to provide the schools and teachers to carry out programs of compulsory education. Only the state could raise the money and the manpower to equip and maintain modern armies and navies. For all these purposes the state required money, which could only be raised through an elaborate state-operated taxation system.

The Extension of Bureaucratic Government

The steadily growing demands on the services of the state, and the corresponding growth of the state's demands on its citizenry, necessitated the recruitment of ever larger numbers of civil servants and resulted everywhere in an enormous expansion of the bureaucracy. The extension of bureaucratic government was not only required but also made easier by the economic and technological developments of the era. Improved business methods and accounting systems made for more efficient taxation procedures; improved methods of transportation and communication permitted governments to supervise more effectively the activities of their agents, especially those concerned with taxation. And the general increase in productivity made more money available to be taxed and to pay for the increasing costs of government.

The Army and the New Arsenal

Behind the government agent and the tax collector stood the army, equipped with weapons embodying the scientific and technological developments of the age. Since only the state could afford the large-scale purchase of the new armaments, the increasing effectiveness of weapons contributed primarily to the augmentation of the power of the state.

The breech-loading gun, which allowed for a much faster rate of fire than the old muzzle-loader and permitted reloading and firing from a prone position, was introduced in the Prussian army in 1840. The grooved-bore rifle, with far greater range and accuracy than smoothbore guns, was invented soon afterwards. A repeater rifle came into use toward the end of the American Civil War. In artillery, too, rifled and breech-loading weapons replaced smoothbore muzzle-loaders, and shells replaced round shot. The Gatling gun, a primitive machine gun, was developed during the American Civil War, and in 1867 the French army acquired the *mitrailleuse,* an artillery weapon capable of firing 125 rounds a minute. Meanwhile, the telegraph provided a means of coordinating the movements of mass armies, and the railroad made possible a new strategy of mobility that compelled planners in all countries to reorganize existing military installations and draw up new mobilization and campaign programs. A large number of the new railway lines in Europe were laid down primarily for military reasons.

Navies changed even more fundamentally than armies. Sail gave way to steam, wood to iron and steel. Like the armies, the navies adopted rifled, breech-loading guns; the resulting offensive advantage was partly offset by the iron and steel plating that became standard armor for all ships of war. The invention of the mine, the torpedo, and the submarine should have created even greater changes in the navies, but not until the First World War was the significance of these new weapons fully appreciated by naval strategists.

To secure the manpower to utilize the quantities of weapons made available by mass production, and to train their citizens in the workings of the new types of armament, all the major continental states of Europe adopted programs of compulsory military service soon after 1871, when Prussia's victory over France seemed to demonstrate the necessity of such a system.

Mass armies and the introduction of more lethal weapons made war more costly in human lives and in money than it had ever been before. As the century drew to a close a number of statesmen and military men, alarmed at the prospect of war and at the danger that the involvement of mass armies might set off social revolution, began to search for effective means to preserve peace. Others believed that a balance of terror might be maintained indefinitely among the great powers because none would dare risk a major conflict. On the whole, however, there was still a general acceptance of war as a feasible, legitimate, and honorable method of prosecuting national policies.

Whatever their views on war, military strategists were agreed on the need for careful defensive and offensive military preparations. Great importance was attached to strategy, on the assumption that the state that mobilized first and struck most speedily against its enemy would win the next war. Almost nobody considered the possibility of a long war; it seemed inconceivable that any national economy could bear the cost, or any people the sacrifices, of such a conflict.

On the domestic scene, the new arsenal made it easy for a small body of trained men to deal with undisciplined mobs. Between 1850 and 1890 no successful revolution took place in any of the great European states except after a government and its army had been defeated in foreign war, as in France in 1870.

Compulsory Education

Governments did not depend altogether on physical force to maintain themselves. Through official censorship, and manipulation of the press, they had means to control the minds as well as the bodies of men. But their most effective instrument for this purpose was compulsory education, which was instituted in all major European states during the second half of the nineteenth century.

The introduction of compulsory education was not necessarily the result of cynical political calculation. Among people of all countries there was widespread faith in the elevating and remedial powers of education, and sponsors of education programs were often motivated by a spirit of altruism. Liberals and democrats looked upon education as the most effective means of providing all people with equality of opportunity, and even such a conservative as the French statesman and historian François Guizot (1787–1874), declared that "the opening of every schoolhouse closes a jail." In countries with representative governments there was a growing belief that education was essential to train men to make intelligent and responsible use of their political rights. Everywhere men of affairs began to recognize that education had become a practical necessity for workers in the industrial age and for soldiers who had to cope with the increasing complexities of modern warfare.

From the beginning, however, there were those who saw in state control of education an ideal instrument for indoctrination, and in practice government-sponsored education programs (in which compulsory military service played an important part) generally instilled in the citizen a feeling of loyalty toward the state. This feature of state education was at once apparent to leaders of the Christian churches, which prior to the nineteenth century had been the major and often the sole source of education in Europe. As the state assumed more and more educational functions, the struggle for the control of education, and hence for the minds and loyalties of men, became crucial in conflicts between church and state.

The state was to discover, as had the church on numerous occasions, that education could produce unexpected and not always desired results. In Austria-Hungary, for example, it did much to arouse national self-conciousness among the various peoples of the empire, as it was to do later in the British and French colonial territories. In all countries, education made the masses accessible to socialist, revolutionary, and every other kind of antigovernment propaganda, and thus facilitated the development of subversive political organizations.

An important aspect of compulsory education was the provision for the schooling of girls as well as boys, which not only helped women become literate but opened teaching as a new profession for women. These developments were major steps in the political and social emancipation of women.

All programs of compulsory education were originally limited to the elementary level. By the end of the nineteenth century only a beginning had been made in extending compulsory education beyond this level and in establishing free trade and technical schools.

IMPERIALISM

The most impressive demonstration of the power of the European states in the nineteenth century was the continued expansion of that power over territories outside Europe, an imperialism on so vast a scale that by the eve of the First World War European or Europeanized states had succeeded in establishing their control, directly or indirectly, over almost every other part of the world.

There is a commonly held theory that there was a marked decline in European imperialist activity during the first three-quarters of the century, followed by a new burst of expansionism during the century's final decades. This theory has a certain validity only if imperialism is narrowly defined as the establishment of formal rule over *overseas* territory, but even then it is riddled with exceptions. For in fact a great deal of imperialist activity, including the seizure of overseas territory, took place during the first three-quarters of the nineteenth century. The British took over the Cape Colony from the Dutch, they occupied or annexed New Zealand, the Malay states, Hong Kong, Sierra Leone, Gambia, Lagos, and the Gold Coast. From their bases in British India they expanded into the Punjab, Sind, Berar, Oudh, Kashmir, and Lower Burma; from the Cape Colony they expanded into Basutoland, Griqualand, and Natal. During this same period the French annexed Algeria, the Marquesas, Tahiti, and other islands in the Pacific; they began their conquest of Indo china; and they attempted to establish an empire in Mexico.

If the definition of imperialism is extended to include expansion into contiguous territories and economic imperialism, then the theory of a decline in European imperialist activity in the first three-quarters of the nineteenth century becomes patently absurd. For during those years the Russians conquered and annexed immense stretches of territory in central and eastern Asia, and on the east and west coasts of the Black Sea. In North America, Australia, and New Zealand, the white settlers continued a steady process of expansion at the expense of the indigenous population.

Everywhere in the world, with the British leading the way, Europeans continued to extend their influence through various forms of economic imperialism. By gaining a strategic foothold in the trade of another country and a mortgage on its revenues, Europeans established their influence in many of the countries of Central and South America recently liberated from formal Spanish and Portuguese rule; in the Ottoman Empire and its quasi-independent vassal states in the Balkans and North Africa; and in many parts of Asia. Where their influence was resisted, Europeans did not hesitate to use political or military measures to force their way into foreign markets. The British and the French forced the opening of several Chinese ports to gain entry into the China market, and the Europeanized Americans did the same in Japan. The entire process came to be known as the "imperialism of free trade," and because it was cheaper and less dangerous than direct rule it was the preferred system of control so long as it remained effective. It was only when informal means failed to provide the necessary framework of security for European enterprise (civil strife, refusal to honor debts to European investors) that the question of establishing formal rule arose.

During the final decades of the nineteenth century there was a marked increase in the establishment of formal rule over non-European territories and an intensification of interest in expansionist enterprises on the part of all European peoples and governments that has been called the "new" imperialism.

The change in the nature of European imperialism was a reflection of the change in the political situation in Europe itself, the increase of nationalist sentiment that accompanied the national revolutions, the new national rivalries, and a greater preoccupation with national security, military power, and national prestige. Before 1871, especially in the period of flux following the revolutions of 1848, the attention of the continental powers, including Russia, had been focused on Europe. After 1871, as it gradually became clear that no major readjustments of the western European boundaries were imminent, national ambitions were diverted into the territories beyond Europe. The British, who had enjoyed a virtual monopoly in overseas expansion earlier in the century, were faced with more intense and embittered competition from France and Russia. Two new European powers, Germany and Italy, entered the field, and even small states such as Belgium joined in the scramble for empire. The new imperialism was thus a manifestation of the new nationalism, an extension of European national rivalries into every other part of the world.

A steadily increasing and at times almost pathological concern about national security gave rise to theories that a country's survival as a great power (which was assumed to be an essential condition for its survival as a free and sovereign state) depended on the extent of its territorial possessions and on the strategic advantages and economic resources such territories could provide. Colonies were deemed essential as sources of raw materials for the manufacture of modern weapons, and as naval bases to protect trade routes and strategic supply lines. Moreover, the need to acquire such territories was growing more pressing with each passing day. Because the total amount of land in the world was limited, a state had to acquire as much territory as possible as quickly as possible while there was still territory left to take, if only to prevent it from falling into the hands of rival powers. Colonization, said the eminent French political economist Paul Leroy Beaulieu (1843–1916), had become for France "a matter of life and death: either France will become a great African power, or in a century or two she will be no more than a secondary European power and will count for about as much in the world as Greece or Rumania in Europe." Similar arguments were advanced by the historian Sir John Seeley (1834–1895) in England, who predicted that within fifty years the power of states like France and Germany would be dwarfed by Russia and the United States, and he warned that a similar fate would befall England if it failed to maintain and expand its empire. The entire process, in the words of the British statesmen Lord Rosebery, was one of "pegging out claims for the future."

Competitive economic nationalism, combined with the fear that protectionism on the part of rival European states would eventually spell ruin for one's own national economy, provided further incentive for the acquisition of a colonial empire which seemed to promise free and secure access to markets and raw materials. During the long economic slump following the financial crash of 1873, all the major European states with the exception of Britain had abandoned free trade and put up tariff barriers to ward off foreign competition, and foreign observers were confident that Britain too would resort to tariffs as soon as British industrialists, with their enormous head start in the world's markets, began to feel the hot breath of foreign competition.

Not to be overlooked as motives in European imperialism were religious and humanitarian idealism. European missionaries by the thousand journeyed to every part of the world, often at the risk of their lives and

A German view of British imperialism, from the German satirical magazine *Simplicissimus. The cartoon shows an Englishman pouring whiskey into a black man, while a colleague squeezes all possible wealth out of him; a Christian missionary stands by piously reading the Bible, with one eye cocked on the profits that are being made.*

A German view of their own imperialism. *This cartoon satirizes the German passion for order and regimentation.*

health, to convert the heathen to Christianity, to found schools and hospitals. Many European administrators were imbued with a missionary zeal of their own and were genuinely concerned with abolishing the slave trade, introducing what they believed to be higher standards of law and government in areas under their jurisdiction, and in general bringing the benefits of European civilization to those who had not yet had the good fortune to share in them.

By the end of the nineteenth century imperialism, like nationalism, had developed into a mass cult. Colonies became symbols of national greatness and prestige, and were desired by nationalists of every economic and social class. The imperial idea, like nationalism itself, had been stirred into flame by visionaries, theorists, and prophets; it was subsequently nourished by the systematic propaganda of interest groups, patriotic and colonial societies, and by the nationalist press. But, again like nationalism, imperialism appears to have met some profound psychological need for vicarious excitement, to feel oneself the member of a national team that was making its mark in the world and proving its superiority over other peoples and races. For millions of Europeans, the need for empire became a matter of faith, and no European government, democratic or otherwise, could afford to ignore the clamor of its public opinion—not isolated individuals or small interest groups, but the masses with no immediate political or economic stake in imperialism—for a vigorous expansionist policy.

The prime ingredient in European imperialism, however, and certainly the most important reason for its success, was that feature of European civilization stressed at the beginning of this discussion: European power. For several centuries Europeans had enjoyed a power advantage over other peoples of the world which had enabled them to engage in large-scale and successful imperialist enterprises, but that advantage had increased immeasurably with the coming of the industrial and technological revolutions. Never in the history of mankind had any group of people possessed such a superiority of power as did the nineteenth-century Europeans—power not only in the form of superior weaponry, but power stemming from the political, economic, and military organization provided by the machinery of the modern European state.

Armed with repeating rifles, machine guns, and artillery, conveyed to foreign shores in ironclad gunboats, a small number of Europeans could easily defeat large armies of Asians and Africans equipped with more primitive weapons. So formidable was European power that the use of force was sometimes not even necessary. The mere presence of a gunboat, or a European emissary backed up by European guns, was often sufficient to persuade a local potentate to sign a treaty or ultimatum giving Europeans complete or partial control over his peoples and territories.

As the Europeans demonstrated in the nineteenth century, there were many ways of using power and many different methods for establishing control over another people or territory: by outright conquest, as in Russia's seizure of the khanates of central Asia and parts of the Ottoman Empire; by setting up a "protectorate" over a native government, as the British did in Egypt and the French in Tunis; by establishing an outright colonial government, as the British, French, and Germans did in central Africa; by governing through a commercial enterprise, as the British did until 1858 in India and the Belgians until 1908 in the Congo; by dominating the economy of a region, as the British did in South America; by large-scale immigration, as the white settlers did in North America, Australia, and Siberia; by establishing a "sphere of influence" in a country, usually after treaty agreements with other European powers, as several European states did in China.

During the heyday of European imperialist activity, imperialism was not only a reflection of European power; it made a major contribution to that power. This does not mean that all European colonial ventures were profitable. Most of the overseas colonies acquired in the era of the "new" imperialism were losing propositions. Although a small number of traders and investors extracted profits from them, they generally cost the mother country and its citizens a great deal more to pacify and administer than they brought in by way of revenue. Trade with these new colonies was minimal (Germany's trade with its colonies, for example, amounted to only one-half of one per cent of its total foreign trade), they did not attract investments, and most of them were unsuitable for large-scale European immigration.

For Europe as a whole, however, imperialism in all its forms was unquestionably enormously profitable. Europe became the foremost supplier of manufactured goods and capital to the world, the foremost shipper and insurer, and from its visible and invisible exports it derived immense revenues. Far more important, Europe drew on the resources of the world and received the benefit of the cheap labor that produced those resources. Meat and grain, coffee and tea, sugar, tin, rubber, cotton, petroleum poured into Europe from every corner of the world to feed Europe's burgeoning population and stoke its ever-expanding industrial economy.

In terms of national security, the benefit of overseas colonies in wartime was restricted to those European states with a navy powerful enough to keep open the routes of access to them, which in the event proved to be only Britain and its allies. Britain's ability to draw on the resources of its colonial empire (formal and informal) was a major factor in the Allied victory in the First World War. Overseas colonies were useless to Germany during that war, and the international ill-will Germany aroused in the process of acquiring them was diplomatically disastrous.

The most significant and permanent form of European imperialism, whether in terms of economic profitability or national security, was the acquisition of territories which were not only conquered but *settled* by Europeans. The Russian empire, acquired through expansion into contiguous territories, is the only European empire which is still intact and the only European state which remains one of the world's great powers. Europeanized countries such as the United States and Australia are not even regarded as empires by the majority of their inhabitants, but in the eyes of the people from whom these lands were conquered they stand out as particularly vicious examples of European imperialism, for their conquest and settlement was accompanied by the large-scale extermination of the existing population.

For the world as a whole the most important result of European expansion has been Europe's cultural imperialism, which non-European peoples will never shake off. Europeans brought the industrial revolution to the rest of the world; they built factories and railroads; they opened mines; they introduced new methods of agriculture. To administer colonies effectively they introduced European methods of government, bureaucratic centralization, efficient systems of taxation. They trained native soldiers in the use of European arms and military methods. Above all, they brought with them their ideologies, and of these the most influential were not the Christian faith or the principles of law or self-government which European missionaries, religious and secular, tried to impart, but nationalism and Marxian socialism, which had an automatic appeal to people living under foreign political or economic domination.

It was in Europe itself, however, that the impact of the modern European state, its power nourished by industrialization and imperialism, was most immediate and pervasive. Although its influence was not always resented and in many cases not even recognized, the state was encroaching to an ever-increasing extent upon all aspects of the lives of its citizens. Increased bureaucratic authority, compulsory military service, compulsory education, the new weapons for mass destruction, and the flourishing mass media provided the governments of Europe with means to control and manipulate their populations more effectively than ever before. Pessimistic prophets such as the historian Jakob Burckhardt (1818–1897) wondered how long it would be before all aspects of human endeavor were absorbed or utilized as tools by the new Leviathan.

For most people, however, material progress obscured all evil portents. So impressive were the products of human ingenuity that they seemed to overshadow politics and political ideas. But precisely because of the power for good or evil now placed in the hands of the state, politics and political ideas had never been more important.

CHAPTER 4

The Disruption of the Concert of Europe

AFTER THE defeat of Napoleon in 1815, there was no major war in Europe until 1853. The Concert of Europe established after 1815, with all its weaknesses and defects, proved to be an effective league of princes, who recognized their common interests and stood together against the revolutionary forces of the era. They supported the international settlements of 1815 with considerable consistency and united against attempts to disturb the *status quo*. As a means of maintaining stability in Europe, the policy of monarchical solidarity represented a sense of realism in politics far more profound than that of the so-called realistic statesmen who emerged after 1848—men like Schwarzenberg, Cavour, and Bismarck. The policies of these later realists were revolutionary; they permanently shattered the confidence of the monarchs in one another, and nothing they could do could restore that confidence or reestablish a genuine harmony among them.

The revolutions of 1848 should have given the Concert of Europe a new lease on life by warning the princes of the developing threats to their authority and of the greater need for unity and vigilance. Furthermore, a new and uncertain factor had been introduced into European politics in the person of Louis Napoleon of France. The Concert of Europe had originally been formed to safeguard the states of Europe from French domination, and the rise of a new Napoleon, like the revolutions themselves, might have been expected to encourage the other monarchs to close ranks. That this did not happen was due above all to fear of the growing power of Russia, which obscured the emergence in France of a renewed threat to the old order.

LOUIS NAPOLEON AND THE NEW ASCENDANCY OF FRANCE

When Charles Louis Napoleon Bonaparte, nephew of the first Napoleon, became president of the Second French Republic in December, 1848, he

Louis Napoleon taking the oath of office as president of the Second Republic, December 20, 1848. *An eyewitness sketch by Constantin Guys.*

was contemptuously dismissed by many of his contemporaries as a nonentity. Dull, heavy-lidded eyes and an expressionless face gave him an appearance of stupidity, and his refusal to reveal his thoughts gained him the reputation of being a man of mystery without any secret. By the most famous writer of the age, Victor Hugo, he was branded indelibly as *Napoléon le Petit.*

This low estimate proved to be a serious error. Louis Napoleon (1808–1873) was never a great statesman, but he was one of the most able politicians of the nineteenth century. He possessed a remarkable flair for sensing and exploiting the popular forces of his age, and a stubborn tenacity in pursuing his goals. He also had an unshakable faith in his mission to rule France.

It was neither political ability nor faith, however, that catapulted Louis Napoleon into the presidency of the newly created republic. It was his name. The republican legislators, with more idealism than political wisdom, had included a provision for universal suffrage in their constitution of November, 1848. In the subsequent elections, Louis Napoleon was the only candidate whose name was familiar to the majority of French voters. But the name Napoleon, although a major political asset, was also a fateful legacy, for it possessed a dynamism of its own. "Napoleon" stood for political stability, for law and order; but to a far greater extent it stood for military triumph, for glory, and for empire. In the attempt to live up to his name, Louis Napoleon was to reestablish the empire at home and to engage in foreign adventures that would plunge France into political catastrophe.

Although he concealed his thoughts so well that some people wondered whether he had any ideas at all, there can be little doubt that from the time he became president he intended to do away with the republic and revive his uncle's empire. "We are not at the summit yet," he told an old friend on the day he took the presidential oath of office. "This is only a stop on the way, a terrace where we may rest a moment to gaze at the horizon." It was some time before Louis Napoleon took a further step. In the first period of his presidency he trod warily through the unfamiliar fields of French politics, not yet ready to challenge the recently created republican institutions.

President and Parliament

Louis Napoleon's most obvious political opponents were to be found among the deputies in the legislature. In January, 1849, the predominantly republican assembly that had drawn up the 1848 constitution reluctantly voted to dissolve. New elections in May resulted in the return of a large conservative-monarchist majority, a reflection of the people's general fear of radicalism and political unrest. Victory for the monarchists did not mean a victory for Bonapartism, however. On the contrary, most of the new deputies favored the restoration of a Bourbon or Orleanist candidate, and were decidedly hostile to the pretensions of the new Napoleon.

For three years Louis Napoleon worked steadily to build up his personal following and political power by placing trusted lieutenants in key positions in the government, the army, and the police; by distributing political favors astutely; and by convincing the people of France that he represented their best guarantee of order against the forces of revolution. In the manner of a modern political campaigner he made frequent public appearances on national holidays, at military reviews, at the opening of new bridges and railway lines. His speeches on these occasions were calculated to appeal to the interests and prejudices of the particular audience he was addressing. He spoke to financiers and industrialists about building projects and commercial expansion; to landowners and peasants about agricultural subsidies and higher farm prices; to military men about past glories and the prospect of new ones; and to all he emphasized the virtues of public order and good government.

On a more practical level he won over an important number of army officers by key promotions; he ensured the loyalty of the army rank and file by pay increases and extra rations; he gained favor with the Church by sending an army to Rome to support the pope against republican revolutionaries and by backing legislation to give the Church greater control over education at home. He suppressed every threat of social revolution or political unrest. "It is time that the good should be reassured and that the wicked should tremble," he declared.

By the end of October, 1849, Louis Napoleon felt strong enough to dismiss the Orleanist ministry he had selected the previous December, when the legislature was still predominantly republican, and to appoint a ministry "devoted to his own person." In January, 1851, he relieved an outspoken champion of the legislature, General Nicolas Changarnier (1793–1877), as military commander in Paris. Later in the year he appointed his own henchmen to the crucial posts of minister of war, prefect of police, and minister of the interior.

The monarchist-dominated Legislative Assembly meanwhile was conducting a campaign against the president. Recognizing the advantages to Louis Napoleon of universal suffrage, the monarchists passed legislation that deprived some three million men of the franchise and imposed numerous restrictions on freedom of assembly and of the press. Louis Napoleon acquiesced to these measures and at the time made no move to abrogate the power of the legislature. Instead, he allowed the monarchists by their actions to discredit themselves with liberals and republicans, the natural supporters of parliamentary government. The president's request in May, 1850, for repeal of the new electoral law and a return to universal suffrage was denied by the conservative majority in the assembly. On July 15, 1851, the legislature directly challenged the president by rejecting a proposal to revise the constitution to allow him to stand for reelection. This meant that Louis Napoleon would be compelled to relinquish office in 1852 at the end of his four-year term, and that his career as head of state would be over.

The Coup d'État of 1851

The refusal of the legislature to let him stand for reelection ended whatever intentions Louis Napoleon may have had of trying to extend his power by legal means. On the night of December 1, 1851, Paris was occupied by troops loyal to the president. The main government buildings, military installations, and strategic points were seized; police agents arrested seventy-eight key political figures who might have become leaders of an opposition movement. On the morning of December 2, the anniversary of the coronation of Napoleon I and of his great victory at the Battle of Austerlitz, Paris was placarded with announcements that the president had dissolved the legislature, which—the notices alleged—had robbed the people of their right to vote and throttled their political liberties. It was declared that the president was restoring universal suffrage and would seek the people's approval of fundamental changes in the constitution.

The *coup d'état* of December 2, 1851, made Louis Napoleon dictator of France. Opposition was ruthlessly suppressed in Paris and in the provinces.

Throughout the country approximately a hundred thousand people were arrested; by the end of the year about twenty thousand had been sentenced to terms of imprisonment or exile. On December 21 a plebiscite was held asking the French people to approve the *coup d'état* and grant the president the right to draw up a new constitution. Napoleon made full use of his powers to influence the voters, but there is no reason to doubt that the overwhelming preponderance of "Yes" votes represented the sentiments of the majority of the French people.

The new constitution of January 14, 1852, was modeled directly on the constitution of the Consulate of the first Napoleon. It declared that the chief of state was "responsible to the nation," but at the same time it gave him "free and unfettered authority" to conduct the nation's affairs. There was to be a Council of State, appointed by the president, to draw up laws proposed by the president; a Senate, appointed by the president, had the duty to guard and amend the constitution. A legislative body was to be elected by universal manhood suffrage, but its presiding officers were to be appointed by the president. No public debate was permitted, and only government-approved summaries of the legislature's proceedings could be released to the press. One of Napoleon's ministers and the chief author of the constitution informed the Austrian ambassador: "I am willing enough to be baptized with the water of universal suffrage, but I don't intend to live with my feet in it."

The actual administration of France was carried on by the professional civil service through the highly centralized bureaucratic system created during the French Revolution and perfected by Napoleon I. The prefects, appointed by the central government, were the administrative heads of the departments into which the nation was divided. Through the prefects and their departmental bureaucrats, the legislation of the central government was transmitted to the entire country. As in Prussia, the government was based fundamentally on the civil service and on the army.

THE CRIMEAN WAR, 1854–1856

Louis Napoleon had yet to fulfill the promises of national glory associated with his name. The French ruler recognized that to gain this glory and to restore France's old position of ascendancy in Europe, he would have to break the restrictions imposed on France by the treaties of 1815. He also recognized that the chief supporter of those treaties in the mid-nineteenth century was Russia, which was using them to establish its own ascendancy on the Continent. It was Napoleon's good fortune that he came to power at a time when fear of Russia overshadowed fear of France among the states of Europe, and he soon discovered that France would not lack allies in pursuing an anti-Russian policy.

Fear of Russia was no new phenomenon in European history. Since the days of Peter the Great, European statesmen had looked with increasing apprehension at the mammoth power rising in the east and at the gradual but steady extension of Russia's frontiers in every direction. Finland, the east coast of the Baltic, and a large part of Poland came under Russian control in the late eighteenth and early nineteenth centuries. For two centuries there had been a war between Russia and Turkey almost every twenty years, as Russia extended its influence at the expense of the Ottoman Empire into the Middle East, the Balkans, and the Mediterranean. As long as Russia was economically and technically backward, containment by the smaller states of Europe remained feasible. But were this backwardness to be overcome, Russia, with great natural resources and a large population, might prove more than a match for the countries of western Europe, especially if by that time its power had been solidly established not only on the Baltic but in the Balkans and at the great strategic base of Constantinople, from which the entire Mediterranean basin could be dominated.

It was to prevent Russia from controlling the Balkans and Constantinople that the Crimean War was fought. The tragedy of the war was that its purpose could have been, and in fact was, accomplished by diplomacy. The one significant result of the Crimean War was that it permanently destroyed the Concert of Europe.

Russia had emerged from the revolutionary era of 1848 as the apparent arbiter of Europe: the friend of Prussia, the protector of Austria, the reservoir of support for all monarchical and conservative governments. Russia's strength, or semblance of strength, was to prove a serious political handicap, for it tended to make other countries suspicious of Russian policies and anxious to prevent any extension of Russian influence. Austria, though deeply indebted to Russia for military aid against Hungary in 1849 and for diplomatic support against Prussia in 1850, had no desire to become a Russian protectorate. To maintain their country's political independence, Austria's leaders sought to strengthen their diplomatic ties with other powers. Their attitude toward Russia was summed up by the Austrian prime minister, Prince Schwarzenberg: "We will astonish the world by our ingratitude." Prussia, under the irresolute leadership of King Frederick William IV (ruled 1840–1861), played a negligible role in the diplomacy of the period, but Prussia too had reason to fear Russian power, and was resentful of Russia's support of Austria in German affairs.

Curiously enough it was Great Britain, farthest away and least menaced, that was to become the most rabid opponent of Russia in Europe. The British feared the Russian threat to the European balance of power, the possible establishment of Russian control over the Ottoman Empire, and the consequent danger to their routes to India, their trade in the Near East, and their sea power in the Mediterranean. These British fears were compounded by the belief that Russia had gained control of the Concert of Europe and that Austria, Prussia, and the other conservative powers had fallen under its domination. The British therefore welcomed Louis Napoleon's anti-Russian policy and his efforts in 1851 to challenge Russia as the chief protector of the Christian holy places in the Ottoman Empire.

The dispute over the holy places was no empty issue of national prestige but a question of power and influence in the Near East. By establishing its role as protector of the holy places and the Christian population, a state could obtain an excuse to intervene in the internal affairs of the Ottoman Empire and thus gain a valuable means of improving its position in areas under Turkish control.

France already exerted considerable influence in the Near East through trade, missionary work, and financial assistance to the Turkish government. In 1851 Napoleon took advantage of this influence to press for special privileges in connection with the holy places. These were granted by the sultan, who was not blind to the fact that faraway France was a less dangerous protector of Christianity than neighboring Russia. The tsar retaliated by demanding new concessions for Russia. When the Turks, on the advice of Britain, rejected the Russian demands, the tsar occupied the Turkish provinces of Moldavia and Walachia (later reunited as the state of Rumania) to back up his claims. The French and British replied by sending their fleets into the eastern Mediterranean. The situation was tense, but it seemed the difficulties could be resolved by diplomacy as they had been so often since 1815. After complicated negotiations, the tsar promised to evacuate Moldavia and Walachia and to refrain from direct intervention in Turkey; he insisted only that Russia's existing treaty rights in the Ottoman Empire be observed. So moderate were the Russian conditions that Louis Napoleon could find no good reason for rejecting them. But the British cabinet was divided on the question, and anti-Russian influences in London prevailed. The Russian proposal was rejected, and at the end of September, 1853, the British fleet was ordered to Constantinople. Confident of British support, the Turks declared war on Russia on October 4, 1853.

The Turkish armies temporarily held their own against Russia, but on November 30 a Turkish naval squadron was destroyed by the Russians at Sinop, a port on the Black Sea. The battle at Sinop demonstrated conclusively the obsolescence of wooden warships; a Russian fleet equipped with the most recent type of shell-firing guns blasted the Turkish ships to pieces. But the Russians themselves failed to learn the lesson of Sinop; otherwise, the course and outcome of the Crimean War might have been very different. British and French naval vessels were still built entirely of wood. Had the Russians blocked the entry of a hostile fleet into the Black Sea and taken up a defensive position at the mouth of the Bosporus, they might have prevented, or at least rendered far more difficult, allied domination of the sea-lanes to the Crimea.

As it was, the most important result of Sinop was its effect on British public opinion. Russia's perfectly legitimate act of war was denounced in Britain as a treacherous massacre; British newspapers called for war against the "inhuman" Russians and demanded the reinstatement of Lord Palmerston, the most bellicose and anti-Russian member of the cabinet, who had resigned (in opposition to a franchise-reform bill) on the day the news of Sinop arrived in London. The French reaction was more restrained, but Napoleon could not afford to neglect this opportunity to move against Russia in alliance with Britain.

In December, 1853, the British and the French fleets were sent into the Black Sea to protect the Turkish coast and clear the Black Sea of Russian warships. On March 28, 1854, Great Britain and France formally declared war on Russia.

The greatest puzzle in the origin of the Crimean War is the attitude of Britain. For France the war was a blow against the peace treaties of 1815 and a step in the reestablishment of French political predominance in Europe. For Turkey the support of Britain and France provided a unique opportunity to open a counteroffensive against Russia, which had long been encroaching on Ottoman territory. But why should Britain have sought war after the tsar had agreed to Britain's principal conditions for the settlement of the Near Eastern question? Even after Sinop, the tsar offered to withdraw his troops from Moldavia and Walachia and to negotiate a settlement satisfactory to the powers, and still Britain went to war.

There were two obvious reasons for this British behavior. The first was the fervent desire for war by a British public that wished to see the nation reassert its influence on the Continent. The second was the attitude of a few influential British statesmen, notably Palmerston and the British ambassador in Constantinople, Lord Stratford de Redcliffe, who had no faith in Russian promises and believed war was the only certain means of restoring the European balance of power. On May 26, 1854, Palmerston wrote to Lord John Russell, a member of the cabinet, that just to expel the Russians from Moldavia and Walachia "would be only like turning a burglar out of your house, to break in again at a more fitting opportunity. The best and most effectual security for the future peace of Europe would be the severance from Russia of some of the frontier territories acquired by her in later times, Georgia, Circassia, the Crimea, Bessarabia, Poland and Finland . . . she would still remain an enormous Power, but far less advantageously posted for aggression on her neighbors." Palmerston's reasoning resembles that of most advocates of preventive war. He forgot, however, that Britain and its allies might not have the strength to impose such terms on Russia, and that even if Russia could be permanently deprived of the power of aggression, which was practically impossible, there would be other states to take its place. Palmerston himself was one of the

Group of 8th Hussars preparing a meal. *A photograph by Roger Fenton, who took the first successful war pictures. Although Fenton had ample material to show the horrors of war in the Crimea, he was uncertain whether the British public would buy pictures of mutilated bodies and unsanitary field hospitals. He concentrated instead on officers and groups of soldiers. The woman in the picture is a* cantinière *who sold refreshments.*

first to be dismayed by the emergence of French power after the Crimean War, and was soon talking in terms of preventive war against France.

The Conduct of the War

The strategy of the Crimean War was as senseless as its causes. The major problem for Britain and France in a war against Russia was to find a geographical target for an offensive. In August, 1854, under diplomatic pressure from Austria, the Russians withdrew from Moldavia and Walachia. The provinces were promptly occupied by Austria, which remained neutral, thereby making impossible either an allied campaign against Russia or a Russian campaign against Turkey through the Balkans. The British sent a naval squadron to attack Russian strongholds in the Baltic and White seas, and an allied fleet threatened Russian possessions in the Pacific, but nothing significant was accomplished. The allies finally settled on an attack on Russia's Crimean peninsula, which was accessible to allied armies because their navies controlled the Black Sea.

The allied leaders, presumably after a superficial study of maps of the Crimea, reasoned that their fleets could easily cut the peninsula off from the mainland by dominating the narrow isthmus with their guns. The strategy

The harbor of Balaclava. *The first military railroad was built here in 1855, transporting men and supplies from the harbor to the front lines before Sebastopol.*

might have worked but for the fact that the waters on either side of the isthmus were only two to three feet deep. When this awkward fact was discovered, it became evident that an actual invasion of the Crimea would be necessary.

Allied forces landed in the Crimea on September 14, 1854, and on September 20 they defeated a Russian army on the Alma River. Had they pressed home their victory they might well have captured Sevastopol, the great Russian naval base in the Crimea, which was the major objective of the campaign. As it proved, however, the failure to capture Sevastopol in the first offensive was a stroke of luck for the allies. Their delay gave the Russians time to strengthen the city's defenses and bring up reinforcements. The resulting siege of Sevastopol was probably the most effective drain on Russian resources that could have been devised. The allies could be supplied and reinforced relatively easily by sea, whereas the Russians, although fighting on their own territory, were forced to deal with the problems of long supply lines, bad roads, and weather. Men and materiel were sent overland to the Crimea at fearful cost. So severe were the rigors of the long journey, especially in winter, that only one Russian soldier in ten actually reached the front, after a three-month march. The Russian medical department estimated the nation's losses at half a million men; in comparison, the British and French lost about sixty thousand, two thirds of whom died of disease. The drain on the Russian economy was on a comparable scale. The defense of Sevastopol bled the country white. The allies could have adopted no better strategy, but it was unplanned and undesired, for the politicians in London and Paris wanted dramatic victories to satisfy the public. A tedious siege offers few opportunities for glory.

No military commander emerged from the war with credit except the Russian engineer Count Eduard Ivanovich Totleben (1818–1884), who organized the defense of Sevastopol. The first French commander was a dying man when he arrived in the Crimea; his successor, though a competent general, lacked sufficient drive and authority to impose any kind of joint strategy on his British allies. The British commander, Lord Raglan (1788–1855), who had lost an arm at Waterloo, had seen no action for forty years and persisted in calling the enemy "the French." Symptomatic of the low quality of military leadership was the disastrous charge of the British Light Brigade, whose slaughter resulted from confused orders transmitted by a confused orderly to an officer foolish enough to carry them out. Only one person, a woman, gained a heroic reputation from the Crimean War—Florence Nightingale (1820–1910), the nurse who reorganized the military field hospitals and later inspired the reorganization of the entire British hospital system. Her activity led to the opening of the

The famous English nurse Florence Nightingale tending the sick in a hospital at Scutari, near Constantinople. *In subsequent years she was to provide the initiative and leadership to bring about a reorganization of the entire British hospital system.*

nursing profession as a respected public career for women, the first big step toward the more equal status of women in public life.

The Crimean War had a significant effect on methods of warfare. Indeed, it brought about a revolution in naval procedures. The operations in the Black Sea demonstrated conclusively the superiority of steam over sail and of the ship driven by a screw propeller over the side-wheeler. They also revealed the inability of wooden warships to withstand the firepower of rifled, shell-firing cannon. To meet this difficulty, the French developed the first ironclad warships, which they used as floating fortresses in the siege of Sevastopol.

The innovations in land warfare were less dramatic. The allies had the advantage of being equipped with Minié breech-loading rifles, while the Russians still used smoothbore muzzle-loaders. The railroad was used for the first time for military purposes, to bring allied troops and equipment to the front lines before Sevastopol. An attempt was made to employ another new invention, the telegraph, to direct military operations in the Crimea from London and Paris, but the results of such long-distance leadership were sufficiently unfortunate to end this experiment quickly. The telegraph was put to more significant use by British war correspondents, whose descriptions of the inadequacies of the military supply system and the consequent suffering of the soldiers aroused public opinion and led to a demand for large-scale reforms in the military system.

Tsar Nicholas I died in March, 1855; Sevastopol fell in September; and in December, Austria threatened to join the allies unless Russia surrendered. The new tsar, Alexander II, his resources exhausted, faced with revolt at home and the prospect of an Austrian invasion, decided to yield. An armistice was arranged on February 25, 1856.

The Aftermath of the War

In the Treaty of Paris of March 30, 1856, the Russians surrendered only one piece of territory that they had not been willing to renounce before the war began—a strategic section of Bessarabia, at the mouth of the Danube. They agreed to the internationalization of the Danube and relinquished their claim to the right to protect Christians in the Ottoman Empire. Most important of all, they accepted the neutralization of the Black Sea, which meant that Russia could not maintain a navy or naval bases on the Black Sea and was consequently deprived of offensive and defensive weapons in this area. They also agreed to leave the Aaland Islands in the Gulf of Bothnia unfortified and to restore to Turkey the fortress city of Kars, near the east coast of the Black Sea, which they had captured in the course of the war. The Danubian principalities of Moldavia and Walachia were placed under the protection of the signatory powers, who further promised to respect the independence and territorial integrity of the Ottoman Empire.

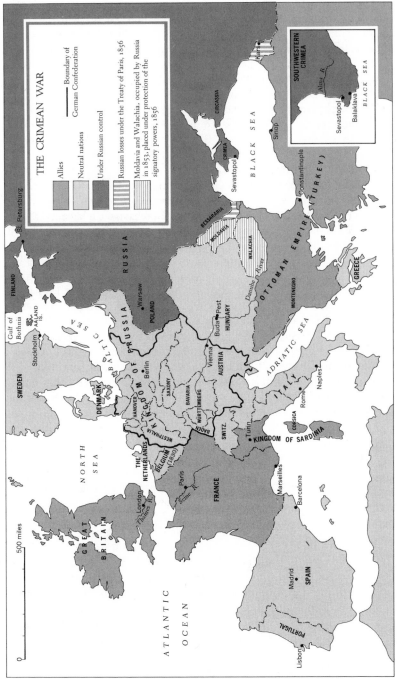

THE CRIMEAN WAR

Allies

Neutral nations

Under Russian control

Russian losses under the Treaty of Paris, 1856

Moldavia and Walachia, occupied by Russia in 1853; placed under protection of the signatory powers, 1856

Boundary of German Confederation

These provisions might have created a permanent obstacle to further Russian expansion at the expense of Europe and Turkey had they been permanently enforced, but international settlements are never permanent. The coalition that imposed the Treaty of Paris on Russia had already begun to break apart during the peace negotiations. Russia repudiated the Black Sea clauses of the treaty in 1870, was again at war with Turkey in 1877, and had regained both Bessarabia and Kars by 1878.

The most permanent result of the Crimean War was the disruption of the Concert of Europe. Forty years of peace were now followed by four wars (1859–1871) that revolutionized the power structure of the Continent. Defeated and humiliated, Russia was determined to break the restrictions imposed by the Treaty of Paris, and thus became a revisionist state, although it refrained from active intervention in European affairs during the next two decades, while setting its own house in order. "Russia is not sulking," the Russian chancellor Prince Gorchakov explained. "She is quietly gathering her forces—*la Russie se recueille*." Great Britain, disillusioned by an inglorious war and an inconclusive peace, adopted an attitude similar to that of Russia by withdrawing from European affairs. Austria was isolated. During the Crimean War both sides had confidently anticipated Austrian backing: Russia had expected Austria to support the 1815 peace settlement against France and to repay a debt of gratitude for recent military and diplomatic aid; Britain and France had been certain that Austria would recognize the necessity of halting Russian expansion in southeastern Europe, where vital Austrian interests were at stake. Austria's neutrality antagonized all the belligerents, with the result that until 1879 Austria was without friends among the great powers. Prussia's policy during the war was so flaccid and its strength seemed so inconsequential that it was almost dismissed as a major power.

France was the state that seemed to have gained most from the war. French armies had won the most impressive victories in the final attacks on Sevastopol; the international system of 1815 and its restrictions had been swept away; France had supplanted Russia as the dominant power in Europe. But France's position was not so strong as it appeared. Britain was apprehensive about the revival of French power and the renewed danger of French hegemony on the Continent. Russia, already antagonized by the Crimean War, was further alarmed by Napoleon's talk of an independent Polish state, which would deprive Russia of its Polish provinces. A similar reaction occurred in Austria and Prussia, with large Polish minorities of their own, and these states also resented Napoleon's interference in German and Italian affairs. France was as isolated among the great powers as Austria, a situation Napoleon never seemed to understand. He pursued an ambitious foreign policy, confident that French strength and prestige could overcome all obstacles. He was to be cruelly disillusioned.

Only one state gained a diplomatic advantage from the Crimean War. The north Italian kingdom of Sardinia had entered the war on the side of the allies in January, 1855, as a move in its struggle against Austria for supremacy in Italy. Cavour, the astute Sardinian prime minister, had seen clearly that his country's Italian ambitions might be permanently jeopardized if an exclusive alliance between Austria and the western powers were formed. To forestall this danger and to stay in favor with his sovereign, who was eager to win military glory, Cavour had agreed to send Sardinian troops to the Crimea. "Once our soldiers are aligned alongside yours," King Victor Emmanuel II told the French ambassador, "I'll snap my fingers at Austria."

Cavour's policy was successful. In the eyes of Britain and France, Sardinia's unconditional participation in the war contrasted favorably with Austria's neutrality. Sardinia was therefore admitted to the peace conference on an equal footing with the great powers. The British and French delegates supported Cavour's denunciation of political conditions in Italy, which was, in effect, an indictment of Austrian influence in that country. Although Sardinia gained nothing concrete from the Crimean War, it established goodwill with France and Britain which would prove of considerable value in subsequent maneuvers against Austria.

With the Concert of Europe in shambles, Russia and Britain temporarily withdrawing from the international scene, and Austria in isolation, the field was open to political opportunists of every kind. Foremost among them was Louis Napoleon, whose ambitious but ill-defined and inconsistent policies kept European politics in ferment until the fall of his regime.

THE SECOND EMPIRE

In 1852, while the Crimean War was brewing, Napoleon finally dropped the mask of republicanism. On November 21 another plebiscite was held, to ask public approval for the restoration of the empire. Again the government secured an enormous majority, and on December 2, 1852, the anniversary of the *coup d'état*, Louis Napoleon was proclaimed emperor of the French. He took the title Napoleon III, thus recognizing the reign of the first Napoleon's little son, in whose favor Napoleon I had abdicated on April 6, 1814.

On January 30, 1853, Napoleon III married Eugénie de Montijo (1826–1920), the daughter of an impoverished Spanish-Scots family. Beautiful, pious, and an increasingly conservative influence toward the end of her husband's reign, the Empress Eugénie was never really popular in France, but she provided the empire with a male heir. She also provided French society with a glittering court, the most dazzling, if not the most exclusive or cultivated, in Europe. Women enjoyed a special eminence there, as did the representatives of the bourgeoisie—the stock promoters and business

Emperor Napoleon III, Empress Eugénie, and their son, the prince imperial, who was killed fighting with British forces against the Zulus in 1879.

magnates who played so prominent a part in the economic life of the Second Empire. It was a court of the *nouveaux riches*, whose vitality and self-indulgence is well reflected in the music of Jacques Offenbach (1819–1880), the most popular composer of the time.

Economic Policy

The first half decade of the reign of Napoleon III was, on the whole, a period of prosperity for France, as it was for the other countries of western Europe. The policies of the imperial government undoubtedly contributed to the French economic revival. The emperor took a genuine interest in economic questions, especially as they related to social welfare. As head of state he put the power and authority of the central government behind programs to stimulate the national economy and improve the standard of living of the French worker. The emperor was strongly influenced by the socialist theories of Henri de Saint-Simon (1760–1825), a leading advocate of economic planning. Napoleon III believed with Saint-Simon that society should organize its resources scientifically for the benefit of its members. His was a program of state socialism, but to fulfill it he employed all the resources of the rapidly developing capitalist system.

The basis of this imperial economic program was the expansion of credit: money was made available on easy terms to entrepreneurs of every kind—

farmers, manufacturers, builders, shippers—to permit them to take full advantage of the developments of the agricultural and industrial revolutions. They, in turn, were expected to produce more goods and services for the French people, to provide employment for French labor, and to create an expanding market for French products. The government floated public bond issues for major construction programs and encouraged private investment by providing state guarantees for government-sponsored credit companies. The Crédit Mobilier was founded with official backing in 1852 to promote large-scale industrial enterprises: railroad and harbor construction, the installation of gas-lighting in urban centers, the expansion of mining and shipping companies. The Crédit Foncier, also founded in 1852, was originally conceived as a national mortgage bank to provide long-term loans to peasants for agricultural improvements, but the conservative French peasant was suspicious of the innovation. The Crédit Foncier became instead a major source of capital for public and private building, above all for the great urban-reconstruction programs of the Second Empire.

The government's easy-credit policy provided a breeding ground for shady speculators and financial manipulators, but it did indeed stimulate the national economy. During the first years of the empire, the French rate of economic growth surpassed that of all other states. The major French railway lines, planned during the reign of Louis Philippe, were built or completed, together with an impressive network of branch lines. The harbors of Marseilles, Le Havre, Brest, and Cherbourg were developed into centers of world shipping. French shipyards were equipped to build iron steamboats in place of wooden sailing ships. The Suez Canal, largely a product of French enterprise, was built between 1859 and 1869. The adoption of new inventions and methods of manufacture stimulated a boom in the mining and metallurgical industries. Coal production doubled. France remained behind Britain in steel production, but in 1870 was still ahead of the states of Germany in this crucial industry. In foreign trade, too, the rate of French expansion exceeded that of all other European states, as the combined value of French exports and imports almost trebled in the course of Napoleon's reign.

The economic policies of the Second Empire prompted the greatest building boom up to that time in French history. Under the direction of Baron Georges Eugène Haussmann (1809–1891), the prefect of the Seine, Paris was transformed from a picturesque medieval city of narrow, winding streets into the present city of air and light, with broad, straight boulevards, great circular plazas with avenues radiating from them, and superb architectural vistas. Paris was provided with an adequate public water supply, an underground sewage system, gas illumination. A new central market was built, construction on the lavish opera house was begun, a public park was created in the Bois de Boulogne. The rebuilding of Paris was a major enterprise in city planning. The vast construction program supplied employ-

The grand staircase of the new Paris opera house (1862–74), designed by Charles Garnier. *The opera was one of the most spectacular of the new public buildings included in the plans for the reconstruction of Paris.*

The new Paris sewers. *As important as the landscaping and architectural plans for the reconstruction of Paris was the building of a gigantic network of underground sewers, which also housed water mains, conduits for natural gas, and later, electric, telegraph, and telephone wires. It was said of Napoleon III that he had "found Paris stinking and left it sweet."*

ment to large numbers of skilled and unskilled workers, and materially improved the living conditions of Parisians. The new city plan also facilitated the suppression of revolts and street fighting by making the erection of barricades more difficult and by providing easy access to every quarter of the city for artillery and troops. As one observer put it, the new broad streets were beautifully accessible to light, air—and infantry. Paris is the best-known example of civic reconstruction undertaken during the Second Empire, but the work of the emperor's planners in other cities, especially Marseilles, was equally noteworthy.

As a further stimulus to the French economy, Napoleon lowered import duties to provide industry with cheaper raw materials and labor with cheaper food. This policy was also designed to compel French producers, including the peasants, to adopt more efficient and economic methods in order to compete with foreign manufacturers and growers. In 1853 tariffs were lowered on food and on basic raw materials such as iron and coal. In 1860 the Cobden-Chevalier trade treaty with Britain significantly reduced French tariffs on British goods and opened the British market to French products. In the next six years France concluded similar reciprocal-trade agreements with Belgium, the German customs union, Italy, Austria, Sweden, Switzerland, the Netherlands, Spain and Turkey.

Napoleon's trade treaties provoked the first widespread opposition to the imperial regime. This arose even though the government provided subsidies for agriculture and industries that had been injured by the tariff agreements, thereby undercutting its own efforts to compel French producers to adopt more efficient methods. The emperor was unlucky in that his reciprocal-trade program was instituted at a time when the general prosperity in Europe was in sharp decline after the financial crash of 1857 and the French economy itself was suffering a succession of severe blows. Crop failures at the end of the 1850's were accompanied by the incidence of a disease of the silkworm, which badly damaged the silk industry, and of the attack of the phylloxera plant louse on French vineyards, which temporarily ruined the French wine industry. The blockade of southern United States ports by the Union navy during the American Civil War cut off a vital source of raw cotton and seriously hurt the French textile industry.

The French economy in the 1860's was also affected by a change in government financial policy. In 1859 Pierre Magne (1806–1879) was replaced as minister of finance by Achille Fould (1800–1867), a conservative banker who favored tighter credit, a balanced national budget, and severe curtailment of government spending. Fould's policies did put an end to loose speculation, but at the same time they ruined many marginal enterprises and depressed the national economy just when it was in need of stimulus. Drastic retrenchments were also made in expenditures for the army. The government did allocate 113 million francs to equip the army with a rapid-firing breech-loading rifle, the *chassepot*, but it did not provide adequate funds to modernize the artillery, a serious oversight. For the inferiority of French artillery was to be a major factor in France's defeat by Prussia in 1870–1871. The ministry of finance was not alone to blame for the cuts in the French military budget; a program of government economy was a prominent feature of the period of political liberalization in the final years of the empire.

The Liberal Empire

Opposition to the imperial regime aroused by government tariff policies, the economic slump, and various aspects of the imperial foreign policy prompted Napoleon III to seek new bases of popular support. His efforts to secure this support did not really represent a fundamental change in his approach, but rather constituted an extension of methods he had used since the beginning of his reign. As he had once won over landlords and businessmen by offering them political stability and economic opportunity, he now attempted to win over republicans, workers, and other disaffected groups by a lavish use of the spoils system and by political and economic concessions. During the 1860's many restrictions on personal freedom were relaxed, trade unions were legalized, workers were granted the right to strike.

To gain more active parliamentary support for his regime, the emperor increased the voice of the legislature in affairs of state and enlarged its control over the budget. Publication of the complete records of legislative debates was authorized, and members of parliament were granted the right to question government ministers on official policies. In making these concessions, Napoleon appears to have been motivated primarily by a desire to find men of talent to support his regime: politicians willing and able to aid him in governing France, ministers who might assume some of the work and responsibility now burdening him.

One fateful result of the liberalization policies was that the emperor was rendered powerless to force through reforms in the French army to match recent military reforms in Prussia. Many members of the legislature objected on principle to strengthening the army and to the higher taxes which doing so would entail. They looked upon the army as a bulwark of the Napoleonic dictatorship and upon compulsory military service as an instrument of political indoctrination and oppression. Between 1863 and 1870 the legislature relentlessly pared military expenditures. But a large share of the responsibility for the inadequate reorganization of the French army belonged to government and military leaders: an economy-minded ministry of finance; conservative generals reluctant to accept innovations; high-ranking imperial officials who, fearing the revolutionary outlook of the population, hesitated to arm what might eventually become the instrument of their own downfall.

The so-called Liberal Empire did not last long enough to make possible a sound evaluation of its ultimate aims and potential. Over the short run the emperor's liberalization policies evidently produced the results he desired. Opposition was undercut; the government strengthened its hold on old supporters and won important new ones; republicans and socialists as well as financiers and industrialists gained an interest in preserving the imperial regime. In January, 1870, Émile Ollivier (1825–1913), former leader of the radical opposition in the legislature, became the chief minister in the imperial government. Ollivier was told that the emperor needed his assistance in "organizing liberty." In May, 1870, the French people were asked to approve by plebiscite the recent liberalizing legislation, and thus, in effect, to cast a vote of confidence in the imperial regime. The returns gave Napoleon III a victory as great as any he had scored at the beginning of his reign.

These triumphs in the domestic arena were short-lived. Five months later the Second Empire was swept away as a result of mistakes in the conduct of foreign affairs.

Imperial Foreign Policy

In foreign policy, as in domestic, Napoleon III showed a rare ability to understand the popular forces of his day, but his efforts to exploit or placate these forces, instead of increasing his power or improving the international position of his country, involved him in ruinous political adventures. It was above all in international relations that the name Napoleon played him false. The French people had given him their overwhelming endorsement in the 1848 elections and had enthusiastically approved the restoration of the empire in 1852, but with that restoration they anticipated a new succession of military victories, a revival of French glory, the reestablishment of France as the Great Nation of Europe. These expectations too Napoleon understood, and fatefully, he undertook to satisfy them.

The most astute feature of the emperor's foreign policy was his effort to improve relations with Great Britain. Having brooded long over the history of the First Empire, Napoleon III had concluded that Britain had been the greatest obstacle to his uncle's success and that Britain's opposition to France's freedom of action on the Continent should be removed by winning its friendship. Accordingly, he sought to break down tariff barriers and establish closer trade relations with Britain. He backed British policy in the Near East, and during the Crimean War, French troops fought alongside instead of against British troops in a European campaign for the first time since the days of Cromwell. In 1860, in cooperation with Britain, France brought pressure to bear on China to open eleven new treaty ports to European commerce. In 1861, again in cooperation with Britain, France compelled the Mexican government to recognize European property rights, a prelude to the ill-fated Mexican expedition shortly thereafter.

Especially after the experiences of the Crimean War, Napoleon recognized that he had neither the military nor the organizing genius of his uncle, but he believed that there were other ways to European leadership than military conquest. Just as he was one of the first modern statesmen to exploit mass public opinion, so he was one of the first to appreciate the power that the explosive force of nationalism might give to the man who could harness it to his own interests. His uncle had supplied the formula: "The first ruler who appeals to the peoples of Europe will be able to accomplish anything he wishes." But Napoleon I had failed to apply his own ideas, and the peoples of Europe had overthrown him. The opportunity now fell to the new Napoleon. If he became the champion of the cause of nationalism, if he led the peoples of Europe to freedom from foreign and domestic tyranny, he, the emperor of the French, would be regarded as the natural leader of a free Europe, and France would acquire a political and moral ascendancy on the Continent unmatched in history. Napoleon III's program to liberate the peoples of Europe was not the product of cynical calculation. Inspired by the Italian nationalist Giuseppe Mazzini, he believed in the cause of national liberation as ardently as he believed in the cause of eradicating poverty, and he looked forward to an era when free nations would live together harmoniously—under the leadership of France.

Napoleon's vision of a society of free nations under French leadership was undeniably a grand conception. As a program of foreign policy, however, it was not only impractical but also directly contrary to French national interests. His encouragement of the Polish rebellion against Russia in 1863 gave rise to cruelly false hopes among Polish patriots, to whom he was unable to give effective aid. At the same time he gratuitously drew upon France the wrath of the tsar. The encouragement of nationalism, and hence inevitably of national unification movements in Germany and Italy, proved disastrous, for it contributed to the creation of great powers directly on the French border in place of weak and impotent neighbors.

In 1859, Napoleon went to war with Austria in support of the efforts of the Italian kingdom of Sardinia to drive Austria out of Italy. The French emperor undoubtedly sympathized with the Italian national cause, and he was grateful to Sardinia for its recent participation in the Crimean War. But he also had more selfish reasons for entering the Italian arena. The situation in Italy offered him a dramatic opportunity to place himself at the head of the European nationalist movement. On a more practical level, it gave him a chance to supplant Austrian by French influence in Italy.

As a move to establish paramount French influence in Italy, Napoleon's action made sense, but in all other respects his Italian policies were ill-conceived, ill-executed, and inconsistent. His armies failed to score a quick victory over the Austrians, and in the Italian nationalist movement he found he had released passions he was unable to control. Alarmed at what was happening in Italy and fearful that Prussia and other German states might come to the aid of Austria, he made peace with Austria without consulting his Italian allies. He left Venetia under Austrian rule and at first refused to permit the states of central Italy, which had revolted against their Austrian-supported rulers, to unite with Sardinia. Unable to stem the tide of national feeling without resorting to force, he finally agreed to this union, but forced Sardinia in return to give up Nice and Savoy to France.

All this time French troops had remained in Rome, where they had been sent in 1849 to support the Pope against republican revolutionaries. These troops now blocked the aspirations of Italian nationalists, who looked upon Rome as the natural capital of a united Italy. Thus Napoleon was cast in the ridiculous position of simultaneously supporting Italian nationalists against Austria and thwarting them in Rome. As a result of his separate treaty with Austria, his acquisition of Nice and Savoy, and his policy concerning Rome, Napoleon found that instead of winning the gratitude of Italian patriots for his aid against Austria, he had reaped hatred and abuse. It was an inauspicious beginning to France's spiritual conquest of Europe.

The emperor's policy with respect to Germany was even less fortunate and more confused. Napoleon saw the danger of a Germany united into one strong state, but he believed he could maintain a balance of power between the two major states of Germany—Prussia and Austria. As in the case of Italy, he hoped to establish in Germany a loose national confederation in which the weaker states would look to France for protection. In pursuing this policy he believed he would be able to round out France's "natural frontiers" by gaining control of the territory on the left bank of the Rhine. His calculations went completely awry. Prussia's victory over Austria in 1866 ended any hope for a balance of power. To compensate for the fiasco of his German policy and to offset the increase in Prussian strength, Napoleon now made territorial demands hardly befitting the champion of national freedom. Ineptly and unsuccessfully he claimed for France the Rhineland, Belgium, and Luxembourg.

Napoleon's search for successes in foreign policy became all the more frantic after the Second Empire suffered a serious setback in Mexico. Napoleon's Mexican expedition began after a joint diplomatic campaign by Great Britain, France, and Spain to force the revolutionary government of Benito Juárez (1806–1872) to recognize European property rights. Taking advantage of the fact that the Civil War left the United States government unable to intervene in Mexico, Napoleon sent an army to establish Archduke Maximilian (1832–1867), brother of the emperor of Austria, as emperor of Mexico. Napoleon appears to have been motivated by the desire to curry favor with the Catholic Church by overthrowing Juárez's anticlerical regime, to conciliate Austria, which had been antagonized by his Italian

Autograph letter of Napoleon III to King William of Prussia, September 1, 1870, after the French defeat at Sedan. *The text reads: "Not having been able to die in the midst of my troops, there is nothing left for me to do but place my sword in the hands of your Majesty."*

policy, and to give France a great new political and economic sphere of influence in the western hemisphere. (The first Napoleon, too, had dreamed of a Mexican empire.) With the end of the Civil War, the United States government forced Napoleon to withdraw his troops from Mexico, and the French Mexican empire collapsed. In 1867 the unfortunate Maximilian was executed by Juárez's troops at Querétaro.

The Fall of the Second Empire

"There are no mistakes left to commit," said the veteran Orleanist statesman Adolphe Thiers, but he was wrong. In 1870, after scoring a diplomatic victory by persuading the Prussian king to withdraw the candidacy of a member of his family for the Spanish throne, Napoleon III yielded to the demands of French public opinion, and of his empress and his ministers, and posed further conditions, which Prussia found unacceptable. The result was war and national disaster. Poorly organized, poorly equipped, and miserably led, the French armies went down to defeat; at Sedan on September 2, 1870, the Second Empire collapsed under the pounding blows of the Prussian artillery.

Napoleon III left France with better railroads, better ships, better harbors, a stronger economy—and with two new great powers, Italy and Germany, on its frontiers. This was a heavy price to pay.

CHAPTER 5

The National Revolutions, 1850–1870

AFTER THE withdrawal of Russia from the Concert of Europe, the principal defender of the *status quo* on the Continent was Austria, the multinational empire of the Habsburgs, which was to be the major victim of the disruption of the 1815 treaty system and Napoleon III's policy of encouraging nationalism. The 1815 treaties had restored the Habsburgs' control over much of central Europe and had given them preponderant influence in Italy and Germany. In the later years of the century their favorable position in these various areas was either destroyed or seriously undermined by nationalist revolution and agitation. The unification of Italy and Germany was achieved largely at the Habsburgs' expense; within what was left of their territories they were obliged to recognize the quasi-independent national status of the Hungarians; and the agitation of other nationalities for special rights or outright independence threatened the empire's very existence.

THE HABSBURG EMPIRE

So serious was the nationalities problem that many historians have tended to regard the Habsburg empire as an anachronism, an institution containing within itself forces that would bring about its inevitable collapse. It is well, however, to be cautious about the concept of inevitability in history. The Habsburgs had been emperors in Europe since the thirteenth century, and their empire had already faced and survived many disasters—the rending effects of the Reformation, the Thirty Years' War, Turkish invasions that had reached the gates of Vienna, the program of dismemberment of Frederick the Great, four decisive defeats by Napoleon, and the revolutions of 1848. By its very survival the empire had demonstrated that there was an unusual resilience in its character and institutions, and throughout its worst crises it had managed to retain to a remarkable degree the loyalty of its diverse peoples.

The unifying forces within the empire were the crown, the army, the bureaucracy, the Roman Catholic Church, and to a limited extent, the economy and the culture.

The imperial idea, associated with the Habsburgs for six hundred years, held sway over members of all nations and all classes. Until the empire was swept away after the First World War it was possible to undertake the most drastic kind of political and social reform under the imperial banner. The house of Habsburg had developed its own mystique, a belief that its rulers were not only kings by divine right but executors of a divine will. This certainty of its right to rule helps explain the impersonal quality of so many of its leaders, the unscrupulousness of their policies, their cold-blooded use of men and nations which made "the ingratitude of the house of Habsburg" proverbial over the centuries.

The army was the main pillar of the Habsburg state, the force which protected the empire from foreign foes and imposed internal political unity. It was also an effective instrument for indoctrinating a large body of men of every class and nationality with dynastic sentiments and the idea of imperial unity, especially after the introduction of compulsory military service in 1868. To the army, the fatherland was the whole empire, not some province or region, and more particularly it was embodied in the sovereign himself, a concept underlying the maxim "If my emperor is in Baden, then my fatherland is there also." Officers and men were rotated regularly from one part of the empire to another to promote the feeling of unity and overcome regional loyalties.

The bureaucracy, including the police and the secret service, was the civilian army of the Habsburgs. Through this administrative apparatus the central government could bypass feudal magnates and local governments, and impose imperial policies on every part of the empire. Careers in the imperial civil service, including the highest posts, were open to men of talent of every class and nationality and attracted some of the ablest people in the empire. Like all bureaucracies, that of the Habsburgs was characterized by pedantry, thoughtless routine, and secrecy, and not infrequently, by haughty incompetence and inefficiency. "An absolutism tempered by slovenliness," a prominent socialist leader called it. Yet even the severest critics of the imperial bureaucracy admitted that it was far superior to former feudal administrations, and that, compared with other governments of the nineteenth century, especially those of eastern and southern Europe, it represented an honorable degree of integrity and humanitarianism. It remained remarkably free of corruption and could seldom be accused of brutality toward the poor and oppressed.

The Roman Catholic Church had acted as a unifying influence in the empire in the years following the Reformation, when Church and state had cooperated to stamp out Protestantism and impose a considerable measure of religious unity on the realm. Since the eighteenth century, the Church had lost some of its political influence and it was often in conflict with the government, but it remained a strong force in society, and on the whole considered that its interests were served by supporting rather than undermining imperial rule.

The empire was never a natural economic unit—few states are—but by its very size it formed a large free-trade area in central Europe, particularly after the abolition of tariff barriers between Hungary and the other parts of the realm in 1850. The agricultural regions formed a valuable hinterland for the developing industries of German Austria, Bohemia, and Galicia.

Finally, there was the unifying quality of Viennese culture. In Vienna, melting pot of the empire, years of synthesis had produced a predominantly German culture with a strong admixture of Slav, Magyar, Italian, and other ethnic influences. German was still the lingua franca of the empire in 1850, but even after German gave way to local national languages later in the century, Vienna remained the cultural heart of the monarchy. For generations the imperial court had been the chief sponsor of talent and ambition. To Vienna flocked Czechs and Magyars, Rumanians and Croatians, Poles and Slovenes, representatives of every class and profession, all with a desire to make a name in the world. These people were absorbed into Viennese culture and in turn made their contributions to it.

The greatest weakness of the empire was its lack of organic unity in administration and in the composition of its population. It was a patchwork of provinces brought together over the centuries by conquest, diplomacy, or marriage alliances. Each province retained in large measure its local government, rights, traditions, and customs. The empire included the seventeen hereditary lands of Austria; the territories inhabited by the Slovenes in the south; the predominantly Czech lands of the crown of Bohemia, including Moravia and part of Silesia; the Polish province of Galicia, acquired in the partitions of Poland; the provinces of Venetia and Lombardy with their distinctly Italian population; and the lands of the crown of St. Stephen (Hungary, Transylvania, Croatia). Within this conglomerate of provinces there were some twenty more or less distinct nationalities.

The awakening of self-consciousness among the many nationalities of the Habsburg dominions was the most disruptive force in the empire in the nineteenth century. It is important to remember, however, that nationalism was not a mass movement in central Europe in 1850. In most parts of the empire the peasantry and town laborers were hardly touched by the nationalist spirit; to many members of the nobility espousal of the nationalist cause was little more than a means of safeguarding or extending local privileges. The Hungarian nationalist movement, for instance, attracted Magyar nobles who resented the restraints on their authority imposed by the Vienna government. The same motives characterized many members of the Polish nobility. During the Polish revolt in 1846 and the Hungarian revolt in 1848 it was the house of Habsburg that enjoyed the "popular" support of the peasants, who looked to the imperial government for protection against the local landlords of their own nationality. Once the rights of the Polish and Hungarian nobles had been guaranteed by the Vienna government, many of them became staunch supporters of the monarchy. Having secured "freedom" for themselves, they proved far more intolerant of national minorities within their own territories than the Habsburgs had been, and their policy toward the peasantry was often one of harsh oppression. In Italy, too, the common people still supported the Habsburgs in the mid-nineteenth century. The Italian patriot Giuseppe Garibaldi saw with dismay how the peasants of Lombardy rejoiced when the Austrians returned after a brief period of national "liberation" in 1849. The unimaginative but honest Austrian administration had treated them only with rough justice, but at least not with the crass injustice displayed by the kingdom of Sardinia. Nationalist sentiment was to become a steadily stronger disruptive force, however, and was undoubtedly the single greatest threat to imperial unity during the later nineteenth century.

The persistence of traditions confined to particular regions or groups, the jealous guarding of feudal and local privileges, the presence of economic inequalities and of dissension among the various social classes as well as the several nationalities, made for further weaknesses in the imperial structure. These weaknesses were clearly recognized at the time. Many Austrian leaders were infected with pessimism and accepted the general view that their empire was doomed. This opinion was already prevalent in the period following the French Revolution and the Napoleonic Wars. Prince Metternich, the chief engineer of political reconstruction after 1815, was so obsessed with fear of revolution that he has been described as suffering from a "dissolution complex." The gloom persisted and became more widespread as the signs of national disaffection increased and the problems of government seemed to grow more difficult. Pessimism permeated the entire population. Austrians accepted crisis at home and defeat abroad with a certain fatalism, an attitude summed up in the expression *Es ist passiert* ("well, it has happened"), suggesting that they had expected "it" all along.

The revolutions of 1848 seemed to confirm the view of the worst pessimists. The process of dissolution went forward rapidly, and Metternich, long a prophet of disaster, fled the country. But recovery followed, national and social revolts were suppressed, and in 1850 the empire seemed to have emerged from its agonies stronger than ever.

The Emancipation of the Peasants and the Industrial Revolution

The most important and lasting result of the revolution of 1848 was the final emancipation of the serfs. The act of emancipation of September 7, 1848, put an end to all rights of the lords over the peasants and abolished the compulsory labor service (the *robota*). Compensation to the lords for the loss of this free labor was paid in part by the state, in part by the peasants who held the land.

The emancipation of the peasants gave great impetus to agricultural production and economic life generally. The peasants worked harder for themselves than they had for their landlords, produced more than ever before, and became consumers with significant purchasing power. The great estates, freed from the wasteful system of forced peasant labor, could be run more efficiently and economically. The compensation paid to the great lords allowed them to develop their estates as capitalistic enterprises, to invest in mechanical farm equipment, to build breweries, beet-sugar factories, and sawmills, to exploit mines. The petty nobles, on the other hand, did not own enough land to run their estates profitably without free labor, nor did they receive enough money in compensation to become agricultural entrepreneurs. For many of them the emancipation of the serfs meant economic ruin, and they became competitors for positions in the service of the state. Because these poorer nobles were of many nationalities, their competition did much to intensify national antagonism in the empire.

The richer peasants, like the great landlords, profited from the emancipation. An act of Emperor Joseph II (ruled 1780–1790) had forbidden the acquisition by the nobility of traditional peasant holdings ("rustic land"). This measure was still in force, not so much to protect the peasants as to prevent this rustic land from falling into the hands of the nobility, who paid lower taxes than the peasants, or, as in Hungary, no taxes at all. The land law gave the peasant class security of tenure, but it did not prevent richer peasants from buying out poorer ones. Like their counterparts in western Europe, the richer peasants tended toward political conservatism, but during this period they also became more nationality-conscious and began to identify their interests with those of their national groups. The poorer peasants, with little or no land, supplemented their incomes by working on the land of others or subsisted altogether as farm laborers. Many were attracted to the towns, where they supplied the manpower for industry and swelled the ranks of the industrial proletariat. The great influx of unskilled peasant labor to the towns after 1848 laid the basis for future class antagonisms and also contributed to the conflict of nationalities. Before 1848 the majority of the townspeople in the empire were Germans. The arrival of Czech, Polish, or Croatian peasants destroyed the predominantly German character of the towns, but the Germans generally remained in control of the economy and were the chief employers of labor. Thus the class and nationality struggles reinforced each other, and laborers too, became nationality-conscious.

Perhaps the most significant result of peasant emancipation in Austria was the creation of a supply of mobile labor, which sped the progress of the industrial revolution. The industrial revolution was the great force behind economic change in the Habsburg empire, as it was everywhere in Europe at this time. The government stimulated industrial development by abolishing trade and tariff barriers within the empire in 1850, by sponsoring a large-scale program of public works and railroad building, by providing official encouragement to manufacturing and trade. The main impetus for the industrial boom that took place after 1850, however, appears to have been the rapid growth of finance capitalism. Before 1848 the chief sources of capital in the empire had been the Austrian National Bank, which dealt almost exclusively with the state, and the house of Rothschild, which still operated conservatively and was far from generous with loans and credit.

The first bank to make credit available on a large scale in Austria was the Crédit Mobilier, founded in Paris in 1852 to promote industrial joint-stock enterprises and open new fields of business. In 1853 the first private Austrian bank, the Diskonto-Gesellschaft, was established for the same purpose. In 1855 the Rothschilds opened the Creditanstalt to compete with the highly successful Crédit Mobilier. These institutions provided the financial stimulus for the expansion of Austrian industry, which flourished particularly in Vienna and in the provinces of Bohemia and Galicia.

The industrial revolution brought to Austria the usual problems of city growth: an urban proletariat, slums, and labor unrest. But it also brought wealth and prosperity to a large section of the population and created a new middle class. Above all, it provided the money and material required by the administration and the army. And the strength of the army enabled Austria to remain among the great powers in spite of the disruptive forces operating within the empire.

Francis Joseph

At the head of the heterogeneous Habsburg realm was Emperor Francis Joseph I (ruled 1848–1916), who had been summoned to the throne during the revolutions of 1848 at the age of eighteen, with little preparation for his complicated duties. Despite his consequent need for good advisers, he seldom appointed men of outstanding ability to top government positions. Fearful of delegating authority, he insisted on himself formulating the major policy decisions affecting his empire. And because he was ponderously slow in making up his mind, important decisions might be delayed for months or even years. Yet when he did see the necessity for quick action, he could move with thoughtless haste. His life was a long record of misfortune.

The Emperor Francis Joseph of Austria and his brothers. *From left to right:
Archduke Charles Louis, a passionately pious man who died of dysentery after
drinking water straight out of the River Jordan on a trip to the Holy Land;
Archduke Louis Victor, who retired in a cloud of scandal to the castle of
Klessheim near Salzburg; the emperor; Archduke Ferdinand Maximilian, the
ill-fated Emperor Maximilian of Mexico.*

His only son killed himself; his wife was assassinated; his empire was in a
chronic state of crisis; his foreign policy led from defeat to defeat. After his
first major setback in the Italian war of 1859, he never regained his
self-confidence. "I have an unlucky hand," he once confessed.

Yet Francis Joseph, through his office and through his personal qualities,
probably did more than any other man or institution to hold the Habsburg
empire together. His dignity and his unwavering sense of obligation to his
position made him the embodiment of the imperial idea; during the
sixty-eight years of his reign he won and retained deep personal loyalty
among the many peoples of his empire. His profound consciousness of his
imperial mission, of the tradition and greatness of his house, gave him the
moral strength to push on through a lifetime of difficulties and personal
tragedies. It is symbolic that his empire did not collapse until after his
death.

Upon becoming emperor of Austria in 1848, the young monarch attached to his original name of Francis the name of his popular predecessor, Joseph II. This, too, was symbolic, for in his rule Francis Joseph was to fluctuate between the principles of Francis I, whose chief minister, Metternich, had defended the *status quo*, and of Joseph, who had pressed ruthlessly for change, seeking a more rational, centralized system of government of the kind advocated by the political theorists of the Enlightenment. The outstanding characteristic of Francis Joseph's reign was his experimentation with a variety of governmental techniques in the interest of preserving his empire. Far from being rigid in his political ideas, as his critics have frequently maintained, he was all too ready to jettison a system when it met with setbacks and to experiment freely with the process of government.

The Schwarzenberg Government and the Bach System

The first governmental system adopted after Francis Joseph came to the throne on December 2, 1848, was introduced not by the emperor, but by the ministers who had restored order in Austria during the last months of 1848 under the leadership of Prince Felix zu Schwarzenberg (1800–1852). In 1851 the Schwarzenberg government formally abolished the various constitutions introduced as a result of the 1848 revolutions and instituted a system of imperial autocracy.

Schwarzenberg's attention was devoted primarily to foreign affairs. The chief architect of Austrian domestic policy after 1848 was Alexander von Bach (1813–1893), a German lawyer and former liberal, who was more interested in efficient government than in political freedom. To break the power of the feudal nobility and overcome regional particularism, he flooded the empire with German, Czech, and Polish officials, the notorious Bach "hussars." Behind the bureaucracy stood the army, the police, and a network of spies and informers as extensive as Metternich's. Unlike Joseph II, Bach did not hesitate to use the Roman Catholic Church as an instrument for consolidating state power. In an 1855 Concordat the Church was given extensive control over education and censorship, ecclesiastical courts were restored, the property of the Church was declared sacred and inviolable, civil marriage was abolished, and the government agreed not to alter confessional laws without the consent of the Vatican; in return, the government expected clerical support in carrying out its unification policies. The Bach regime, according to a bitter socialist critic, consisted of "a standing army of soldiers, a sitting army of officials, a kneeling army of priests, and a creeping army of denunciators."

Under Bach the Habsburg empire became for the first, and last, time a centralized state. He ruthlessly swept aside local rights and privileges and introduced a unified administration, a single system of law and taxation. He made German the official language of government in order to simplify administration and at the same time utilize language as a means of unification. The judiciary was separated from the executive branch of government to give it greater independence. Trial by jury was introduced. Every citizen was accorded equal rights and could move about within the empire without a passport. Bach's bureaucracy enforced the legislation freeing the serfs, a move that required strong pressure on the part of the central government to overcome the opposition and inertia of the nobility in every part of the realm.

The economy, too, was centralized. In 1850 all tariff barriers within the empire were removed, and for the first time the entire empire became a free-trade area. Karl Ludwig von Bruck (1798–1860), the minister of commerce, tried to extend this customs union to include all of Germany and to establish a central European empire of seventy million people under Habsburg leadership. His plans failed because of the opposition of Prussia and the smaller German states, and of Russia, which feared so great an increase in Habsburg power.

The state took over the construction of railways; communications were generally improved; the merchant fleet was expanded; the postal services were reorganized. Chambers of trade and industry were founded in an attempt to expand industry and encourage exports. Extensive public works and a stepped-up armaments program provided workers with employment and industry with lucrative contracts.

The economy nevertheless remained the weakest and most vulnerable aspect of the Bach regime. Mounting expenditures for the army and the bureaucracy, the outlays for the large-scale public works, the compensation paid to landowners for the emancipation of the serfs, produced a staggering rise in the costs of government. Mobilization during the Crimean War was unexpectedly expensive. At the same time, Bach's officials found it increasingly difficult to collect taxes. In the many parts of the empire where the centralization policies were unpopular, especially in Hungary, rich and poor alike displayed unexampled ingenuity in evading payment of taxes, and the costs of collection rose sharply. To secure the necessary funds to run the government, the state borrowed from the National Bank, sold crown property and the state railways, generally on very unfavorable terms, and floated loans at ever higher rates of interest. A stock-exchange crash in 1857 plunged the empire into economic depression. The Bach regime was in serious economic trouble by the end of the 1850's.

It was also in serious political trouble. The Bach system aroused widespread hostility in many segments of the population. The policy of centralization clashed with local administrative, legal, and economic rights. Non-German peoples objected to the German character of the government. The German middle classes, who welcomed the predominance given to the German language and German officialdom, resented the antiliberalism of the government, its concessions to the Church, and the heavy tax burden it imposed.

But it was blunders in foreign policy that brought the Bach system to an end. Under Schwarzenberg's forceful leadership the Habsburg empire had recovered from the shock of 1848 with remarkable speed and once again ranked as a great power in Europe. But Austrian leaders forgot that their recovery had been due in large measure to Russian support, and that to maintain their position they would have to retain the goodwill of Russia or secure similar backing from other states. Austrian diplomats did neither, with grave consequences for the realm.

With the sudden and unexpected death of Schwarzenberg in April, 1852, foreign affairs were placed in the hands of Count Karl Ferdinand von Buol-Schauenstein (1797–1865). His appointment proved to be disastrous. His policy of irresolute neutrality during the Crimean War cost Austria the friendship not only of Russia but of Britain and France as well. Then in 1859 he fell into the trap the Italian statesman Cavour had set for Austria in Italy.

THE UNIFICATION OF ITALY

At the midpoint of the nineteenth century, Austria was the chief power blocking Italian unification. Besides controlling the wealthy and populous provinces of Lombardy and Venetia, the Habsburg empire stood behind the "legitimate" rulers of the Italian petty states, and behind the pope, who governed Rome and much of central Italy. The ruling families of Modena and Tuscany were members of Austria's house of Habsburg, and after the 1848 revolutions even the Bourbon rulers of Parma and Naples looked to Austria for protection.

In Italy, as in many other parts of Europe in the mid-nineteenth century, the concept of national freedom and unification was meaningful to only a minority of politically conscious people. Neither nationalism nor liberalism was in any sense a mass movement at this time. Successful national revolts in Italy were organized by small groups, and generally won widespread popular support only when they were able to exploit local grievances.

The most striking achievement of the Italian nationalists was their propaganda, by which they convinced others, Italian princes as well as foreign powers, of the deep-seated desire of the whole Italian people for political freedom and national unification, and of the inevitable triumph of these causes.

Although Italian patriots generally agreed about the broad goals of their movement, they differed widely on how Italian unification was to be achieved and on what form of government the new Italian nation should assume. Some favored a confederation of Italian states under the leadership of the pope, others a republic. After 1848, however, a growing number of Italian nationalists looked for leadership to the state of Sardinia.

The kingdom of Sardinia, which included the island of Sardinia and the mainland provinces of Piedmont, Nice, and Savoy, was ruled by the house of Savoy, the only native Italian dynasty. In 1848 Sardinia had been granted a constitution by its sovereign, and had attempted to wrest Lombardy and Venetia from Austria. Despite the far from liberal nature of its new constitution and its utter defeat in the conflict with Austria, Sardinia emerged from the 1848 revolutions as the foremost standard-bearer of Italian liberal-nationalist aspirations. Shortly afterward, the Sardinian government came under the leadership of one of the outstanding statesmen of the nineteenth century, Count Camillo Benso di Cavour.

Cavour

Before devoting himself entirely to politics, Cavour (1810–1861) enjoyed a highly successful career in several fields. By employing scientific and efficient methods of farming on his private estates, he made a fortune in agriculture. He acquired additional wealth in banking, railroads, and shipping. He traveled much and learned much, especially from the political and economic system of England.

Cavour's entry into political life began with the publication in December, 1847, of his newspaper, *Il Risorgimento* ("The Resurgence"), which gave its name to the entire Italian nationalist movement of the nineteenth century. Cavour was no revolutionary firebrand, but rather an aloof and somewhat detached intellectual. In his political orientation he was a moderate liberal and a moderate nationalist. He believed in constitutional

Count Camillo Benso di Cavour, the principal political architect of Italian unification.

government and sought to improve the existing social system by means of orderly reform. As a nationalist, he wished to free Italy of foreign domination and to bring about some kind of political unification of the peninsula, but he had no rigid views on how Italian liberty and unification were to be achieved and was doubtful whether these ideals could be realized in his lifetime.

Cavour's moderate political views and his cold intellectuality did not make him popular with his king or with the majority of Sardinia's politicians, but Cavour did not depend on popularity for political influence. His energy and resourcefulness were combined with a rare ability to take advantage of political opportunities. He displayed exceptional skill as a parliamentarian. His speeches, replete with facts and statistics, conveyed a sense of inevitability which, as a rule, won support for his policies. He was at his best in debate: after summing up all the arguments on a question, he would present his views with such cogency that his own conclusion seemed the only one possible. In the course of his life Cavour not only dominated his own government but changed the political configuration of most of the Italian peninsula. By the time of his death in 1861, all of Italy with the exception of Rome and the province of Venetia had been united under the leadership of Sardinia.

Cavour's first concern when he became prime minister of Sardinia in 1852 was to strenghten the country economically and militarily. He reorganized the treasury, reformed the taxation system, and borrowed heavily from abroad to stimulate the national economy and raise the funds to maintain and equip a large modern army. He concluded trade treaties with foreign governments and sponsored the construction of highways and railroads, harbors and canals. He reformed the banking system, encouraged the expansion of credit, and stimulated investment in new industrial and agricultural enterprises. The result was a remarkable spurt in Sardinia's economy and a considerable rise in the state's revenues.

Despite the kingdom's increased power and prosperity, Cavour, unlike many of his countrymen, realized that Sardinia alone could not vie with Austria for supremacy in Italy. His country had failed to defeat Austria in 1848, when the entire Habsburg empire was in revolt; its chances against a stabilized Austria would be considerably worse. Sardinia needed powerful allies. To secure them, Cavour engaged in a series of brilliant diplomatic maneuvers.

Cavour's Diplomacy

Although Cavour failed to secure any territorial gains or even promises of support from Britain and France in return for Sardinia's entry into the Crimean War, he made skillful use of his country's participation in the subsequent peace negotiations with Russia to win recognition among the great powers and draw attention to the Italian problem. "We have gained two things," he announced to the Sardinian Chamber of Deputies upon his return from the Paris peace conference. "In the first place, the unhappy and abnormal condition of Italy has been denounced to Europe, not by demagogues, not by hot-headed revolutionaries or passionate journalists, but by representatives of the foremost powers of Europe. . . ˙. In the second place, those very powers have declared that it was not only useful to Italy but to Europe to apply some remedy to the ills of Italy. I cannot believe that the judgments expressed, the counsels given, by powers like France and England can long remain sterile."

Four years after the Crimean War, Cavour succeeded in forming an alliance with Napoleon III against Austria. This alliance was arranged in a secret and informal agreement on July 20, 1858, at the spa of Plombières. Napoleon promised to join Sardinia in a war against Austria provided the war "could be justified in the eyes of diplomacy and even more in the eyes of the public opinion of France and Europe." The first objective of the conflict would be to drive the Austrians out of Italy once and for all. After that, Italy was to be reorganized as a confederation of four states under the presidency of the pope. Sardinia was to become the kingdom of Upper Italy and would annex the Austrian provinces of Lombardy and Venetia, along with the duchies of Parma and Modena and a large section of the Papal States. In central Italy a new state would be created, envisaged by Napoleon as a kingdom for his cousin Prince Napoleon Bonaparte (1822–1891), who would form an alliance with the house of Savoy by marrying the daughter of King Victor Emmanuel II of Sardinia. Evidently the pope was expected to be satisfied with the presidency of the new confederation, for he was to be stripped of most of his territories, those not turned over to Sardinia going to Prince Napoleon Bonaparte's new kingdom. The pope's temporal authority was to be restricted to Rome and its immediate surroundings. The boundaries of the fourth member of the confederation, the kingdom of the Two Sicilies, were to remain unchanged.

On the face of it, the Plombières agreement, which was confirmed but rendered somewhat more vague by later treaties, gave Napoleon a variety of means for exercising future control over Italy: he would be able to do so through the pope, who depended on French military support to maintain his temporal power; through Sardinia, which would need French aid against a vengeful Austria; through his cousin, who would be king of central Italy; and through his hold on the sentiments of the Italian nation, which would be grateful for French aid against Austria and look to France for leadership. To cap these advantages, Cavour agreed to cede to France the Sardinian provinces of Nice and Savoy, which lay on the French side of the Alps and which the French had long desired to round out their "natural frontiers"—the Alps, the Pyrenees, and the Rhine.

Great as were the apparent advantages of the pact of Plombières for France, the real winner in the negotiations was Cavour. The agreement gave him the alliance he needed against Austria and assured him of the support of the strongest military power in Europe. Nice and Savoy, the price to be paid for French aid, could not be compared in value to Lombardy and Venetia, Parma and Modena, and the large section of the Papal States that Sardinia would acquire. Cavour's only problem now was to "justify" a war with Austria in order to realize the terms of the agreement. This could be done most easily by making Austria appear as the aggressor. Cavour accordingly did his best to goad Austria by such tactics as encouraging revolt in Austria's Italian provinces and sheltering deserters from the Austrian army on Sardinian territory. The Austrians foolishly played into his hands, and on April 23, 1859, sent an ultimatum to Sardinia, which Cavour naturally rejected. The Austrian invasion of Sardinia four days later brought France into the war.

The War of 1859 and Its Aftermath

Napoleon III soon found that he had made serious miscalculations in his Italian policy. The war with Austria proved to be more costly and more difficult than he had expected. After two major battles, at Magenta and Solferino, the Austrians had still not been decisively defeated, and France was faced with grave danger from another quarter. The war in Italy had aroused anti-French sentiment in Germany, and it seemed likely that public opinion in Prussia and other German states would compel their governments to come to Austria's aid. Prussia mobilized its army; with the bulk of the French forces in Italy, the road to Paris from the east lay open.

Events in Italy also took an unexpected turn. Shortly after the war began, nationalist revolts broke out against the Austrian-supported governments in central Italy. These revolts were encouraged by Cavour, who had sent Sardinian commissioners into the central Italian states to organize them for the war effort against Austria and to bring them into a closer political relationship with Sardinia. The rapid spread of the Italian nationalist movement alarmed Napoleon, who feared that Sardinia might absorb enough territory to become a rival instead of a satellite state. Faced with this accumulation of dangers, Napoleon decided that his best course was to make peace with Austria as soon as possible. On July 11, 1859, he concluded an armistice with Austria at Villafranca, in northeastern Italy, without troubling to consult his Italian allies.

At Villafranca, Austria agreed to give up the greater part of Lombardy, but kept Venetia and the strategic Lombard fortresses. The various rulers who had been deposed by the revolts in central Italy were to be restored to their thrones. Napoleon turned Lombardy over to Sardinia, and with considerable restraint relinquished his claim to Nice and Savoy, but these gestures failed to win him the gratitude of Italian nationalists, who were indignant that Venetia had been left under Austrian rule and that the

Giuseppe Garibaldi. *The uniform, which he habitually wore, derived from his days as guerrilla fighter in South America.*

Austrian-supported governments of central Italy were to be restored. Even the normally cool Cavour was furious at being deprived of the full fruits of the Plombières agreement, and he resigned his prime-ministership in a rage.

It was soon evident to Napoleon that, short of using force, he would be unable to restore the rulers of the central Italian states or prevent the union of these states with Sardinia. To make the best of the situation he concluded another bargain with Cavour, who had returned as prime minister in January, 1860. By the Treaty of Turin of March 24, 1860, Napoleon secured Nice and Savoy for France in return for his consent to Sardinia's annexation of the states of central Italy. Thus Napoleon finally achieved some gains for France, but at the price of further antagonizing Italian nationalists.

Garibaldi and the Conquest of Southern Italy

The next chapter in the history of Italian unification was written by a man whose character and methods differed in almost every respect from those of Cavour. Giuseppe Garibaldi (1807–1882) was a single-minded Italian patriot: simple, blunt, devoid of guile or selfish ambition. A colorful and romantic military hero, he was capable of arousing immense enthusiasm in the men who served under him. Whereas Cavour applied a highly sophisticated intelligence to politics and prepared every political move with extreme care, Garibaldi believed in direct action; and he had the courage to take such action no matter how great the odds against him. He professed to be a radical republican and a believer in the freedom of the individual, but like many men of action he was willing to employ dictatorial methods to achieve his ends.

In 1833, at the age of twenty-six, he had fallen under the influence of Mazzini and had joined the Young Italy movement, taking an oath to fight against injustice and tyranny and for the unification of Italy. Exiled from Sardinia in the following year for revolutionary activity, he became a soldier of fortune in South America, where he acquired exceptional skill as a guerrilla leader. During the revolutions of 1848–1849 he led an army of volunteers against Austria in Lombardy. In 1849, after the republican revolution in Rome which had expelled the pope, he conducted the defense of the newly established Roman Republic with ability and courage.

Garibaldi was back on the battlefield in the 1859 war with Austria. He shared the disgust of most Italian patriots at the Peace of Villafranca. The subsequent transfer to France of Savoy and Nice, the place of his birth, again spurred him to action. He organized an army of volunteers to defend these provinces against the French, at the same time initiating preparations to free Venetia from Austria and to expel the French forces from Rome. These activities were most embarrassing to Cavour. After vainly trying to dissuade Garibaldi from taking action of any kind, he appears to have contrived to divert him from northern Italy by secretly encouraging him to take his volunteer army to Sicily in support of a revolt that had broken out against King Francis II (ruled 1859–1861), the Bourbon monarch of Naples and Sicily. If this was indeed Cavour's policy, it was a clever move. If Garibaldi succeeded, Sardinia might profit from his victory. If he failed, Sardinia could disavow him, for officially the government knew nothing about the Sicilian undertaking. Cavour even alleged that he had done his best to stop it, but the fact remains that the entire project was organized (and with a good deal of publicity at that) on territory under Sardinian control, and that the Sardinian fleet did nothing to prevent the expedition from sailing. On May 11, 1860, Garibaldi and his volunteer army—the Thousand Red Shirts—landed in Sicily.

Garibaldi advanced against an organized army that outnumbered his twenty to one. By daring and resourceful tactics, and with the support of revolutionaries on the island, he outmaneuvered the Neapolitan forces. On May 27 he captured the Sicilian capital of Palermo. Success led to success.

Thousands of volunteers and deserters from the Neapolitan army joined his forces. The Sicilian peasants, most of whom had little or no feeling for the Italian nationalist movement, were converted into enthusiastic Garibaldians by the dramatic personality of Garibaldi himself and by his promises of land and tax reforms.

Widespread peasant unrest in Sicily played an important part in Garibaldi's victory. Many of the peasant bands that had terrorized the island and in some areas had brought local government to a standstill joined Garibaldi's army. At the same time, many property owners also found it necessary to support him, since he offered their only hope for the reestablishment of law and order. They, at least, were not disappointed. Garibaldi proclaimed himself dictator of Sicily in the name of Victor Emmanuel II, "the constitutional king of Italy." If only for reasons of military necessity, he at once set about establishing effective control over the country. To facilitate the requisitioning of supplies for his troops, he restored the authority of local government, and his edict conscripting all male Sicilians between the ages of seventeen and fifty into his army temporarily drained the area of the manpower heretofore available to terrorist bands.

By the end of July, 1860, most of Sicily had been conquered. On August 22 Garibaldi crossed to the mainland and began a triumphal campaign up the Italian peninsula. The city of Naples fell on September 7, and Francis II withdrew with what remained of his army to the fortress of Gaeta, in the northern part of his kingdom.

Cavour and Garibaldi

Garibaldi's success placed Cavour once again in an awkward position. The general's exploits had captured the imagination of people in every part of the peninsula, and it was conceivable that he might establish permanent authority over southern Italy. As a power and an ideal, Garibaldi had become a dangerous rival to King Victor Emmanuel II and the state of Sardinia, despite his professions of allegiance to the house of Savoy. Garibaldi had also become a danger in the field of diplomacy. If he continued his drive to the north and attacked Rome, as he had announced intentions of doing, war with France would result. An attack on Venetia, which Garibaldi also envisaged, would mean renewal of the conflict with Austria— this time without French support. Cavour realized that war with France or Austria would hardly be as simple as war with the demoralized forces of Francis II. He accordingly decided to take measures to put a decisive check on Garibaldi's activity by sending a Sardinian army to join Garibaldi in the south. On the flimsiest of excuses, Cavour invaded the Papal States, having convinced Napoleon that it was preferable for Sardinian rather than French troops to deal with Garibaldi. Napoleon warned that the diplomatic complications would be serious and that he himself would be placed in a

THE UNIFICATION OF ITALY

Kingdom of Sardinia at the time of
the Congress of Vienna, 1815

Territories acquired, 1859–1860

Territories acquired, 1860–1870

difficult position, but he nevertheless approved Cavour's plan. "Act, but act quickly," he told the Sardinian leader.

The Sardinians easily defeated the papal army. They then moved into the kingdom of Naples, where they joined Garibaldi in the final stages of the campaign against the Bourbon regime. By this action Cavour not only checked Garibaldi but also regained the initiative in the Italian unification movement. On October 21 and 22, 1860, plebiscites were held in Naples and Sicily, and the people voted overwhelmingly—according to the official count—for union with Sardinia. Similar plebiscites were held in the former papal states of Umbria and the Marches, with similar results. Only the city of Rome, garrisoned by French troops, was left to the pope. Garibaldi might have attempted to resist Sardinia's absorption of the fruits of his exploits, but he chose to subordinate himself to the cause of Italian unity. He went into temporary retirement at Caprera, his island home off the coast of Sardinia, leaving to others the political reorganization of the areas he had conquered.

On March 17, 1861, the kingdom of Italy was proclaimed by an Italian parliament, and King Victor Emmanuel II of Sardinia became the first king of Italy. On June 6 of the same year Cavour died at the age of fifty-one. His death was a grievous loss to the new state, which badly needed his leadership and political resourcefulness during the period of its consolidation.

The final steps in the unification of Italy were primarily the result of Prussian rather than Italian enterprise. In 1866 Italy was Prussia's ally in the war with Austria and was given Venetia in the wake of Prussia's military victories—the Italians themselves had been defeated on land and sea. On September 20, 1870, after the withdrawal of French troops from Rome in the course of the Franco-Prussian War, Italian forces occupied Rome, which was henceforth to be the capital of the united Italy. Thus, almost from the start, the new Italian nation was dwarfed by the rising power of Bismarck's Germany.

THE UNIFICATION OF GERMANY

The Germanic Confederation and the Austro-Prussian Rivalry

The Germanic Confederation established in 1815 consisted almost exclusively of the states inhabited by German-speaking people; thus in an ethnic sense at least it came close to being a perfect German union. Austria exercised a preponderant influence in the affairs of the Confederation during the first half of the nineteenth century, but was never able to impinge seriously on the sovereignty of its members. Even the smallest of the German states jealously guarded its independence, and joined with the others to prevent effective domination of the Confederation by either Austria or Prussia, Austria's only serious rival to predominance in Germany.

Toward the middle of the nineteenth century this balance of power among the German states was threatened by the rise of national feeling among politically conscious members of the German population, many of whom desired the unification of the entire German people under a single government. In Germany, as in Italy, nationalists disagreed widely about how unification was to be achieved and about what form of government was desirable for their country. There were advocates of a stronger confederation, of union under Austria or Prussia, of union through an all-German, popularly elected parliament. It should be emphasized once again, however, that national feeling was not an irresistible force sweeping all before it, and that there remained powerful as well as widespread opposition to the unification movement no matter what form it might take.

During the revolutions of 1848, the Germanic Confederation was discredited by its inability to give effective support to the German national cause in a quarrel with Denmark over Schleswig-Holstein; in the same period an attempt to achieve German unity through the popularly elected Frankfurt Parliament failed. The result was that after 1850 the hopes of German nationalists came to focus on Austria and Prussia, which alone seemed to possess the power to bring the rest of the country under their dominion.

In the rivalry between these two states, Austria had the advantage of a long tradition of supremacy; it dominated the existing confederation, and as a Catholic country appealed to the largely Catholic population of southern Germany. Above all, Austria was commonly believed to possess a stronger army and greater natural resources than Prussia. Austria's weakness lay in the multinational character of the empire; it had barely survived the recent revolutionary crises, and most of its subjects were not Germans at all. Further, although Austria's Catholicism was attractive to the Catholics of southern Germany, it alienated the Protestants of the north.

Prussia had the advantage of possessing an almost exclusively German population, its own autocratic tradition had been sufficiently tempered by reform to make its leadership more acceptable to German liberals, and its Protestantism was an asset with respect to Germany's Protestant population. Prussia's greatest strength lay in its economic domination of Germany through the customs union (*Zollverein*), and in the rapid development of its own economic power, especially in the Rhineland provinces.

So important was Prussia's economic strength that a number of scholars regard it as the decisive factor in the struggle for supremacy in Germany. It is argued, for example, that Prussia's economic policies and its successful defense of the *Zollverein* against Austrian attacks were far more crucial to Prussia's ultimate triumph in Germany than the more spectacular activities of Prussian diplomats and generals, who are generally given major credit for this achievement. Such economic arguments, although a valuable corrective to the usual political emphasis, seriously underestimate the strength and range of the opposition to Prussia and to the German unification movement in general. In the final war for supremacy in Germany, for instance, all members of the *Zollverein* with any freedom of choice sided with Austria against Prussia; moreover, it is extremely doubtful whether Prussia could have won this war, or even fought it, if Prussian *diplomacy* had not precluded the intervention of France and Russia, which had every interest in preventing German unification of any kind. It is not necessary to accept these economic arguments in their entirety, however, to recognize the fundamental importance of the economic and social forces released by the industrial revolution in Germany in breaking down traditional modes of thought and behavior, and in bringing about conditions conducive to revolutionary political change.

Prussia to 1862

As the nucleus of a future great power, few states could have been more unpromising than Brandenburg-Prussia in the seventeenth century, when its rise began. Its territories were scattered, its population sparse; it lacked both natural resources and natural frontiers. These weaknesses, typical of most German states in this period, were overcome in Prussia by a few strong rulers, who with unusual firmness of purpose centralized the government and built up a strong army, thereafter devoting a large part of the state's resources to its maintenance. In carrying out their aims, they ruthlessly crushed the power of the landowning nobility (the *Junkers*), and channeled the energies of the members of this class into the service of the state. *Junkers* became the chief ministers of the Prussian government, the mainstays of the bureaucracy, and the officers of the army.

By the late eighteenth century, the rulers of Prussia had expanded their territories and raised their country to the status of a great power. Their success was the result of skillful and often unscrupulous leadership, aided by a bureaucracy that had become proverbial for its honesty, efficiency, and willingness to work hard for little pay. Most obviously significant in Prussia's rise, however, was the army, which was regarded as the central pillar of the state, its main line of defense, its only true frontier. This importance in the development of Prussia makes understandable the high status enjoyed by the army in that country, and the corresponding prestige of its leaders, almost all of them members of the *Junker* aristocracy.

After the Napoleonic wars, Prussia was given a large part of the Rhineland, the territory that was to become the principal center of the industrial revolution in Germany, and thus obtained unprecedented economic strength to harness to the Prussian political-military organization. With the Rhineland, Prussia also acquired a population with a more liberal political tradition, including an influential group of financiers, industrialists, and professional men who resented the monopolization of political power by the landed aristocracy and who joined forces with the rising middle classes in other parts of the state. These people desired the establishment in Prussia of parliamentary government on the English model, and during the early years of the reign of King Frederick William IV (ruled 1840–1861) it seemed that this desire might be fulfilled.

Frederick William, however, proved to be an unstable romantic visionary, whose impractical schemes and political vacillation were to be recalled during the reign of his great-nephew Emperor William II. He was one of the few nineteenth-century monarchs who still appears to have believed sincerely in the divine right of kings. Upon coming to the throne, he spoke of satisfying the desires of the middle classes for representative government, but what he actually had in mind was a revival of medieval estates—which had never existed in Prussia. In 1848, submitting ignominiously to the demands of revolutionaries for genuine representative government, he

King Frederick William IV of Prussia in his study in the palace in Berlin. *Painting by Franz Krüger. The paintings and artifacts in the background reflect the king's varied and far from military tastes, an atmosphere that was to change during the reign of his brother William.*

granted his country a constitution. But once the revolution was crushed, he failed to honor the most important provisions of this constitution, and ruled autocratically, with a small group of reactionary advisers. In domestic affairs, his reign was characterized by repressive legislation. In foreign affairs, his pusillanimity and inconsistency led to a marked decline in Prussia's international influence.

That the reign of Frederick William IV was not totally barren of constructive action was due in large measure to the efforts of the Prussian bureaucracy, especially with respect to economic affairs. Prussia's control of the German customs union was successfully defended against a vigorous Austrian attack, and some important legislation was enacted to implement provisions for freeing the serfs. For Prussia, as for the rest of Europe, the early 1850's were years of prosperity, of economic and industrial expansion, and the Prussian government did much to foster this growth. In these years was inaugurated the remarkable cooperation between industry and universities and technical schools under government auspices that contributed significantly to Germany's later economic progress. Within Prussia and the area of the customs union, tolls on rivers and roads were abolished to encourage the free flow of trade, while a system of tariffs protected Prussia's infant industries from competition by states outside the union. Roads were improved, rivers and canals widened and deepened. The government sponsored banking programs on a limited scale to provide the capital for these projects. Although Prussia, unlike other German states, relied mainly on private enterprise to finance and manage its railroads, it did encourage the building of lines that were economically and militarily essential by guaranteeing interest on investments in them and by other financial devices. Furthermore, the government exercised close supervision over the construction of all railroads in order to prevent wasteful competition and to ensure that they would meet strategic requirements. Throughout the territory of the German customs union the rate of railroad construction was more rapid than in any other part of the Continent.

In the struggle for leadership in Germany, the Prussian government had attempted to take advantage of Austria's weakness during the 1848 revolutions by putting forward a proposal for unification through a federal union of German princes under Prussian domination. Austria soon recovered, however, and in November, 1850, compelled Prussia to withdraw the proposal through the Treaty of Olmütz, which patriotic Prussians subsequently branded as the Humiliation of Olmütz.

In the Olmütz treaty, Austria scored a major diplomatic victory over Prussia. Yet Austria was no more successful than Prussia in establishing control over the smaller German states. The stalemate between Austria and Prussia in Germany might have continued indefinitely, with the smaller states throwing their support from one side to the other to prevent either from gaining a decisive advantage. Above all, both France and Russia were vitally interested in preventing the unification of Germany under a single great power. Actually, the stalemate persisted for sixteen years after Olmütz. Then the struggle was decisively settled in Prussia's favor through the political genius of Otto von Bismarck, who became prime minister of Prussia in 1862.

The Constitutional Conflict in Prussia

The political history of Prussia after the revolutions of 1848 turned largely on the constitution granted to his people by King Frederick William IV in December, 1848, but subjected to several conservative revisions before its final promulgation in 1850. The constitution established a system of government very different from that desired by most Prussian liberals. The government remained authoritarian; executive power was vested in the king, and the royal ministers were responsible to the king alone. The constitution did provide for a parliament, but it was obviously intended to be little more than a façade. The upper house could be packed by royal appointments. Voting for representatives to the lower house, although ostensibly based on universal suffrage, was weighted to favor the biggest taxpayers. The establishment of this system of weighted votes proved to be a serious miscalculation on the part of the conservatives: it gave little voting strength to peasants and artisans, who by and large remained conservative during this period, and accorded the major representation to the rising middle classes, who wanted more political power to match their new economic status.

Despite its authoritarian character, the constitution had given parliament important legislative and taxation powers, which liberal representatives might have used to acquire a strategic position in the government if the king and his ministers had honestly respected their own constitution. But they did not. The most important constitutional rights and guarantees were simply disregarded. Freedom of the press was curtailed, public meetings and demonstrations were forbidden, liberal political clubs were dissolved, and the government removed inconvenient critics by arbitrary arrest and imprisonment.

The situation changed when, in September, 1858, King Frederick William IV suffered a mental breakdown and was declared insane. He was succeeded by his brother William, first as regent, then, upon the death of Frederick William in 1861, as king. William was a direct contrast to his dreamy and impractical brother. He possessed what family chroniclers liked to think were typical Hohenzollern virtues: industry, sound common sense, and a profound feeling of responsibility for the welfare of his people. He was also a man of honor. Although a staunch conservative and certainly no champion of constitutional government, he regarded the constitution granted to Prussia by the crown as a contract between the king and his people that was as inviolable as any other moral obligation. He accordingly put an end to many of the restrictive measures introduced during the last years of his brother's reign, dismissed his brother's ministers, and selected a cabinet that included men with liberal sympathies. It seemed as though a profound change were about to take place in Prussian politics, and hopeful liberals designated this first period of William's rule as the New Era.

Those who believed the prince regent would move in the direction of genuine parliamentary government were sorely disappointed. Although he meant to respect the constitution, he had no intention of surrendering his executive authority to parliament. His defense of his royal powers led to one of the bitterest and most important constitutional conflicts in German history. The issue was clear-cut: would the country be governed by king or by parliament?

The constitutional conflict in Prussia centered on control of taxation and of the army. Before becoming head of state, William had made his career in the Prussian army, and the army remained the chief object of his concern. It seemed to the prince and his military advisers that Prussia's main weakness in dealing with Austria in 1850 and in its overall foreign policy during the past decade had stemmed from military inadequacy. No important changes had been made in the Prussian army since 1815, and both its organization and its equipment were in dire need of renovation. Mobilization in 1859 during the war in Italy between France and Austria had glaringly exposed Prussia's military deficiencies. A drastic reform of the army seemed essential if Prussia were to return to the ranks of the great powers. In December, 1859, William appointed Albrecht von Roon (1803–1879) minister of war and authorized him to execute the necessary reforms. With the assistance of Helmuth von Moltke (1800–1891), chief of the army general staff, Roon was to make the Prussian army the most effective military machine in Europe.

It was over the question of army reform that the Prussian parliament came into direct conflict with the crown. According to the constitution, parliament's consent was required for the additional taxes needed to pay for the reorganization and reequipment of Prussian forces. Besides sharing the usual reluctance of legislative representatives to vote new taxes, liberals in the Prussian parliament feared that the proposed reforms, with their provisions extending the period of compulsory military service, would bolster the authority of the monarchy and strengthen the influence of the conservative-military clique, which might use the reformed army as much against domestic as against foreign foes.

Despite the opposition of many liberals, the Prussian parliament did agree to new taxes in 1860 and 1861, but in order to retain its strategic control over the government's powers of taxation, it refused to vote for a permanent increase in military appropriations. Elections in December, 1861, brought a more determined group of liberals into the Prussian parliament, and the new military budget submitted in March, 1862, was rejected. A dissolution of parliament and new elections failed to return more pliant representatives. The conflict between crown and parliament had reached a deadlock.

William, who had become King William I in January, 1861, could have dealt with the situation most easily by basing his authority squarely on the army, repudiating the constitution, and ordering the parliamentary deputies to go home. But this was a course William could not bring himself to pursue. He seriously considered abdicating in favor of his son, Crown Prince Frederick William, who sympathized with the liberal cause and under the influence of his strong-minded English wife (the daughter of Queen Victoria), favored the establishment of English parliamentary institutions in Prussia. But Frederick William was destined not to come to the throne for another twenty-six years; by that time the cause of genuine representative government in Prussia had been lost.

Bismarck

It was Roon, the minister of war, who persuaded William I to remain on the throne and to entrust the government leadership to the conservative statesman apparently offering the last hope for a solution of the constitutional conflict on terms acceptable to the monarchy. On September 23, 1862, Otto von Bismarck (1815–1898) was made provisional head of the Prussian government. His official appointment as prime minister followed on October 8.

The decision was difficult for the king because he distrusted Bismarck, who at this time was generally known only as an extreme conservative. So audacious were his views that even men who sympathized with his opinions feared he might plunge Prussia into civil war. Others, among them many liberals, refused to take him seriously. They reasoned that a man with such extreme ideas, so out of step with the times, would soon face political bankruptcy and be forced to yield to more moderate elements. Bismarck's political genius became apparent only after he had been in office for several years.

Bismarck was born in 1815, the son of a dull, unenterprising Prussian *Junker*, from whom he inherited his massive physique and prodigious strength. His middle-class mother was the daughter of a distinguished Prussian civil servant, whose sponsorship of reform had earned him a reputation for Jacobinism. In contrast to her stolid husband, she was high-strung, often ill-tempered, with a restless, inquisitive mind. It was from his mother that Bismarck inherited his temperament—and his brains.

The young Bismarck did not distinguish himself at school, but he did acquire a solid background in Greek and Latin, a fluent command of French and English, and a lively interest in history and literature. At the university he adopted the current pose of rebellious romanticism, joined briefly one of the radical *Burschenschaften*, engaged in passionate love affairs, drank, and dueled. Yet, while affecting to scorn his studies, he read widely in history and the German classics. After taking a degree in law, he entered the service of the Prussian state, but he resented the tedium and discipline of a bureaucratic career and soon resigned to manage his country estates. Still bored, he found release in wild escapades, which earned him local notoriety as "the mad Bismarck."

At this stage of his life he came into contact with a group of Pietists, among them Johanna von Puttkamer (1824–1894), whom he later married. Under their influence he appears to have experienced a genuine religious conversion. The belief that he was an instrument of God's will gave him a new feeling of confidence and purpose, but also a sense of responsibility for his actions to which he was to refer at many major crises of his life.

Bismarck entered public life in 1847, but was given little opportunity to prove himself until 1851, when the king appointed him Prussian delegate to the diet of the Germanic Confederation in Frankfurt. Here he gained his first experience in diplomacy and a detailed knowledge of German affairs. Later, as Prussian ambassador to St. Petersburg, and then to Paris, he had an opportunity to study the political situation in Russia and France and to size up the character of the rulers of these states.

Bismarck has been called a realist in politics, the exponent of a peculiarly modern and amoral *Realpolitik*. But most statesmen, even the most self-consciously idealistic, look upon themselves as realists. The distinctive quality of Bismarck's realism resulted from his ability to recognize the limita-

Bismarck in 1859.

tions of his own powers and those of the state he governed. In the tradition of Richelieu and Talleyrand, he regarded politics as the art of the possible, and his maneuvers to achieve the possible were masterful.

Bismarck was an artist in statecraft as Napoleon had been an artist in war. Like Napoleon's campaign strategy, Bismarck's policy was never bound by fixed rules or preconceptions. While remaining aware of long-term goals and broad perspectives, he concentrated on the exigencies of the moment. His plans retained a resilience which allowed for error, for misinformation, for accident—the *imponderabilia,* as Bismarck called them. He did not only take into account the most obvious moves of his opponents; he was prepared to deal with every conceivable move, even the most stupid, which if unanticipated might upset the cleverest calculations. Much of his success depended on patience and timing. He once compared himself to a hunter inching forward through a swamp to shoot a grouse while one false step might cause him to sink into a bog.

Bismarck's outstanding quality, and the one he himself valued most highly in a statesman, was the ability to choose the most opportune and least dangerous political course. He was keenly aware that politics presents a constant succession of alternatives, that there is rarely a single solution to a specific political problem; and he would explore simultaneously a wide range of possibilities until the moment came for a final choice. Even then, except when the choice was war, he left alternatives open and never committed himself irretrievably. Although frequently checked, Bismarck thus always remained in a position to abandon an unsuccessful policy and embark on some new course by which he might regain the political initiative and recoup his losses.

The absence of doctrinaire rigidity in Bismarck's politics is reflected in the shifts his personal values underwent in the course of his career. He was born a Pomeranian *Junker* into a society not distinguished for its political sophistication or breadth of vision. Bismarck's fellow squires were loyal to the king, to the kingdom of Prussia, and to the *Junker* class. Bismarck gradually emancipated himself from the standards of this society, and in due time moved from a Prussian, to a German, to a European, and ultimately even to a global, point of view. But it would be a mistake to think that Bismarck had no fixed values or loyalties. He was loyal to the Prussian state, which provided the means of his self-realization. At the height of his career, the keystone of his system of values was the German empire, which he regarded as his creation. To maintain and defend that creation became the aim of all his policies and the focus of all his energies.

Bismarck possessed that most rare quality of men of political genius—moderation, the ability to recognize where to draw the line. Unlike Napoleon, he was never a political gambler; he never staked the future of the state or his own career on the outcome of a battle or a political experiment. He did not wage war until he had ascertained that all other means had been exhausted and that all possible odds—military, diplomatic, and moral—were on his side. Each of his wars was fought with a clear, limited purpose. When he decided that the advantages to be gained by war no longer justified the risks involved, he became Europe's staunchest defender of peace.

Bismarck's Policies

Bismarck's most immediate problem upon becoming head of the Prussian government was the conflict with parliament. His approach to this crisis was characteristic. He first tried to compromise, and literally offered parliament an olive branch he had plucked at Avignon. When his various proposals for a compromise were rejected, he seized the moral initiative and accused parliament of violating the constitution by claiming exclusive control over the budget. By refusing to negotiate with the crown, which had also been given budgetary powers in the constitution, parliament itself had caused the breakdown of constitutional government. Therefore the crown had both the right and the duty to carry on the business of state without parliamentary cooperation.

From 1863 to 1866 Bismarck simply ignored parliament. He solved the financial problem by collecting the taxes already voted in 1861 and 1862. From these funds money was allocated to the army to carry through the projected military reforms.

To counteract Bismarck's tactics, parliament would have had either to engage in open revolt or to persuade a majority of the citizens to refuse to pay taxes. The weakness of the parliamentary position was immediately apparent. As long as the army remained loyal to the king, no revolt could be successful; and as long as the army stood behind the tax collector, it was inconceivable that any large number of Prussian citizens would withhold their taxes. Furthermore, the liberals of the 1860's, mindful of the grim lessons of 1848, were not prone to violence. Most of them were confident that human reason and the inevitable march of progress were on their side; they had only to wait until Bismarck's policies had been discredited. While they waited, Bismarck was free to concentrate on foreign affairs, which, he was convinced, would decide the crucial questions of Prussia's future.

Bismarck was well aware that most politically conscious Germans craved some kind of national unification; in his youth he himself had fallen under the influence of romantic nationalism. He therefore could not fail to see the advantage to Prussia of gaining the leadership of the nationalist movement. He also recognized that there were two major obstacles to Prussia's domination of Germany: Austria and France. Neither of these powers could be expected to concede Prussia the leadership of a united Germany unless compelled to do so, and such compulsion would very probably involve armed conflict.

Unlike many of the German liberals, Bismarck did not eschew the use of force. In one of his first speeches as prime minister—an appeal to the parliamentary finance committee to grant funds for army reforms—Bismarck said: "Germany is not looking to Prussia's liberalism but to her power . . . The great questions of our time will not be decided by speeches and majority resolutions—that was the mistake of 1848–1849—but by iron and blood." This statement, the most famous of all Bismarck's political pronouncements, disclosed a crucial aspect of his thinking. But it did not mean that Bismarck considered iron and blood the only means of establishing Prussia's leadership in Germany. The speech was primarily an appeal for military appropriations, and necessarily its emphasis fell on the importance of military power. Bismarck was aware of the hazards of war, and of the danger that victories on the battlefield might create military heroes who could become serious political rivals. Moreover, he realized that Prussia needed more than military power. It needed allies, and a diplomacy that would undercut the alliances of its opponents and secure the maximum moral advantage in any international controversy. Iron and blood, if used at all, should be employed only under the most favorable possible circumstances. Even then he believed the risks to be so great that he never abandoned his efforts to attain his ends by peaceful means.

The Polish Revolt

A revolt in the Russian part of Poland in February, 1863, gave Bismarck an opportunity to secure the goodwill of Russia. European public opinion was generally sympathetic to the Poles. France, Great Britain, and Austria made motions to intervene on behalf of the rebels. The pro-Polish position of France and Britain was understandable, especially since the French sympathized with the Polish Catholics and the British felt concern for an oppressed people. Austria's support of the rebels was motivated by a desire to conciliate its own large Polish population and to establish closer diplomatic ties with Britain and France. But in view of its festering minority problems and its need for Russian goodwill to bolster its position in central Europe, Austria's policy was a piece of arch-foolishness.

Bismarck made no such error. Disregarding the protests of liberals in the parliament, Bismarck sent a mission to St. Petersburg to assure the tsar of Prussian support, and he dispatched four army corps to the frontier. Prussian interests in any case demanded cooperation with Russia in order to prevent the revolt from spreading to Prussia's Polish provinces. The revolt was quelled, and as a result of these events, Prussia supplanted Austria as Russia's protégé in German affairs.

The Schleswig-Holstein Question and the Danish War

The revival of the complicated Schleswig-Holstein question in 1863 provided Bismarck further and far broader scope for maneuvering in foreign affairs. In 1848 the two duchies had rebelled against their dynastic overlord, the king of Denmark, who had tried to integrate Schleswig, with its large German population, into Denmark. An international treaty signed in London in 1852 restored Schleswig and Holstein to the king of Denmark on a dynastic (personal) basis but specifically forbade their integration with Denmark. In 1863 the Danish government enacted a new constitution which was widely interpreted as a step toward the incorporation of Schleswig into Denmark. The Danish action aroused the anger of German nationalists, who regarded both Schleswig and Holstein as German states. In response to the pressure of nationalist opinion, the diet of the Germanic Confederation resolved to send troops into Holstein, which was a member of the Confederation, to defend the independence of both duchies. Since both Austria and Prussia were also members of the Confederation, the action of the diet automatically involved them in the controversy.

Bismarck had no intention of subordinating Prussian policy to the decisions of the Austrian-dominated German federal diet, but neither could he afford to alienate German opinion by remaining aloof from the Schleswig-Holstein question. To secure independence of action and to gain the political initiative, he came forward in defense of international law as represented by the treaty concluded in London in 1852, which had been violated by both Denmark and the German federal diet. He then maneuvered Austria into joining Prussia in sending an ultimatum, on January 16, 1864, demanding that Denmark abide by the terms of the London treaty by abrogating its new constitution within forty-eight hours, a condition he

A Prussian coastal battery at Almor during the Austro-Prussian war against Denmark, 1864.

knew the Danes could not fulfill. Thus he dissociated himself from the action of the federal diet, destroyed Austria's advantage as leader of that body, and appeared in Germany as the champion of the German national cause. At the same time, by making impossible demands on Denmark, he obtained a reason for war while posing as the champion of international law.

But the Danes, too, were anxious for a showdown on the Schleswig-Holstein question. They rejected the ultimatum not only because of its impossible conditions but because they had confidence in the strength of their military and diplomatic position. They believed that they could contain an Austro-Prussian invasion until they received aid from other powers. And they had no doubt that such aid would be forthcoming, being convinced that neither Great Britain nor Russia would tolerate the conquest of the strategic Danish peninsula by the most powerful German states, and expecting support from Sweden and possibly from France as well. The Danes seriously misjudged the situation. Austria and Prussia declared war on Denmark on February 1, 1864. The Danes received no outside military support, and alone they were no match for the German powers. On April 18 German troops stormed the strategic fortifications at Düppel, which guarded the crossing to the principal Danish islands.

The British tried to rescue the Danes by diplomatic intervention. On April 25 an international conference met in London to deal with the Schleswig-Holstein question. Bismarck, in possession of the disputed territories, was in a strong bargaining position. His proposals for a settlement were rejected by the Danes, who thus incurred the blame for the failure of the conference. The war was renewed at the end of June, and by the middle of

July the Danes had been completely defeated. In the Treaty of Vienna of October 30, 1864, they surrendered both Schleswig and Holstein to Austria and Prussia.

In determining the final status of the duchies, Bismarck again persuaded Austria to ignore the German federal diet. In the Convention of Gastein of August 14, 1865, Austria and Prussia agreed to maintain joint sovereignty, with Prussia administering Schleswig and Austria administering Holstein, which lay between Schleswig and Prussia. A situation was thereby created which would make it possible to engineer an incident between Austria and Prussia whenever it might be required.

The Austro-Prussian War of 1866

There can be no doubt that when Bismarck arranged the Convention of Gastein in the summer of 1865, he had in mind the possibility that war with Austria for the leadership of Germany might become necessary. In the months that followed, his policies, as usual, were flexible and he tested a variety of possible courses. He tried to persuade Austria to agree to a division of influence in Germany, with Prussia dominating the area north of the Main, and he conducted a vigorous political campaign to persuade the German population and the governments of the smaller German states to accept Prussian leadership peacefully. At the same time, he began to lay the groundwork for success in a future conflict by securing support for Prussia among the great powers and by isolating Austria.

He had no difficulty with Russia. The Russians had no desire to see a single power dominate Germany, but they did not expect a complete Prussian victory; moreover, they welcomed a war likely to weaken their German neighbors. Tsar Alexander II remained grateful for Prussian support during the recent Polish insurrection and resentful of Austria's position in the Polish crisis and in the Crimean War. After ascertaining the tsar's attitude, Bismarck concluded that he could count on the benevolent neutrality of Russia in a war with Austria, at least during its first stages. Great Britain, which had not actively intervened in the Danish war even though important British interests were at stake, might be expected to stay out of a conflict over Germany.

The main problem was the attitude of France. In dealing with Napoleon III, Bismarck played a brilliant diplomatic game. He realized that the French emperor badly needed an international success to balance the increasingly obvious failure of the Mexican expedition and to quiet mounting criticism of his regime at home. Napoleon could only welcome a war between Prussia and Austria, which might be expected to exhaust the two major German powers, and give France the opportunity to extend its influence into the Rhineland and perhaps into the Low Countries as well. In October, 1865, Bismarck met Napoleon at Biarritz, where he appears to have hinted that Prussia would agree to France's acquisition of territory in the Rhineland or Belgium in exchange for Napoleon's promise of benevolent neutrality in the event of an Austro-Prussian war. Napoleon was most willing to give this assurance. His only fear was that Prussia would be defeated by Austria before France could gain sufficient advantage from the conflict, for his military observers during the Danish war had reported that the Austrian army was far superior to the Prussian. To balance the opposing forces, Napoleon helped Bismarck arrange an alliance with the new kingdom of Italy, which was looking for an opportunity to wrest Venetia from Austria as a further step toward Italian unification. To make sure of winning no matter what the outcome of the conflict in Germany, Napoleon concluded a secret treaty with Austria on June 12, 1866, whereby Austria agreed that, even if victorious, it would cede Venetia to France (which would receive the province on Italy's behalf), and consented to the establishment of a new independent state along the Rhine, which would presumably be a French protectorate.

By the spring of 1866 Bismarck had evidently decided that a war with Austria was unavoidable. His attempts to extend Prussian authority in Germany were being steadfastly opposed by Austria, which had strong backing from the smaller German states. Meanwhile, Bismarck had completed his diplomatic preparations, and the Prussian army had been reorganized and modernized. So far as Bismarck was concerned, everything now depended on timing; his alliance with Italy, signed on April 8, 1866, assured him of Italian support only if war with Austria broke out within three months.

Immediately after concluding the Italian alliance Bismarck set about forcing a crisis in German affairs. The Austrians were not reluctant to take up the challenge. They believed their army was superior, and they were assured of the support of the most important of the smaller German states. Early in June, 1866, using as a pretext the Austrian effort to reorganize the government of Holstein, Bismarck declared that Austria had violated the Convention of Gastein and sent Prussian troops into the duchy. Austria replied by persuading the diet of the Germanic Confederation to order federal mobilization against Prussia for violating the federal territory of Holstein. War between Prussia and Austria was now certain, and the smaller German states with any freedom of choice hastened to align themselves with Austria, which they expected to be the victor.

None of the prophets of Prussian defeat had reckoned with the new Prussian army. In training and equipment the Prussian army was now far superior to the Austrian. The Prussian breech-loading needle gun, which could be loaded and fired in a prone position, was more accurate and had a higher rate of fire than the Austrian muzzle-loader. In addition, the Prussian network of strategic military railroads gave the army a high degree of mobility.

Helmuth von Moltke, shown here in his office in Berlin. *The famous Prussian general represented a new type of professional army officer: a scholar far more than a man of action, who worked out his campaign plans and coordinated the operations of modern mass armies from his desk far behind the front lines.*

The Prussians also possessed superior leadership. The nerve center of the Prussian military organization was the army general staff, a body of carefully selected and highly trained experts, who applied to the conduct of war a continuous study based on the experience of the past and an analysis of contemporary military developments. General staff officers drew up detailed plans to meet every conceivable military emergency and to ensure the rapid mobilization and deployment of their forces—an important consideration in view of Prussia's long and exposed frontiers. The general staff included specialists to coordinate the movements of the unprecedentedly large armies raised by compulsory conscription, and to deal with the technical problems of transportation, communication, and supply. Once the armies were in the field, the general staff provided field commanders with a steady flow of information and advice, and readjusted tactics to correspond with the progress of the fighting.

Chief of the army general staff since 1857 was General Helmuth von Moltke, who in manner and appearance seemed far more a scholar than a soldier. In directing the preparation of Prussia's campaign plans, Moltke had employed bold new conceptions in strategy—among them the use of technical innovations such as the railroad and the telegraph—in his attempt to solve the problem of military operations with mass armies. Instead of adhering to the traditional strategy of concentrating forces at one point to achieve a military decision, he divided his troops, but kept them in a position to converge on a single point at the opportune time. "The main task of good army leadership is to keep the masses separate without losing the possibility of uniting them at the right moment," he said. "If on the day of battle the forces can be brought from separate points and concentrated on the battlefield itself; if the operations are directed in such a way that from different sides a last short march strikes simultaneously against the enemy's front and flank: then strategy has achieved the most that it can achieve, and great results must follow."

With all their plans and preparations made long in advance, the Prussians were able to seize the initiative from the beginning of the war. On June 15, 1866, the day after the diet of the German Confederation voted federal mobilization against Prussia, a Prussian army invaded Hanover, Saxony, and Hesse-Cassel, which had entered the conflict on the side of Austria. Meanwhile, the bulk of the Prussian forces advanced against the Austrians, who had been forced to divide their armies to meet a simultaneous invasion by Prussia's ally, Italy. On June 29 the Hanoverian army capitulated following its defeat at the Battle of Langensalza. Four days later, on July 3, 1866, the Austrian army was decisively beaten in the Battle of Königgrätz (or Sadowa). In just over two weeks the Prussians had scored a complete victory. It was one of the shortest and most decisive wars in history.

Moltke's strategy was much criticized by military experts despite the crushing victories of his armies. The Prussian triumph was ascribed to the needle gun, to the superior quality of the Prussian troops, to the incompetence of the Austrian commanders, to luck. Only a few military observers appreciated the significance of Moltke's handling of mass armies. Although both Austria and Prussia had been obliged to divide their forces, each side had sent almost half a million men into the field at Königgrätz, which in terms of numbers, remained the biggest battle in history until the First World War. Moltke's method of deploying so large a force to encircle and destroy an army maneuvered according to conventional tactics was a military innovation quite as important as the needle gun. The cast-steel rifled cannon developed by the great armaments firm of Alfred Krupp (1812–1887) were badly handled at Königgrätz, and would not demonstrate their worth until the war with France in 1870.

Bismarck's superb sense of proportion in international affairs was never more evident than in the period following the Battle of Königgrätz. Before the war, Bismarck had been obliged to overcome the doubts of his king and several of his military advisers about undertaking a conflict with Austria. Now he had to restrain their desire to exploit their victory by annexing vast stretches of Austrian territory and staging a triumphal march through Vienna. With Russia on one side and France on the other, Prussia could not afford to prolong the war, giving these great powers a chance to intervene, or to make Austria and the other defeated German states into bitter and irreconcilable opponents. Bismarck's one big aim in the war had been the expulsion of Austria from German affairs. This aim could be realized without annexing Austrian territory and without a victory march through Vienna, which would wound Austrian pride while accomplishing no political purpose.

The preliminary Peace of Nikolsburg of July 26, 1866, was followed on August 23 by the final Peace of Prague. Austria was deprived of all influence among the other German states, and the states of northern Germany, while retaining their old identities, were organized into the North German Confederation under Prussian leadership. The vanquished states of southern Germany were allowed to remain independent, but they were forced to sign treaties with Prussia that would bring their armies under Prussian leadership in the event of war with a foreign power. Only the rulers of Hanover and Hesse-Cassel, who refused to accept the Prussian terms, were deposed and deprived of their territories. These areas, together with Schleswig and Holstein and the free city of Frankfurt, were annexed by Prussia.

The End of the Constitutional Conflict in Prussia

The Prussian victory over Austria decided more than the question of supremacy in Germany. It also marked the final victory of authoritarian over representative government in Prussia. Bismarck was the hero of the hour. Now, at the height of his success and popularity, he came before the Prussian parliament to end the constitutional conflict. He appealed to the liberal majority for a bill of indemnity retroactively making legal the taxes whose collection had made possible the reorganization of the Prussian army and the consequent victories over Denmark and Austria. A surprisingly large number of deputies (75 out of 310) stood by their principles and refused to be swayed by Bismarck's achievements. In so doing, they risked repudiation by their constituents, for public opinion was enthusiastically on Bismarck's side. However, most of the liberals were enthusiastic about the Prussian victories and went over without hesitation to the Bismarck camp. National sentiment had triumphed over liberalism.

At the same time, Bismarck outdid the liberals at their own game. In the constitution of the North German Confederation he provided for a parliament that would be elected by universal manhood suffrage, a political democratization that went beyond most liberal programs. Bismarck made this move in the belief that the peasants and artisans who constituted the majority of the population were more conservative than the middle classes who dominated the existing electoral system in Prussia. The rapid growth of a volatile urban proletariat was to upset Bismarck's calculations, and the parties that appealed to the masses were to become his most determined opponents. Bismarck's concession of universal suffrage also lost him the support of a powerful body of conservatives. Much of his opposition henceforth was to come from his former conservative allies, who felt he had betrayed them. In addition, he was still opposed by discerning liberal idealists, who denounced his concessions as a sham and deplored the fact that the new representative bodies he had created lacked real legislative authority. After 1867 Bismarck's main support came from the nationalists, both liberal and conservative, and from interest groups that were reaping profits as a result of German unification or of governmental policies.

THE FRANCO-PRUSSIAN WAR

Prussia's remarkably rapid victory over Austria in 1866 ruined the plans of Napoleon III, who had counted on a long war in Germany that would exhaust the belligerents and permit France to dictate terms to the German states. Two days after Königgrätz, the French emperor attempted to salvage something from his German policy by offering to mediate between Prussia and Austria. Bismarck's fear that Napoleon might now seek to intervene actively in German affairs was his principal reason for concluding a swift and lenient peace with Austria. The danger from France, however, was slight. Many of Napoleon's troops were still in Mexico; the emperor himself was ill and lacked the strength and will power to pursue an energetic policy. In August, 1866, he tried to persuade Bismarck to honor his vague promise, made in Biarritz in 1865, to give Rhineland territory to France in exchange for French neutrality during the war against Austria. When Bismarck rejected this claim on the ground that such a concession would never be sanctioned by German public opinion, Napoleon put forward a request for Belgium and Luxembourg. At Bismarck's suggestion he made the terrible blunder of allowing his ambassador to put this proposal into writing. Bismarck was to avail himself of this document to influence British opinion during Prussia's war with France in 1870. He made immediate use of Napoleon's request for compensation in the Rhineland to persuade the south German states to enter into a close military alliance with Prussia for their mutual security.

It is commonly assumed that Napoleon's failure to gain compensation for Prussia's victories in 1866, and his need for prestige to bolster his tottering regime, forced him to adopt the desperate expedient of going to war with Prussia, and that Bismarck was eager to meet the emperor's bellicosity halfway. A remarkable amount of popular as well as official opposition to any extension of Prussian authority had manifested itself in southern Germany between 1867 and 1870, and Bismarck is supposed to have concluded that German unification could only be completed by exploiting the patriotic sentiment that would be generated by a national war against France.

This interpretation of the origin of the Franco-Prussian War is plausible, but it again raises the question of Bismarck's ultimate political objective in Germany. Was he consciously aiming to bring about the immediate political unification of Germany under Prussia, or would he have been content with a gradual extension of Prussian influence in southern Germany which would have avoided a direct challenge to France? War with a great power such as France was a hazardous undertaking under any circumstances, no matter how confident of victory the Prussian generals might be. In addition, there was always the possibility of outside intervention. If the war went at all badly for Prussia, a vengeful Austria might be expected to join forces with France. In the event of a Prussian victory, Great Britain, Russia, Austria, and other states might intervene to prevent the creation of the new great power which a united Germany would represent. It is hard to believe that Bismarck, who is credited with so much political realism, would have provoked a war with France that involved so many obvious dangers, especially as there seemed so little to be gained from such a war. By 1867 the south German states were already bound to Prussia by military and economic alliances. The fact that they currently opposed further Prussian encroachments on their sovereignty did not mean that they would always do so, or that their resistance could not be worn down over the years by skillful diplomacy.

There was a chance that the opposition of France, too, might be worn down or neutralized, and in 1868 Bismarck was presented with an opportunity to test this possibility. In that year Prince Leopold of Hohenzollern-Sigmaringen (1835–1905), a member of a Catholic branch of the Protestant ruling house in Prussia, was offered the throne of Spain after a revolution there. The establishment of a Hohenzollern in Spain, which would be another serious blow to the prestige of the French government, might be expected to precipitate a domestic crisis that would prevent effective French intervention in German affairs for some time to come. Furthermore, the presence of a Hohenzollern in Spain would force the French to keep part of their army on guard along the Pyrenees and thus would weaken the pressure they could bring to bear on Germany.

The French were certain to protest the Hohenzollern candidacy, but their objections could be turned aside as unjustifiable interference in the affairs of another country. If they directed their wrath against Prussia, Prussia could be made to appear as the innocent victim of French bullying and aggression.

If they chose to go to war with Prussia over the issue, their diplomatic case and hence their international position would be very weak indeed.

Bismarck's diplomatic campaign built around the Hohenzollern candidacy broke down by sheer accident—a coding error by a clerk in the Prussian legation in Madrid. Bismarck had counted on keeping the matter secret until Prince Leopold was formally elected by the Spanish parliament, so that the cabinets of Europe would be presented with an accomplished fact. Instead, as a result of the coding error, the Spanish parliament was allowed to adjourn. On July 2, 1870, before the *pro forma* vote had been held, the news of Prince Leopold's candidacy leaked out, and the French were given ample opportunity to take countermeasures. They at once brought pressure to bear on the leaders of the Spanish government to withdraw the offer and on the Hohenzollern family to decline it. But powerful elements within the French government wanted more than an elimination of the candidacy; they wanted to exploit the incident to humiliate Prussia and thereby bolster the prestige of their own government.

In the beginning, the French were successful in this endeavor. They totally ignored Spain and thrust Prussia to the fore as their chief target. On July 6 the French foreign minister, the duke of Gramont (1819–1880), set the public tone of the campaign with a statement in the Chamber of Deputies threatening war unless Prussia withdrew the candidacy of Prince Leopold. At the same time the French government urged the king of Prussia, as head of the house of Hohenzollern, to order his relative to abandon the Spanish project in the interests of European peace. To Bismarck's chagrin, the king yielded to the French arguments. On July 12, Prince Karl Anton (1811–1885), father of Prince Leopold, withdrew his son's candidacy.

The French had scored a great diplomatic triumph, but Gramont wanted to underline the fact that this victory had been achieved at the expense of Prussia. The French accordingly demanded that the king of Prussia write Napoleon a letter of apology for the trouble his relative had caused. The letter was to state that the king was animated by feelings of respectful friendship for France; it was specifically to disavow the candidacy of the king's relative to the throne of Spain and promise that this candidacy would never be renewed. On July 13, Count Vincent Benedetti (1817–1900), the French ambassador to Prussia, tried to bring these demands to the attention of the king of Prussia, who was at the spa of Ems. When the king understood the nature of the French proposals, he politely dismissed Benedetti and resisted all further efforts by the French ambassador to see him. On the same day the king sent Bismarck an account of what had happened.

Gramont had overplayed his hand, and in so doing he gave Bismarck the opportunity to turn the tables in the Hohenzollern affair. Upon receiving the royal telegram from Ems describing the incident with Benedetti, Bismarck edited it to make the king's dismissal of the French ambassador seem more brusque and rude than it had been. He then released the edited dispatch to the press. The French effort to inflict humiliation on Prussia was now made to appear the source of humiliation for France.

Bismarck was fully aware of the risk he was taking, but by this time he was evidently convinced that a peaceful settlement was no longer possible. If the French now chose to declare war on Prussia, as Bismarck expected, they would appear to be the aggressors, and Prussia might therefore hope to secure the benevolent neutrality of the moralistic Gladstone government in Great Britain. Bismarck had already arranged for the neutrality of Russia, which engaged to keep Austria uninvolved, and he had military alliances with the states of southern Germany. The Prussian generals assured him of the preparedness of the Prussian army. Diplomatically and militarily, Prussia was ready for war. But to the end Bismarck remained cautious, and he waited for the French to make the decisive move.

In France voices of caution were raised against war with Prussia. The emperor vacillated. He lacked confidence in the French army and feared a long, inconclusive struggle. But French public opinion was clamoring for war, Gramont and the Empress Eugénie declared that the empire could not survive if it accepted the latest humiliation from Prussia, and French military leaders were confident of victory. On July 15, 1870, the French government decided to declare war on Prussia. "The army is ready down to the last gaiter-button," said the French minister of war. "We go to war with a light heart," said Émile Ollivier, the French prime minister.

The ensuing conflict showed that the Prussian political and military calculations had been far more accurate than the French. Napoleon had hoped for support from a vengeful Austria and a grateful Italy, but he had badly misjudged the international situation. The Austrians were still suffering financially from the 1866 war; they were still angry with Napoleon for his support of Italy in 1859; and they were held in check by Russia. The majority of the German Austrians were enthusiastically on the side of their fellow Germans. The Hungarians, too, were opposed to an alliance with France against Prussia, for the reestablishment of Habsburg influence among the German states would diminish their own influence in the newly created Austro-Hungarian empire. In Italy, the king was tempted to help Napoleon, but Italian nationalists had been alienated by the French seizure of Nice and Savoy, and they were now anxious to take advantage of France's war with Prussia to occupy Rome, which was still garrisoned by French troops. Any efforts of the Italian king to side with France would probably have been met by a republican revolt, and Bismarck was in touch with republican leaders to lend support to such a revolt. Russia remained grateful for Prussian support during the Polish insurrection, and was anxious as well

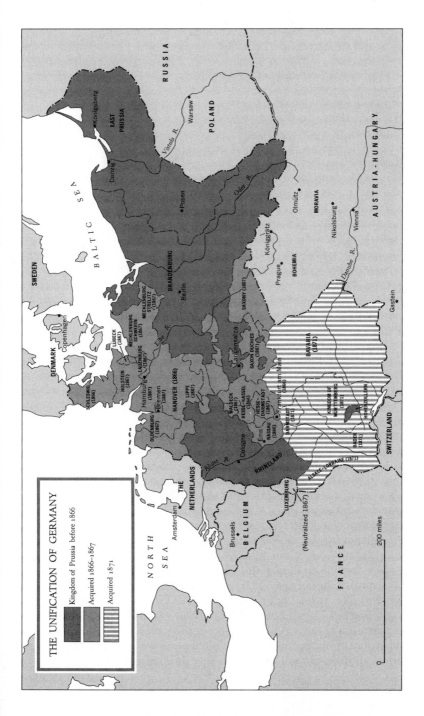

THE UNIFICATION OF GERMANY

Kingdom of Prussia before 1866

Acquired 1866–1867

Acquired 1871

to take advantage of French involvement in war to abrogate the Black Sea clauses of the Treaty of Paris imposed by France and Britain after the Crimean War. Toward the end of the Franco-Prussian War the Russians began to realize that a united Germany might be a greater danger to Russia than France had been, but in the early stages of the war Russian neutrality was assured. The British had for centuries regarded the French as the chief threat to the peace of Europe, and Bismarck reinforced this impression by releasing Napoleon's demands for Belgian territory to the London *Times*, which published them on July 25, 1870. In Britain as in Russia there was grave concern about the change in the balance of power that might result from Prussia's victories, but the Gladstone government was chiefly occupied with domestic reform, so the danger of British intervention was at all times slight.

In the military sphere, too, the Prussian preparations proved to be far superior to the French. The reorganization of the French army had been intelligently conceived, but had barely begun. France's secret weapon, the rapid-firing *mitrailleuse* cannon, had been kept so secret that most of the French troops did not know how to use it. The French *chassepot* rifle was better than the Prussian needle gun, but this advantage was offset by the superiority of the Prussian artillery, which was decisive in a large number of engagements. The Prussian army surpassed the French in organization, mobility, and leadership. As in the war against Austria, the Prussian general staff had prepared careful and detailed plans to ensure the speedy mobilization and deployment of its troops and to make maximum use of the railroad for purposes of transportation and supply. The rapid advance of the Prussian forces through southern Germany prevented the south German governments from even attempting to evade their military commitments, and meant that the war was fought on French rather than on German territory.

The actual conduct of the war, however, showed that Bismarck had been wise to try to accomplish his purposes by peaceful means. Had the French been better led, had they made full use of their superior weapons, had they taken advantage of Prussian errors, they might have fought the war to a stalemate or at least secured foreign mediation. As it was, the French generals made even more mistakes than the Prussian. Within a fortnight after the outbreak of war the Prussian armies had penetrated deeply into French territory and split the French forces. One French army, under General Achille Bazaine (1811–1888), was bottled up in the fortress of Metz. While attempting to relieve Bazaine's forces, a second French army, under Marshal Marie Edmé de MacMahon (1808–1893) was surrounded by the Prussians at Sedan. On September 2, 1870, after a day of heavy fighting, this entire army surrendered and the emperor was captured. The French defeat at Sedan brought the Second French Empire to a close.

King William I of Prussia proclaimed German Emperor in the Hall of Mirrors at Versailles, January 18, 1871. *Painting by Anton von Werner. This self-consciously symbolic act was held in the palace of Louis XIV, who in the opinion of patriotic Germans had inflicted so many humiliations on their country. The painting shows the King of Prussia flanked by his son, Crown Prince Frederick William, and his son-in-law, Frederick I, Grand Duke of Baden, whose hand is raised in calling for a cheer for the new emperor. Bismarck stands prominently in the foreground in a white uniform, with Moltke on his left. German enthusiasm for the new empire was not everywhere so great as suggested by this picture. Many German princes, and their subjects, resented intensely the loss of their sovereignty, and the highest-ranking dignitaries of the realm—the kings of Bavaria, Saxony, and Württemberg—were conspicuous by their absence at the ceremony of the imperial proclamation.*

The collapse of the empire did not end the war. Bazaine's army held out in Metz until October 27, and the French continued a dogged resistance from the provinces. They organized new armies that fought effectively despite their lack of training and equipment. The great French hope at this stage was foreign intervention, but Bismarck had laid his diplomatic foundations well and no aid was forthcoming. On January 28, 1871, after a siege of over four months, Paris capitulated. At the end of February representatives of the provisional French government appealed for an armistice. The final peace treaty between France and Germany was signed at Frankfurt on May 10, 1871. France was compelled to give up Alsace and part of Lorraine, to pay an indemnity of five billion francs, and to support a German army of occupation until the indemnity had been paid.

On January 18, 1871, shortly before the war had come to an end, King William I of Prussia was proclaimed German emperor, or kaiser, in the Hall of Mirrors of Louis XIV's palace at Versailles.

The French defeat, the establishment of the German empire, and the loss of Alsace-Lorraine created a hatred between France and Germany that would prevail until well after the Second World War. Bismarck has been charged with a major political error in aggravating the animosity of the French by annexing territory they regarded as their own, and the question is frequently raised of why he abandoned his restraint in this instance. As in all aspects of Bismarck's statecraft, there is no simple answer. With respect to Alsace-Lorraine, he had German as well as French opinion to consider. To the French the region might be part of their nation's sacred soil, but to the Germans it was a segment of the medieval German empire that had been stolen by France when Germany was weak and divided. Bismarck himself did much to incite German national feeling on this issue, for nationalism was his only weapon in overcoming the religious and political particularism of the German people. There was also the pressing and cogent argument of the army that these provinces were strategically essential. This argument appears to have been the overriding consideration for Bismarck, who was not only concerned about the security of South Germany but anxious to end all possibility of direct French pressure on the south German states. He realized that the loss of Alsace-Lorraine would arouse hostility in France, but he did not foresee how intense and lasting that resentment would be. In any case, he believed that the real reason for future French hostility would not be the loss of territory, but the fact of defeat itself and the creation of a German empire that would represent a constant threat to French security. For the first time since their victory over the Spaniards at Rocroi in 1643, with the exception of the brief interlude after 1814, the French had lost their position of political and military superiority in Europe.

CHAPTER 6

The Course of Reform: Great Britain and Russia

Two STATES at opposite ends of Europe, Great Britain and Russia, were not seriously affected by the revolutions of 1848, and for opposite reasons. In Russia a consistent policy of political repression had succeeded in controlling popular movements; in Britain the institutions of representative government gave men who might otherwise have led revolutionary movements the hope of accomplishing their purposes by legal means.

After 1850 the British continued to meet (if not always to solve) the problems confronting their country by reform legislation enacted by a Parliament that by 1884 represented almost all adult males. But in Russia, too, especially after the Crimean War, it was recognized that repression alone was no longer enough, and that major reforms of government and society were necessary. In Russia, however, reforms were enacted not by a popularly elected parliament, but by the autocratic government of the tsar.

GREAT BRITAIN IN THE MID-NINETEENTH CENTURY

For Britain, a more significant date than 1848 was 1851, the year of the first great international exhibition in London's Crystal Palace, where Britain paraded its prosperity and material achievements before an admiring world. The exhibition reflected a feeling general in the country of satisfaction with the present and confidence in the future, and a belief that given enough time all problems affecting human life and society could be solved by human reason.

The symbol of this mood was Queen Victoria, who ruled Britain and its colonies for sixty-four years (1837–1901). With her strong sense of moral

The Crystal Palace in London. *Designed by a greenhouse builder, it housed England's 1851 exhibition of the technical achievements of the age. With its 300,000 panes of glass and 5,000 columns and girders, it was in itself a monument to the new technology. The photograph shows the interior of the building after it was disassembled and rebuilt at Sydenham.*

respectability, her national pride and self-satisfaction, she represented to a remarkable degree the values and attitudes of her countrymen and of an age that has appropriately been named after her.

The British had grounds for satisfaction with their achievements. Despite the continued existence of widespread poverty, slums, and poor working conditions, the vast majority were better housed and better fed than ever before, and enjoyed more of life's amenities. By 1851 Britain was not only the workshop of the world but also its shipper and trader, insurer, and major investor. During the second half of the nineteenth century the prosperity of the people steadily increased, as did Britain's national wealth and productivity. It is estimated that in the course of these decades, the real wages of all workmen rose as much as 30 per cent, while the increase for skilled workmen was considerably greater. Only toward the end of the century did Britain begin to face serious competition from other parts of the world, especially Germany and the United States.

British politics after 1850 must be viewed against this background of national prosperity and optimism. Although voices were raised against the smug self-satisfaction and philistinism of the era, and although there were prophets of disaster, the prevailing sentiment was one of confidence in the nation and in its institutions.

For British politics in the second half of the nineteenth century, the Reform Bill of 1867 serves as a watershed. In the years before the bill, political parties and political loyalties were in a state of flux; after 1867, the parliamentary system settled firmly into the pattern of two-party government. The terms Whig and Tory gave way to Liberal and Conservative to describe the major British political parties, and it began to seem part of the natural order of things, as a character in a Gilbert-and-Sullivan operetta observed, "that every boy and every gal, that's born into the world alive, is either a little Liberal, or else a little Conservative."

The era of political instability began with the collapse of the Tory (Conservative) Peel government in 1846, when Peel's conversion to free trade and the repeal of the major agricultural tariffs (corn laws) shattered the unity of the Tory party. A period of Whig (Liberal) supremacy followed, but the Whig party too was weakened by internal strife. Between Peel's fall in 1846 and the formation of Gladstone's first government in 1868 there were eight separate ministries, none of them backed by strong party support or committed to carrying out a particular political program. Party ideas and party memberships changed rapidly; politicians who felt betrayed by their leaders formed new political groups or transferred their allegiance to other parties. Individual politicians underwent astounding transformations in their views. Gladstone, the giant of nineteenth-century British liberalism, began his parliamentary career as a high Tory and defender of

Queen Victoria and the Prince Consort, 1854. Roger Fenton's photograph is a far cry from the flattering court portraits of Winterhalter.

slavery and imperialism. His conservative counterpart, Disraeli, began his parliamentary career as something of a radical.

Palmerston

In this period of political confusion and shifting loyalties, of weak governments and lax party discipline, politics tended to be dominated by individuals rather than by parties or principles. The most prominent statesman of the era was Henry John Temple, viscount Palmerston (1784–1865). Although a leader of the Whig party, Palmerston was without fixed political ideas or party loyalties. His strength lay in his astounding energy, his ability to work with men of widely different opinions, and his popularity with the voter. His personality embodied to a remarkable degree the tastes and prejudices of the British: his patriotism coupled with a distrust of foreigners, his good humor and courage, his love of horses and hunting, all combined to make him the most popular statesman of the day. His success was partly the result of longevity and of undiminished vitality in old age. At seventy, he still rode to hounds, he still relished long debates in Parliament, and he astounded younger colleagues by walking home from all-night parliament sessions buoyant, alert, and apparently as fresh as ever.

Palmerston's easygoing manner and willingness to compromise were major assets in conciliating political opponents and in winning personal support in Parliament, but they also aroused the contempt and distrust of men with more rigid opinions. George Canning, Britain's foreign secretary and prime minister earlier in the century, said that Palmerston "almost reached the summit of mediocrity," and Gladstone called him "by far the worst minister the country has had during our time"; yet Canning included Palmerston in his ministry and Gladstone joined a Palmerston government.

In contrast to many of his colleagues, Palmerston recognized the importance of public opinion in British politics, especially after the passage of the Reform Bill of 1832. When he was unable to win support within an existing Parliament he appealed directly to the British voter. Disraeli complained that in the election campaign of 1857 appeals for Palmerston were made "in favor of a *name*, and not a *policy*." The name was sufficient, however. The elections resulted in a great victory for Palmerston.

Palmerston's bombastic foreign policy and his militant defense of British honor and national interests enhanced his popularity at home. His assertion of British rights occasionally became ludicrous. In 1850 he risked war with Greece and France to defend the doubtful claims against the Greek government of a certain Don Pacifico (a Gibraltar-born Portuguese Jew whose house had been burned down by a rioting Athens mob) on the ground that the man had been born a British subject and was therefore entitled to the protection of the British government. Palmerston

Lord Palmerston. *Affectionately called "the most English minister," he was in office five years before the downfall of Napoleon, three years after Bismarck came to power in Prussia, and for all but about ten of the years that lay between.*

shared—and fanned—the bellicose attitude of the British public at the time of the Crimean War, and rode to the premiership on the strength of his war policy. He honestly feared the Russian threat in the Near East, but before the Crimean War was over his apprehensions were focused on the growing strength of his ally Napoleon III. By 1860, with the French annexation of Nice and Savoy, the rapid development of the French Atlantic ports, and the modernization of the French navy, he began to speak about the probable necessity of war with France.

After the disasters and disillusionments of the Crimean War, however, the British were no longer so eager to engage in foreign military adventures, and Palmerston was too shrewd a politician to ignore this sentiment. During the Austro-Prussian war against Denmark in 1864 he wanted to intervene on the side of the Danes to prevent the key to the Baltic Sea from falling into the hands of a great power, but because of the apathy of British public opinion, he restricted his intervention to diplomatic maneuvers and protests. Public sentiment also affected his policies with respect to the American Civil War. Although he professed neutrality, Palmerston in fact supported the South in the belief that an independent Confederacy that could negotiate its own treaties might provide not only raw materials, particularly cotton for the textile mills of England, but also an open market for British manufactured goods. From a long-range point of view perhaps his most important consideration was that the dissolution of the Union would weaken a potential political and economic rival, and create a balance of power in North America comparable to the situation in Europe which had proved so great a benefit to Britain over the centuries.

The American Civil War attracted greater attention and aroused far deeper passions in Britain than the wars that transformed the power structure of Europe in the later nineteenth century. Not only British political and economic interests were involved, but fundamental questions of principle. The British were deeply divided in their views, with some admiring the aristocratic-oligarchic system of government of the South and others favoring the greater degree of democracy that seemed to prevail in the North and feeling a moral and emotional commitment to the abolition of slavery. In the light of theories of economic determinism, it is interesting to note that popular opinion was most fervently on the side of the North in the British textile regions, which were most adversely affected by the northern blockade of southern cotton. Palmerston eventually gave in to the preponderance of British sentiment for the cause of the North, as he was to yield to popular feeling on many other foreign-policy issues following the Crimean War. Britain did not intervene on the side of the South any more than it intervened on the side of Denmark.

Palmerston's domestic policy was aimed at preserving the *status quo.* "One cannot always be legislating," he said. He especially disliked proposals for further franchise reform. "I cannot be a party to the extensive transfer of representation from one class to another . . . We should by such an arrangement increase the number of Bribeable Electors and overpower Intelligence and Property by Ignorance and Poverty." This attitude reflected the views of many middle-class voters emancipated by the 1832 reform bill, who considered their interests safeguarded by the existing laws. They had no desire to see their privileges undermined by new legislation or their political influence diluted by the extension of the franchise which was desired by reformers.

Domestic Reforms before 1867

The period before 1867 was not altogether barren of domestic reform. Palmerston himself, as home secretary, made vigorous efforts to combat air pollution and improve sanitation. He devised a system of tickets-of-leave for convicts (a kind of parole), and adopted the ideas of the great reformer, Lord Ashley, now Earl of Shaftesbury (1801–1885), for combating juvenile delinquency. Shaftesbury said of him: "I have never known any Home Secretary equal to Palmerston for readiness to undertake every good work of kindness, humanity and social good, especially to the child and the working class. No fear of wealth, capital, or election terrors; prepared at all times to run a-tilt if he could do good by it."

At mid-century, during the Whig government of Lord John Russell (1792–1878), the administration of the Poor Law was transferred from arbitrary local control to a government board under the direction of a cabinet minister. A Public Health Act established a central directorate to create local boards of health. In 1850 a Factories Act set a maximum 10½-hour day for factory workers, with a 7½-hour day on Saturday. Workers employed in establishments too small to be subject to government inspection were not affected, nor were shop assistants and domestic servants, whose hours of work were still unlimited. In 1855 a Civil Service Commission was created to obtain candidates for the home civil service by competitive examination instead of through patronage, but since final responsibility for appointments still rested with the heads of the various departments, the effect of the reform was limited. An act of June, 1858, put an end to property qualifications for members of Parliament. An act of the following month removed disabilities on Jews, permitting them to hold seats in Parliament.

Some of the most notable government reforms were undertaken by Gladstone, chancellor of the exchequer in several administrations between 1852 and 1865. By simplifying the taxation system and the collection of various levies, he was able simultaneously to increase the national revenue and to lower taxes. He disapproved of the income tax, believing that the ease with which it could be collected would encourage government extravagance, and thought it should be used only in periods of national emergency; it was in fact levied during the Crimean War. In 1861 Gladstone began to combine all money bills for the year into a single budget bill; henceforth opponents of a particular item could reject it only by opposing the budget as a whole, a step which they might be reluctant to take. By this stratagem he succeeded in abolishing the tax on paper and thereby made possible the publication of cheap newspapers and magazines, the first of the mass media. Gladstone was a champion of free trade, and his influence was decisive in securing the passage of Richard Cobden's trade treaty with France in 1860, a move that did much to ease diplomatic tension with France at this time. Gladstone regarded the trade treaty as the only alternative to the "high probability of war," and he made it an integral part of his 1860 budget, which he conceived as a "European operation." Following in the footsteps of Peel, Gladstone tried to stimulate trade and national productivity by reducing taxes and tariffs of every kind. Using the French treaty as a lever, he abolished or substantially lowered duties on all imports.

The Reform Bill of 1867

These reforms scarcely even began to fulfill the needs of a rapidly changing British society. The remarkable feature of British politics, however, was the confidence of most advocates of reform that necessary changes could be effected through the existing parliamentary institutions, and that what the country required above all was an extension of the franchise. Throughout the nation there were mass meetings—some of the crowds were estimated at 200,000 or more—demanding not revolution, but voting rights. Several attempts were made by governments of both major parties to secure the passage of innocuous franchise-reform bills, but they were regularly defeated. With the death of Palmerston in October, 1865, Gladstone believed the Whig party could at last be transformed into a genuinely liberal body which would push through the necessary reform legislation. The time had come, he said, for a "new commencement."

It was a Conservative government, however, that took the lead in extending the franchise. Although genuinely concerned about social questions, Benjamin Disraeli, the Conservative leader in the House of Commons, was above all a politician, and his attitude toward franchise reform appears to have been determined primarily by expediency. His tactics and expressions of opinion were anything but consistent, being characterized instead by improvisation, and often reflecting his efforts to respond to the political moods of the moment. It is possible, however, as he contended later, that he recognized at an early stage that a radical extension of the franchise, so ardently advocated by the more extreme liberals, would in fact benefit his own party because it would create new voters among the more prosperous artisans and farmers, who would be more likely to vote Conservative than the middle-class citizens enfranchised by the Reform Bill of 1832. If this was the case, his reasoning was similar to that of Bismarck, who in 1867 conceded universal manhood suffrage to the voters of the North German Confederation. Both men were undoubtedly influenced by the success of Napoleon III's plebiscites. The extension of the franchise in Britain would be a gamble for the Conservative party—"a leap in the dark," as Lord Derby (1799–1869), the Conservative prime minister, later described it, but after twenty years in a minority party with only interludes of power as a result of splits among the Liberals, the more realistic among the Conservatives were ready to gamble. At the same time, the huge mass meetings in every part of the country had begun to shake even the more rigid Conservatives, as did a riot that broke out on July 23, 1866, in London's Hyde Park, within full view of the residents of fashionable Park Lane. To many Conservatives it began to appear that the alternative to franchise reform might be revolution. Once Disraeli was certain of the backing of his own party, he was assured of the passage of a franchise-reform bill. The Liberals would be forced to support it, since opposition would be construed as repudiation of their own reform program, and the House of Lords could be expected to pass the measure because a Conservative government had introduced it.

The original franchise bill submitted to Parliament by the Conservatives

Benjamin Disraeli, Earl of Beacons-field. *Conservative party leader and masterful diplomat.*

was a cautious document filled with reservations, but Disraeli apparently expected—and hoped—that the Liberal opposition would eliminate many of these reservations and greatly increase the size of the proposed electorate. This was, in fact, what happened. The final Reform Bill of August 15, 1867, was a major step in the democratization of the country. It provided for a wide extension of the franchise for elections to Parliament and almost doubled the number of voters, which rose from about one million to two million. In the boroughs it gave the vote to all men who paid taxes on property or paid an annual rent of at least ten pounds, and in the counties to all who received an income of five pounds or more from their land or paid an annual rent of at least twelve pounds. The vote was withheld from the urban poor, from domestic servants, from the majority of agricultural workers, and from women (whose political rights John Stuart Mill supported in a spirited plea soon afterward). There was also a large-scale though still inequitable redistribution of parliamentary seats to allow for population increases and movements that had taken place since 1832. Boroughs with populations of less than ten thousand would henceforth send one member to Parliament instead of two; larger towns were given two or three members; nine new boroughs were created; twenty-five additional members were allotted to the counties. In 1868 franchise-reform bills for Scotland and Ireland were enacted. The Scottish bill was very similar to the English bill of 1867. The

Irish bill reduced income requirements for voting in the boroughs, but left the county franchise unaltered.

In 1868 Disraeli succeeded Derby and Gladstone replaced Russell as heads of the Conservative and Liberal parties, respectively. Under the leadership of these powerful personalities the two parties emerged as the only significant political organizations in Britain, and were therefore able to enforce a great degree of party discipline on their members. Parliamentary politics became more than ever a national game, with unwritten rules and procedures that came to be clearly recognized. Parliament itself gained new prestige as a result of its significant accomplishments and of the high intellectual level of its debates during the Gladstone-Disraeli era, and in contrast to parliamentary bodies in Germany after 1871, it attracted exceptionally gifted men to its ranks.

For the Conservatives the Reform Bill of 1867 indeed proved a leap in the dark. Industrial workers did not rally to the Conservative party as anticipated, and the first elections after the passage of the bill resulted in a tremendous victory for the Liberals. In December, 1868, Gladstone formed his first ministry at the head of what was now unequivocally the Liberal party. The power of the right wing of the party had been shattered in the last elections, Palmerston was gone, and the radicals were willing to rally under Gladstone's banner.

With the passage of the 1867 franchise reform bill, the British parliament actually did embark on the kind of "new commencement" Gladstone had envisaged, but the course of reform in Britain was anything but systematic or logical. Because parliamentary representatives always had to consider those influential members of the electorate whose interests would be affected by any significant change in existing institutions, reforms enacted through British parliamentary processes were almost invariably a product of negotiation and compromise. The results seem haphazard, and to proponents of reform they generally seemed inadequate. But, although they rarely satisfied anyone completely, neither did they alienate any significant segment of British society (Ireland always excepted) or arouse the kind of hostility which might have threatened the parliamentary system itself.

Gladstone's First Ministry, 1868–1874

William Ewart Gladstone (1809–1898) served his country in the House of Commons for over sixty years. One of the most efficient administrators of his age and a brilliant financier, he combined personal vigor with remarkable powers of concentration and a retentive memory. He was a superb debater, whose eloquence was backed up by an uncanny mastery of facts and figures. Like many statesmen of his time, he pursued interests which ranged far beyond politics. Fluent in French, Italian, and German, he had read widely and traveled extensively. He was a distinguished classical scholar, author of a three-volume work *Studies on Homer and the Homeric Age* (1859). The chief influence on his life, however, was biblical literature and the writings of Protestant theologians. He earnestly tried to act as a moral and upright Christian in his personal and political life, and his politics frequently took on the nature of a moral crusade. Typical of his seriousness of purpose and humanitarian impulses was his project to redeem prostitutes by persuading them to enter a home for moral rehabilitation maintained by himself and his wife.

During Gladstone's first administration an impressive amount of reform legislation was passed. The prime minister first turned his attention to Ireland, where the need for reform was more desperate than in any other part of the United Kingdom and where hatred of English rule was being manifested in terrorism and open rebellion. "My mission is to pacify Ireland," Gladstone declared before taking office. He did his best to achieve that purpose, and during his four terms as prime minister devoted much time and energy to the matter, finally exposing himself to political defeat and his party to political annihilation for the Irish cause.

The problem was an old one. The Irish had never totally submitted to English rule, and the Act of Union of 1801, which provided for the union of the Irish and English parliaments and for religious union under the Church of England, had not made the Irish more amenable to English leadership. Irish discontent was the product of national self-consciousness, of the religious division between Protestant England and Roman Catholic Ireland, and of sheer economic misery. Englishmen owned a large part of the land of Ireland. In most instances, the landlord lived in England and left the administration of his Irish estate to a local agent, who was expected to obtain for his employer a specified annual income from the property. This system led to many abuses. The refusal of the large majority of landlords and their agents to give long leases or other guarantees of tenure to their landless tenants stifled the initiative of the Irish peasants, who had no incentive to improve property from which they might be evicted at any time without compensation.

Gladstone set out to remove what he believed to be the major causes of Irish discontent. The Disestablishment Act of July 26, 1869, ended the dominion of the Anglican church as the official church in Ireland; henceforth the Irish Roman Catholics were not obliged to support a church they did not attend. The Anglican church was stripped of about half its Irish property, the income from which was subsequently allocated for poor relief, education, and other local needs. Gladstone then attacked the far more difficult problems of land tenure and absentee landlordism, which had become increasingly critical as a result of the large growth of the population of Ireland. The Irish Land Act of August 1, 1870, provided that an evicted tenant receive some compensation for improvements he had made. If, however, his payments were in arrears, he would receive nothing unless the rent could be proved "exorbitant." In practice the new law hardly touched the evils it was supposed to remedy. It failed to establish fair rents or security of land tenure, and landlords soon found they could avoid payment of compensation for improvements by increasing the rent sufficiently to force their tenants into default. Gladstone tried hard to achieve more for Ireland, but was unable to overcome the apathy and opposition in his own party.

Gladstone's reforms in England were more successful. For the many members of his party who believed in human progress and perfectibility, one of the most urgent tasks facing the new government was the improvement of the standard of English elementary education, which was far inferior to that available in France and Prussia. Approximately half the four million children of school age at this time did not attend school at all, and the majority of those who did left by the age of eleven. About a million children went to schools run by the Church of England, which were supported by voluntary contributions supplemented by government grants. Another million attended schools that received no government support and that were not controlled or inspected in any way, a situation that had produced the type of institution represented, apparently without much exaggeration, by Dotheboys Hall in Dickens's *Nicholas Nickleby* (1838–1839).

On August 9, 1870, the government secured the passage of an Education Act, which reflected the conflict of interests and loyalties involved in the issue and the pragmatic attitude with which British legislators approached a problem. The aim of the new act was to make elementary education available to all, and to do so as quickly and as cheaply as possible. Voluntary schools were retained if they could demonstrate their adequacy. Many were given government financial support, and all were subject to government inspection. New schools were set up wherever they were needed under the control of locally elected education boards. They were to be maintained by government grants, local taxes, and fees paid by parents. The great difficulty in connection with the school law was religion. Dissenters (Protestant Christians who did not belong to the Church of England) strongly objected to state support of Church of England schools, especially because the new law permitted these schools to continue their religious instruction. On the other hand, all denominations objected to the secular character of the new board schools, which were not to give religious instruction of any kind. The act itself left much to be desired, for it did not provide for compulsory or free education. It nevertheless represented a big step forward in raising educational standards, and paved the way for further reforms. In 1880 elementary education was made

"The internal economy of Dotheboys Hall." *An illustration by "Phiz" from Dickens'* Nicholas Nickleby.

compulsory, and in 1891 all school fees for public education were abolished. At the university level, a University Tests Act passed in 1871 freed students at Oxford and Cambridge from the need to submit to religious tests in order to obtain degrees.

Besides education, the Gladstone administration turned its attention to the reform of three important branches of the British government: the civil service, the army, and the judiciary. The reform of the civil service, begun in 1855, was extended by an Order in Council of June 4, 1870, which required that the recruitment of civil servants in all government departments be based on competetive examination. The measure was designed to improve the quality of government officials and meant that, in theory at least, membership and promotion in the civil service would no longer be subject to the whims and favors of department heads. Exempted from this provision was the foreign office, where family connections and wealth were still regarded as essential qualifications.

An Army Enlistment Bill of 1870 abolished the long twelve-year period of military service in favor of a six-year enlistment period followed by six years in the reserves. A bill to abolish the purchase of officers' commissions, defeated in the House of Lords, was subsequently put through by royal warrant. By far the most important of the army reforms enacted by the Gladstone government, however, was a measure which subordinated the commander-in-chief of the army to the minister of war in the cabinet; the army was thus removed from the control of the crown and placed directly under the control of parliament.

A Judicature Act of 1873 simplified the British legal system and put an end to abuses such as those described by Dickens in *Bleak House* (1852–1853), which permitted lawyers to consume the bulk of a client's estate before bringing his case to court.

In 1872 the Gladstone government took a big step in the democratization of the franchise with the passage of a Ballot Act, for which reformers had agitated for over half a century. This measure, which made voting secret for the first time, made bribery more difficult and ended the more obvious possibilities for exercising direct pressure on voters.

One of Gladstone's most controversial political moves was his unsuccessful effort to secure the enactment of a temperance bill. In an age when alcohol was clearly the chief opiate of the masses, and when the low price and constant availability of spirits encouraged drunkenness, a moderate bill might have been beneficial. But the advocates of temperance went too far. The licensing bill of 1872 proposed not just a restriction of the consumption of spirits but total prohibition. The bill was defeated, but its mere introduction did much to injure Gladstone at the polls. The powerful brewery and distillery interests united against him, as did the owners of the public houses (pubs), the Englishmen's neighborhood forums. "We have been borne down in a torrent of gin and beer," Gladstone said after his election defeat in 1874.

There were other reasons for the Liberal defeat. The Liberal party was badly split and Gladstone was having trouble holding his cabinet together. Disraeli contemptuously called the Liberal leaders a "range of exhausted volcanoes." The Church of England had been alienated by the Irish Disestablishment Act. Anglicans and dissenters, the latter a major source of Liberal strength at the polls, had been alienated by the Education Act. Advocates of temperance resented the government's failure to pass a temperance bill; their opponents were angry that such a bill had been introduced at all.

Hostility aroused by Gladstone's domestic policies was reinforced by patriotic resentment of his slack foreign policy. Bismarck had been allowed to shift the balance of power on the Continent without the slightest regard for Britain or British interests. In 1872 Gladstone had acceded to the demands of a truculent American government for the settlement of claims in connection with the damage caused by the Confederate raider *Alabama*, a ship which had been equipped in Liverpool and had been allowed to sail from that harbor to prey on Union shipping during the American Civil War. In retrospect, it appears that the fifteen million dollars paid to the United States in settlement of the *Alabama* affair probably constituted one of the best investments Britain ever made; Americans were impressed by the moderation and fairness of the British government, and the incident, which might have had ugly consequences, became instead a landmark in the restoration of goodwill between the two nations. Gladstone's policy was not seen in this light at the time, however, and he was bitterly criticized for his failure to defend British interests more vigorously.

Disraeli's Second Ministry, 1874–1880

The Conservative victory in the elections of February, 1874, the first in which the secret ballot was used, resulted in the formation of Disraeli's second ministry. Now for the first time Disraeli enjoyed an independent majority in the House of Commons; previously he had been associated only with coalition governments.

The great tragedy in the political career of Benjamin Disraeli (1804–1881) was that he came to power so late in life. In 1874 he was seventy and ailing; in two years poor health would force him to give up his leadership of the House of Commons and move to the House of Lords as the earl of Beaconsfield, although he nevertheless stayed on as prime minister. He had long been suspected of being a political opportunist and adventurer, and his dandified dress and social affectations increased the distrust of his critics. Moreover, although he was a baptized Christian, he took considerable pride in his Jewish background. In this age of strong religious feeling and social prejudice, the remarkable thing is that Disraeli ever came to power at all. The fact that he did so suggests something of the tolerance and scope for talent present in the British political system. And Disraeli did have talent. He was a shrewd parliamentary tactician, an able administrator, a match for Gladstone in debate, and a masterful diplomatist. Like Napoleon III he had the ability to sense and exploit the popular movements of his day, but in contrast to the French emperor he did not indulge in chimerical schemes.

As a Conservative, Disraeli thought the primary mission of his party should be to preserve the best features of British society, but he did not believe the party should be merely negative and obstructionist. On the contrary, he felt it should repair and construct; it should accept change—indeed, it should take the leadership in change by building on existing institutions. Its strength should lie in confidence and calm; it should have the moral power to attract idealistic youth as well as traditionalists; it should appeal to intellect as well as to interest.

While injecting new vitality into the Conservative party's philosophy, Disraeli introduced some practical and badly needed reforms into its machinery. During the period of Liberal ascendancy after 1868, the Conservative Central Office was established. Its task was to get in touch with local Conservatives and encourage them to form democratically run local associations which would suggest candidates in preparation for the next elections. The Central Office compiled a classified list of candidates and undertook to supply local associations with the type of candidates required by local conditions. Thus the foundations were laid for the election victory

The Disraeli cabinet in 1876. *Disraeli is standing at the extreme right. Standing, third from the left, is Lord Salisbury, Disraeli's successor as head of the Conservative party and three times prime minister.*

of 1874, and party machinery was created which was to serve as a model for other British parties.

Disraeli did not value political power just for its own sake; he sincerely desired—and in this he again resembled Napoleon III—to use that power to improve the lot of humanity. His concern for social justice is evident in his novels, above all in *Sybil, or The Two Nations* (1845), which contrasts the life of the upper classes and the wretched condition of the workers in the depression of the 1840's. During his parliamentary career Disraeli repeatedly tried to give concrete expression to this concern, and his second ministry (his first with an independent majority) was in many ways as productive of reform as Gladstone's.

In 1875 the Conservative government passed two labor laws, which, Disraeli assured the queen, were the most important pieces of social legislation of her reign. The first, the Employers and Workmen Bill, gave labor the same legal status as the employer with regard to breaches of contract. Previously, a workman who broke a contract with his employer could be sent to prison, whereas an employer who broke a contract with his workman was liable only to a civil action for damages. The second, the Trade Union Act, abolished many restrictions on union activity by giving unions the same rights as individuals. Thus, peaceful picketing and similar labor tactics became legal. The Factory Act, also of 1875, set a maximum fifty-six hour week for factory workers. (Again, shop assistants and employees in plants too small to be inspected were not affected.) Other legislation of 1875 included a Public Health Act, which furnished the nation with a badly needed sanitary code, and an Artisans' Dwellings Act, which established a minimum housing standard and made a start at providing adequate housing for the poor. This act was a new departure, for it called upon public authorities to remedy the defects of housing built by private enterprise, empowering them to raze existing structures for sanitary or other reasons and to replace them with new buildings for the use of artisans (workmen). The year 1875 also saw the passage of a Sale of Food and Drugs Act to prevent adulteration of food and medical quackery, and an Agricultural Holdings Act to give tenants compensation for property improvements in case of eviction. The Merchant Shipping Act of 1876 was an attempt to improve living and working conditions for merchant seamen, and to halt the use of unseaworthy vessels, which were often sent forth so well insured that the owners made a profit when they sank. Sponsored by Samuel Plimsoll (1824–1898), this act sought to prevent the overloading of ships by requiring placement of a mark on the side of every cargo vessel—the "Plimsoll line"—that had to appear above the water level at all times.

Disraeli's most spectacular achievements, however, were in the field of foreign affairs. In November, 1875, he made the brilliant stroke of purchasing the controlling shares in the Suez Canal from the khedive of Egypt, borrowing the money from the Rothschilds and subsequently securing parliamentary approval. The great problem in foreign affairs in the late 1870's was the crisis in the Near East, where Disraeli pursued the traditional British policy of preserving the Ottoman Empire as a bulwark against Russian expansion. By astute negotiations he persuaded Russia to give up substantial gains in the Balkans and a foothold on the Mediterranean, and in 1878 he acquired from Turkey the island of Cyprus as a naval base to protect the Suez Canal and British interests in the Near East. In exchange for Cyprus, Disraeli agreed to guarantee Turkey's Asiatic territories, thereby obtaining for the British an excuse to send troops into the Ottoman Empire whenever they saw fit. In July, 1878, Disraeli returned in triumph from the Congress of Berlin, bringing his country "peace . . . with honour."

Disraeli's last years in office were not so fortunate. Troubles with the Afghans, Zulus, Boers, and Irish discredited the government and were exploited by the opposition. In 1879 Great Britain experienced a severe agricultural depression, accompanied by the worst harvest of the century. The agricultural crisis of 1879 capped several years of economic hardship, which had begun with the general European economic depression of 1873 and had plagued the entire course of the Disraeli administration. In March, 1880, Disraeli dissolved Parliament and called for new elections.

Gladstone made the election campaign of 1880 memorable by abandoning the aloof attitude heretofore considered proper for party leaders, and addressing his constituents in Midlothian in a series of speeches on

Gladstone at the window of a railway carriage during a whistle-stop campaign. *In 1879–80, Gladstone set a new style for politicians by stumping the country to present his party's case directly to the voters.*

the major issues confronting the nation. Gladstone's method of stumping the country and presenting his own and his party's case directly to the voters was a natural outcome of the extension of the franchise, and set a precedent which members of all parties soon found themselves obliged to follow. With ringing eloquence Gladstone denounced Disraeli's imperialistic and aggressive foreign policy and represented the disaffected colonial peoples as victims of Tory oppression. The elections themselves, however, turned far more on the British voters' anxiety over economic depression at home than on their concern with political oppression abroad. The Conservatives suffered the fate of almost every government caught in an economic slump, and were turned out of office.

Gladstone's Second Ministry, 1880–1885

Gladstone's second ministry was not nearly so successful as his first. There was a lack of cohesion and purpose among the members of his cabinet. Within his party he was faced with the task of reconciling right-wing liberals with radicals, Anglicans with dissenters, and of accommodating the aggressive, quasi-socialist new radicalism represented by Joseph Chamberlain (1836–1914), who had built up a reputation as a social reformer while lord mayor of Birmingham.

The administration got off to a poor start when Charles Bradlaugh (1833–1891), an atheist elected to Parliament, refused to take the oath of office because it included the words "so help me God." The Bradlaugh case created a personal dilemma for Gladstone, who was a deeply religious man but believed in freedom of thought. It created an even greater dilemma for the Liberal party. Many uncompromising Christians in the party refused to follow Gladstone's lead in supporting a bill permitting a simple affirmation of allegiance as an alternative to the normal parliamentary oath. The case dragged on until 1888, when the passage of the Affirmation Bill removed the last religious restriction on membership in the House of Commons.

During his second administration Gladstone attempted to achieve passage of additional reform measures, but his efforts were hampered by his difficulty in finding proposals on which the majority of his party could agree. He did succeed in obtaining one major piece of legislation: the Reform Bill of 1884, which gave the vote to all males who paid regular rents or taxes. The largest group to be enfranchised by the new act consisted of agricultural laborers—who generally voted Conservative. Domestic servants, migrant workers, bachelors living under the parental roof, and women were the only sizable groups that still did not have the right to vote. About two million new voters were created, and the total electorate was almost doubled. A redistribution bill of 1885 gave more representation to the larger towns and set up county constituencies with one representative each, putting an end to the traditional two-member constituencies. Inhabitants of boroughs with populations of less than fifteen thousand were deprived of their separate representation and were merged into the electorate of the local county. The historic boroughs and counties thus ceased to be the basis of representation in the House of Commons, and with that the basis of the traditional power of the landed aristocracy was also swept away.

Other domestic reform legislation passed during the second Gladstone ministry included an Employers' Liability Act (1880) which provided compensation to employees injured at work; and a measure of 1883 which initiated electioneering reform by limiting the funds parties and candidates might spend on campaigns.

Ireland remained Gladstone's major concern. His Land Act of 1870 had not succeeded in pacifying Ireland or in stopping the eviction of tenants by absentee landlords. On the contrary, both terrorism and evictions had increased markedly during the agricultural depression of the 1870's. The Irish question was further complicated by the creation of an Irish Home Rule party in the British Parliament, where Irish members had been given the right to sit through the Act of Union of 1801, and where, thanks to the secret ballot granted in 1872, there was now a solid bloc of Irish members dedicated to a radical solution of the Irish problem. In the late 1870's this party came under the leadership of an Irish Protestant named Charles Stewart Parnell (1846–1891), an able politician and a masterful parliamentary strategist. Parnell used two sets of tactics in working for Irish independence. In Parliament he manipulated the solid bloc of Irish votes to extract concessions from both major parties in exchange for Irish support; if concessions were not forthcoming, he used the Irish vote to block legislation altogether. In Ireland, he encouraged local agitation to make British rule as difficult as possible and to keep the Irish question before the public. However, though a fanatic in the cause of Irish independence, Parnell was against the more extreme forms of violence and terrorism. The technique he recommended in dealing with tenant evictions was social ostracism rather than the barn burning, cattle mutilation, and murder adopted on a large scale by his countrymen. Anyone who assisted an unjust eviction or took over a farm made available by such an eviction was to be treated as a social leper. One of the first victims of this treatment was a land agent named Charles Boycott, whose ostracism added a new word to the English language.

To halt the epidemic of terrorist outrages, the British government granted increased coercive powers to its agents in Ireland; the Habeas Corpus Act was suspended, and the executive authority in Ireland was given absolute power of arbitrary and preventive arrest. At the same time, however, Gladstone tried to secure the passage of a new land act for Ireland that would remedy some of the defects of the act of 1870. His new bill, passed in August, 1881, met old Irish demands for the so-called three F's—fair rent, fixity of tenure, and free sale by a tenant of his investment in a rented property. But by this time Irish leaders were no longer satisfied with reform; they wanted political independence. Parnell continued his agitation. In October, 1881, he was sent to jail for his activities, a measure which made Parnell a martyr but did nothing to pacify the Irish. The new and more severe coercive measures of the English government were also ineffective in restraining Irish terrorism. At last Gladstone decided that his only course would be to work with Parnell. By the so-called Kilmainham Treaty of May 2, 1882, named after the prison in which Parnell was held, Gladstone agreed to release Parnell in return for his promise to aid in the pacification of Ireland. In securing the cooperation of Parnell, Gladstone apparently gave him clear indications that he intended to work for home rule for Ireland. Before Gladstone could take action in Parliament, however, all prospects for a peaceful solution of the Irish problem were destroyed by the action of Irish terrorists. On May 6, four days after Parnell's release, the new chief secretary for Ireland, Lord Frederick Cavendish, and the permanent undersecretary, Thomas Burke, were brutally murdered in broad daylight in Phoenix Park, Dublin. The resulting indignation in England made a policy of concession to Ireland impossible. Instead, Parliament passed new coercion acts, which in turn set off a new wave of Irish terrorism. Although Gladstone succeeded in securing a few additional minor reforms for Ireland, his Irish policy as a whole was a failure.

Failure in Ireland was accompanied by failures in foreign policy. To be sure, the Gladstone government scored something of a triumph by securing control of Egypt in 1882. The prime minister gained little credit for this action, however, because he promised that Britain would evacuate Egypt as soon as order had been restored—a promise that only the British voters appear to have believed. In South Africa, British troops were defeated by the Boers, the Dutch settlers in the Transvaal, who had revolted against British rule in 1880. By the Treaty of Pretoria of April 5, 1881, Gladstone conceded independence to the Boers, but they were to remain under British "suzerainty": they would have authority in their internal affairs, but their foreign relations would be controlled by Britain. A dispute with Russia over the frontiers of Afghanistan almost led to war in April, 1885, when Russian forces clashed with Afghan border troops at Penjdeh. Gladstone avoided war by submitting the case to arbitration, and was accused by the opposition and by some members of his own party of truckling to Russia. The worst blow of all came in the Sudan, where Anglo-Egyptian efforts to subdue a revolt against Egyptian overlordship were proving so costly and unsuccessful that the British government decided to evacuate the territory. General Charles George Gordon, who had been sent to the Sudan to investigate the means of evacuation, instead attempted to subdue the area with inadequate forces and found himself besieged in the city of Khartoum. Gladstone hesitated to send a relief army into the Sudan "against a people rightly struggling to be free"—although the people in this case were Moslem fanatics, struggling to maintain the slave trade and a brutal despotism. While Gladstone hesitated, reinforcements for Gordon were delayed. On January 26, 1885, Khartoum fell, and Gordon and his troops were massacred. A censure motion in Parliament failed by just fourteen votes. In June, 1885, Gladstone resigned over a budget amendment, and Lord Salisbury, leader of the Conservative party in the House of Lords since the death of Disraeli in 1881, formed his first ministry.

Gladstone vs. Salisbury, 1885–1895

Lord Robert Cecil, third marquis of Salisbury (1830–1903), was another of the great statesmen of the nineteenth century brought to the fore through the British parliamentary system. A *grand seigneur*, confident of his ability and right to rule, Salisbury had the gift of being able to see political problems in broad historical perspective and refused to be flustered by the crises of the moment. He was never a dedicated reformer like Gladstone or a militant defender of British honor like Palmerston, but neither was he a rigid conservative. He saw the need for change and compromise, and was willing to allow his ministers a good deal of independence in carrying out programs they thought necessary.

Salisbury himself was primarily interested in foreign affairs, and in the 1880's he entered into alliances with continental powers to defend British interests in the Mediterranean and the Near East. Basically,

William E. Gladstone. *A photograph taken shortly before his retirement. To the end of his career he continued to work with energetic moral fervor on behalf of causes in which he believed.*

however, he distrusted agreements with other states and believed that Britain was strong enough to stand alone on its island fortress, shielded by its navy, and that it could always split up a hostile coalition—the only force Britain had to fear—by buying off one or more of its members.

Salisbury's first ministry lasted a mere seven months and was made possible only by an agreement with Parnell, whose Irish votes held the balance in the House of Commons. To get Parnell's support, the Conservatives agreed to make five million pounds available for loans to Irish tenants to permit them to buy their farms on easy terms. But soon Parnell extracted even better terms from Gladstone, who returned to office in February, 1886.

Gladstone's third ministry (February 12 to July 20, 1886) was remarkable chiefly for the introduction of the first Home Rule bill for Ireland, which was bitterly attacked by the Conservatives and was the cause of a permanent rift in the Liberal party as well. Gladstone was deserted by the so-called Liberal Unionists, who favored the preservation of union with Ireland; these included members of both the right and the left wings of the party—the aristocratic Whig faction under Lord Hartington and the young radicals under Joseph Chamberlain.

With the defeat of his Home Rule bill, Gladstone dissolved Parliament and appealed to the British voter. Although now seventy-seven, he stumped the country with his old vigor, full of enthusiasm for what he believed to be a righteous cause. But the forces against him were too great. The sorry record of the Liberal government in foreign affairs, the hostility of public opinion to Ireland as a result of Irish terrorism, the reluctance to desert the Ulster Irish (for the most part Protestants loyal to Britain), and the divisions within the Liberal party all contributed to Gladstone's defeat.

The most significant legislation passed during Salisbury's second ministry (July 26, 1886, to August 13, 1892) was the Local Government Act of 1888, which provided for a system of local self-government under popularly elected County Councils. These councils, which remain the basis of local government in Britain, were to become important centers for the reform of local living conditions, and their activity over the years has in many ways been more significant than any of the more spectacular reform measures passed by the central government.

In Irish affairs the Conservatives were supported by the Liberal Unionists in opposing home rule and pursuing a repressive policy. In 1887 they passed a new coercion act on the strength of letters allegedly written by Parnell which implicated him in the planning of the Phoenix Park murders. These letters were later proved to be forgeries, but it took some time for this fact to come out and when it did another blow struck Parnell. In December, 1889, he was named as the corespondent in a divorce suit against his mistress, Mrs. Kitty O'Shea, a scandal which resulted in his political ruin—even in Ireland this was still the Victorian Age. The scandals surrounding Parnell and the struggle to succeed him as leader split the Irish Home Rule party and seriously reduced its political effectiveness.

A general election in 1892, fought primarily over the issue of home rule, gave the Liberals in alliance with the Irish nationalists a majority of forty in the House of Commons, and on August 18, 1892, Gladstone formed his fourth and last ministry. Now eighty-three, he was almost exclusively concerned with the passage of a Home Rule bill. Overcoming opposition within his own party, he managed to maneuver a bill through the lower house, only to have it overwhelmingly defeated in the House of Lords. Gladstone wanted to take up the challenge, call for new elections, and appeal to the country for support against the Lords, but his colleagues refused to back him up and British public opinion was clearly apathetic over the issue. The defeat of his second Home Rule bill was the final blow for Gladstone personally; he resigned from the premiership and from the leadership of his party on March 3, 1894. But the Irish question had also been disastrous for the Liberal party. A Liberal cabinet under Lord Rosebery managed to carry on until June 21, 1895; the weakened and divided Liberals then gave way to a decade of Conservative-Unionist rule.

The failure to settle the Irish question demonstrated that even the British Parliament, with its powerful traditions and able leadership, had difficulty in dealing with national and economically depressed minorities and was compelled to resort to repression. But for Britain as a whole, the policy of gradual reform through parliamentary institutions was proving its worth. The lot of the average British subject was steadily improving, extremist parties of the right and left found few adherents, and there was never any serious threat of revolution against the established political and social order.

The British system of government was admired and envied by many foreign observers, but it was not generally emulated. The reluctance to adopt British methods was not simply an indication of conservatism or political immaturity, as patriotic Britains often assumed. Many continental statesmen felt that the problems confronting their countries were just too complex to be solved by parliamentary consensus. This was especially true in Russia, where political and social reform took a very different course.

RUSSIA AFTER 1850

In Russia the massive apparatus of autocratic government—army, secret police, censorship, repression—had prevented the outbreak of revolution in 1848. While the thrones of other monarchs crumbled, the Russian autocracy had stood firm and inflexible. The tsar had put his troops at the disposal of the emperor of Austria to crush the revolutions in Hungary and Austrian Poland. He had given his political and diplomatic support to the suppression of liberal movements in every part of Europe. Russia appeared to have taken the place of Austria as the arsenal of autocracy. It was Russian power that had preserved the Austrian empire, that had stood behind the authoritarian governments of Italy and Germany, that had kept the Poles, the Magyars, the Czechs, the Finns, in thrall to foreign despotisms.

The Crimean War exposed the inadequacies behind the imposing façade of Russian autocracy. The mighty empire of Russia was unable to repel a localized invasion on its own soil by two western powers that had invested but a fraction of their potential strength in the conflict. Even the most obscurantist conservative could no longer ignore the fact that Russia's impervious resistance to change had left it far behind the states of western Europe, not only in science and technology but in social and administrative developments. Russia's backwardness was the major problem recognized by most Russians who realistically appraised the lessons of the Crimean War. But in their efforts to overcome this backwardness the advocates of change met enormous inertia in every department of the government and at every level of Russian society.

Alexander II and the Problem of Reform

Tsar Nicholas I (ruled 1825–1855), the standard-bearer of uncompromising autocracy, died during the Crimean War and was succeeded by his son, Alexander II (ruled 1855–1881). Although given the title of Tsar Liberator because of the reforms that took place during his reign, Alexander II was anything but a liberal in the western sense. He was as staunch a believer in autocratic government as his father, and it was as an autocrat that he introduced, or rather imposed, his great reforms. The tsar remained the supreme authority in the state. He ruled through a vast bureaucracy that was responsible to him alone. In a country as large as Russia, with its poor transportation and communications, a good deal of power passed by default to the local authorities, but no changes could be made on a national scale unless they had been initiated or approved by the tsar. There existed no government machinery through which the ordinary Russian citizen could introduce improvements or suggest reforms. This lack of an outlet for the expression of political opinion fostered the development of the many illegal political societies· that flourished in Russia in the nineteenth century, and created an atmosphere of frustration in which politically conscious people turned to extremist ideas and methods, to bombings and assassinations, as the only means of bringing about change.

Alexander II was not a forceful person. He frequently yielded to the pressures around him, and failed to carry through in a consistent or logical manner the reforms that he inaugurated. But the problems he faced were staggeringly complex, and unlike his father, Nicholas I, or his son, Alexander III, he made a determined and on the whole intelligent effort to solve them. His policies met with opposition on every hand: from reformers, who wanted him to do a great deal more; from conservatives, who thought he was undermining the foundations of Russian society; from the peasants, who wanted greater freedom and more land. Alexander himself was disillusioned by the hostility with which his reforms were received, by their failure to stem revolutionary agitation, terrorist outrages, and assassinations of leaders of his government. It was his own fate to be assassinated in 1881. His successors concluded that his efforts at reform had been a mistake and that the only correct course was to revert to a policy of coercion and repression.

Alexander II in his study.

THE EMANCIPATION OF THE SERFS

The most obvious and most pressing problem of Russian society at the accession of Alexander II was serfdom, which in Russia was frequently nothing less than slavery. Plans for the abolition of serfdom had already been under consideration in Nicholas I's reign, not for humanitarian reasons but because the system simply was not working. Compared with the peasant of western Europe, the Russian serf was unenterprising and inefficient, confined to antiquated methods of production. The Russian landowner was having trouble meeting agricultural competition from abroad. Many estates were heavily in debt, the land mortgaged. The detrimental effect of serfdom was especially obvious in the army, where serfs supplied the bulk of the manpower. The Russian serf-soldier was tough and brave, but his was a bravery of stolid acquiescence. He was uneducated, difficult to train, and generally unable to handle the new weapons and technological devices of modern warfare. This problem became grimly evident to Russian officers during the Crimean War.

Moreover, the government was constantly and forcibly reminded of peasant discontent. No major revolution occurred in Russia in 1848, but between 1848 and the outbreak of the Crimean War there were more than a hundred serious local peasant revolts. Such revolts were nothing new in Russia, but they were increasing alarmingly in scope and number. Stressing the need for reform, in a speech to the Moscow nobility, Alexander II said: "The existing order of serfdom cannot remain unchanged. It is better to abolish serfdom from above than to wait until the serfs begin to liberate themselves from below." It was in response to popular agitation and the threat of revolution as much as anything else that the great reforms were at last undertaken and carried through. Not to be overlooked, however, were the humanitarian considerations involved in the abolition of serfdom. "This measure," an enlightened landowner wrote in a memorandum for the tsar, "is even more necessary for the welfare of our class than for the serfs. The abolition of the right to dispose of people like objects or like cattle is as much our liberation as theirs."

The problems of peasant emancipation in so vast and varied a state as Russia were extremely complex, and they were carefully studied by government committees that collected information and evidence from every part of the country and from every class—with the notable exception of the peasants themselves, who made up the overwhelming majority of the population. The emancipation edict itself was largely the work of the bureaucracy, which included many men passionately interested in reform. These zealous bureaucrats were the driving force in the emancipation movement. But it was the tsar who imposed the edict on the reluctant nobility, although not before the members of this class had secured major modifications in the proposals.

The emancipation edict of March 3, 1861 (two years earlier than President Lincoln's), was a massive document that reflected the complexities of the subject. The law gave the serf some personal freedom and attempted to provide a means of livelihood for the liberated peasant in the form of land purchased by the state from the landlord. The division of land between peasant and landlord differed widely in the various regions of Russia, depending on topography, climate, and similar considerations, and was often settled locally because it was necessary to deal with questions concerning rights to water, pasturage, forests, roads, and the like.

The emancipation edict on the whole favored the landlords, who generally secured the best land and the most important rights connected with it. They received generous compensation from the government for the land they relinquished; they were given clear possession of what was left of their property (generally about half); and they were relieved of the responsibility of caring for the serfs on their estates. The landlords, however, were not paid in cash for their lands and serfs, but rather in interest-bearing bonds and redemption certificates. As a result most landlords, many of them deeply in debt already, lacked sufficient capital to purchase farm machinery or introduce scientific farming methods on their estates, a situation which accounts in part for the continuing stagnation of the Russian agricultural economy.

For the peasants, emancipation was a mixed blessing. In theory they were now free to own property, to marry as they pleased, and to resort to law. But from the beginning the great majority of them lacked sufficient land on which to support themselves, especially as the peasant population was increasing rapidly while agricultural productivity remained relatively static.

The most notable defect in the emancipation law was the fact that the majority of the peasants were not granted full personal liberty. The state paid the landowner for the land that was allotted to the peasant. The peasant, in turn, was now expected to reimburse the state for this land, and for the value represented by his person, through long-term installment payments. To make certain that the peasant paid this debt and did not desert the land for a job in the city or another part of the country, the state bound him to the *mir*, or village commune, which was held responsible for the payments the villagers owed, for the collection of taxes, and for supplying recruits for the army. The peasant could not leave the land without the consent of the commune, which in theory was governed by the peasants themselves but in reality was closely supervised by government officials. As there was no dearth of labor in most rural areas, peasants who gave up their share of the land were generally allowed to leave the *mir*. These, on the whole the poorest and least skilled, now moved to the cities to swell the ranks of the urban proletariat.

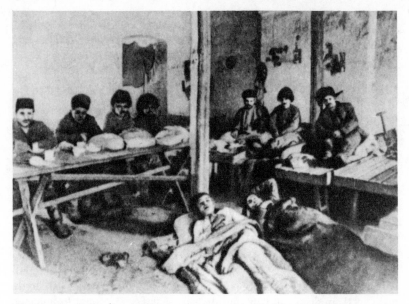

Sleeping berths for Russian laborers in a municipal lodging house, 1890.

Peasants who remained in the commune usually did not own outright the land for which they were paying. The majority of the communes could reallocate the property under their control according to the requirements of their members. Thus the father of a large family might be allocated a comparatively large amount of land, but as his children grew up, some of his fields might be handed over to another member of the commune whose needs were greater. The result was that peasant emancipation in Russia produced not the independent and conservative peasant landowner characteristic of western Europe, but a discontented, land-hungry peasant population still bound to the soil. Not until 1906 were the majority of the peasants allowed to own their land outright and to withdraw from the communes at will. The tradition of a free landowning peasantry therefore never had a proper chance to develop in Russia. In many parts of the country, periodic redistribution of the land deprived the peasants of any incentive to improve their holdings. They continued to follow wasteful timeworn procedures, and almost nothing was done to teach them more efficient methods of agricultural production. The rapid growth of the peasant population in the late nineteenth century, static agricultural production, the fact that the peasants now had to subsist on a smaller land base, meant that emancipation, instead of improving the lot of the peasants, had made their condition worse.

The edict of 1861 was originally intended as only a step toward genuine peasant emancipation. The tragedy for Russia and for the Russian peasant was that this first step was not followed quickly by others giving the peasant complete personal freedom, outright ownership of land, and the means to acquire more land and to cultivate it more effectively. Some additional reforms were enacted, but none of them penetrated to the basic problems of the peasantry until Peter Stolypin's reforms early in the twentieth century.

REFORMS IN LOCAL GOVERNMENT, THE JUDICIARY AND THE ARMY

Inadequate as were the provisions for the emancipation of the serfs, they had a profound effect on the structure of Russian local government. The liberation of the great mass of the rural population from the administration and jurisdiction of the local landlords meant that an entirely new system of local government had to be created. By a law of January 13, 1864, the inhabitants of each rural district were empowered to elect representatives to a zemstvo, or local council, which was to assume responsibility for the maintenance of roads and bridges, poor relief, and later, for primary education and public-health services. To finance these functions, the zemstvos were given the right to levy taxes. Three classes were represented in the zemstvo: landowners, townspeople, and peasants, but a system of voting according to class and landownership assured the gentry a predominant influence.

Even so, the zemstvos constituted a genuine form of self-government and attracted men who had long been anxious to have a voice in local administration. The more enterprising zemstvos established primary schools and hospitals, improved local methods of agriculture, encouraged commerce. To carry out their programs, they engaged teachers and doctors, agronomists, veterinarians, and engineers, many of them liberal or radical in their political outlook. These professionals in turn exerted a strong influence on the political orientation of the zemstvos, which frequently became lively centers of agitation for further reforms by the national government. Important in this connection was the establishment of provincial zemstvos, consisting of representatives from the district councils, to deal with problems beyond the local level. From this point the next logical step would have been a national zemstvo, which would constitute a Russian parliament representing every district and every class in the country. To achieve such national self-government was a goal not only of social reformers, but of noblemen and rich businessmen, whose political instincts and ambitions had long been stifled by the agents of the centralized bureaucracy. Like their counterparts in western Europe, most of these reformers had no wish to overthrow the existing government; they simply wanted a greater share of political power and influence within it.

The effectiveness of the zemstvos as centers of political opinion aroused the suspicion of government bureaucrats. Almost from the start the zemstvos were faced with all sorts of official obstruction. Their powers of taxation were so reduced that they were in constant financial difficulty and lacked the resources to carry out proper education or technical-assistance programs.

Reform of local rural administration was followed by a reorganization of municipal administration in June, 1870. The towns were now also granted a certain measure of self-government in dealing with local problems. Again there was a three-class system of voting, but because representation in the towns was based on the amount of taxes paid rather than on class, the rich, whether members of the nobility or of the middle class, dominated the dumas, or municipal councils. Although these councils were severely limited in their power to levy taxes and were subjected to oppressive restrictions, they were a distinct improvement on the administration that had preceded them. Like the zemstvos, they provided valuable lessons in self-government and built up public services on a scale Russia had never known.

Important reforms in the judicial system were undertaken in 1864. Petty offenses were henceforth to be handled not by local landlords, but by justices of the peace elected by the zemstvos, and the more important cases were to be brought to higher courts whose judges were appointed by the crown. The legal code was revised according to the principles of western jurisprudence; the principles of equality before the law, of legal uniformity, of the independence of law courts, of the irremovability of judges, and of public trial, were recognized. Court proceedings were to be conducted according to a strictly regulated system of prosecution and defense, and trial by jury was introduced for criminal cases.

In 1874 came a reform of the army. Military service was made compulsory for all men of all social classes, although the provisions for exemption were so numerous that only about a third of those eligible actually served. The period of service was reduced from twenty-five to six years, with an additional nine years in the reserves and five in the militia. Training was revised, discipline humanized, the cruelest forms of corporal punishment abolished. The preparation of officers was improved, and all ranks were provided with some form of education to enable them to use the complicated weapons of modern warfare. It was chiefly in the army that the Russian peasant learned to read and write, and it was in the army that an important segment of the Russian population was exposed to the revolutionary propaganda of Russian intellectuals.

The Industrial Revolution in Russia

It was not until 1890 that the great boom in industrialization began in Russia. Until about 1870 industrial development was slow and retarded by frequent depressions. Except in a few industries, manual labor and technical backwardness were the rule; antiquated methods prevailed in such basic enterprises as mining and metal production. The two decades after 1870 have been called the period of the final struggle in Russia's industrial development. By 1890 factory and machine production had won a definite victory over cottage industry and primitive types of manufacture. The foundation had been laid for dramatic industrial growth.

In view of later developments in Russia, it is noteworthy that private enterprise never flourished in that country as it did in western Europe and the United States. The chief entrepreneur in Russia was the state. Government action brought about what was achieved in other countries by the forces of an expanding free market. The state was the principal borrower of foreign capital to finance the new enterprises, the chief builder and operator of railways, the biggest developer of mines. The state founded new industries itself or supplied funds and furnished the necessary guarantees for the development of private industries.

A landmark in Russian economic history was the establishment in May, 1860, of a state bank to take over the assets and liabilities of the many private banks that had foundered in the depression of 1858. The original purpose of the bank was to promote commerce and stabilize the ruble, but in time it became the central financial institution of the empire. It played an important part in financing the emancipation of the serfs, and served as the main channel for the concentration and distribution of capital within Russia and for borrowing funds from abroad. The pace of Russian industrialization can be measured by the flow of foreign capital into the country. In 1850 foreign investments in Russia totaled 2.7 million rubles; by 1880 the figure had risen to 98 million, by 1890 to 215 million, and by 1900 to 911 million.

The state erected tariff barriers to protect Russia's native infant industries. There was a sharp increase in tariffs after 1868, and progressively higher tariffs were imposed in the 1870's and 1880's, until an all-time high was reached in 1891.

The state was also the chief mover in the building of railroads, the barometers of the progress of the Industrial Revolution. Nowhere was the improvement of overland transportation more crucial than in the farflung reaches of Russia. The first major line from Moscow to St. Petersburg was built in 1851, during the reign of Nicholas I. In the next two decades private firms were allowed to dominate the field of railway development. Progress was slow, however, and after 1870 the government assumed the biggest role in railway construction and operation both by acting directly and by giving loans or guarantees to private companies. By 1877 almost 2 billion rubles of government money had been invested in railways, compared with the 698 million rubles of private capital invested in 1870. Government-sponsored foreign loans were essential, for during the early stages of industrialization Russia had to buy almost all its railway equipment abroad.

The emancipation of the serfs and the consequent availability of a large labor supply has often been considered a major factor in the development of the Industrial Revolution in Russia, but this theory is open to question. Between 1850 and 1890 the population of Russia almost doubled. The growth of industry, however, generally appears to have been too slow to absorb the swelling supply of labor. Far from stimulating the process of industrialization, the availability of cheap labor encouraged the continued use of antiquated methods of production. What Russia needed most was not mass labor, but skilled labor, which often had to be hired from abroad.

The government's interest in industrialization was not accompanied by a proportionate concern with the living conditions of industrial laborers. Factories and mines were unsanitary and dangerous. Nothing was done to protect workers from moving machinery; chemical fumes, dust, and smoke dangerous to eyes and lungs polluted the atmosphere. Almost no provision was made for workers' housing. Laborers were frequently obliged to sleep on the floor of the factory, or they were housed in barracks where they slept on the floor or on bare bunks arranged in tiers. A 15-hour working day was the rule; in some cases it was as long as 18 hours. Wages were at a bare subsistence level. Workers were customarily paid only three or four times a year, and wages could be withheld at the whim of the employer. Frequently, payment was made not in cash, but in food or clothing from the company store at prices fixed by the company. Heavy fines were imposed for the most trivial offenses, and a fine of three months wages was not uncommon. Strikes were prohibited by law; striking workers could be fined, imprisoned, or sent to Siberia.

Since the beginning of the reign of Alexander II, government committees had studied the need for factory reform. Nothing was done until 1882, when an epidemic of illegal strikes compelled the government to recognize the need for some kind of legislation. A law of 1882 prohibited the employment of children under twelve, and a corps of factory inspectors was created to enforce it. A law of 1885 prohibited night work in textile mills for women and for children under 17, a restriction later extended to other industries. In 1886 a law concerning labor contracts stipulated that wages be paid at least once a month, in cash. Factory inspectors were given new powers to enforce legislation and arbitrate labor disputes. At the same time, penalties for striking were stiffened.

Even if these labor laws had been strictly enforced—and they were not—they would have been miserably inadequate. The condition of the Russian worker remained deplorable, judged by even the worst standards of the west.

Between 1865 and 1890 the number of workers employed in large factories in Russia doubled (from 706,000 to 1,433,000); between 1890 and 1900 the number almost doubled again (to 2,208,000). This industrial proletariat was small in comparison with that of western Europe or with the

Russian population as a whole. Yet its importance was greater than its numbers indicate, because Russian industry, and consequently Russia's industrial population, was concentrated in relatively limited areas. The members of the Russian industrial proletariat were thus accessible to political agitators and were more readily available for political action than the Russian peasants.

The government did much in the late nineteenth century to encourage the development of industry, but nothing was done on a large scale to improve Russian agriculture. New farm machinery and methods of cultivation were introduced in some areas, but on the whole Russian agriculture remained substantially the same as it had been during previous centuries. Whereas the Russian population rose from about 67 million in 1851 to 125.6 million in 1897 (the first official census), the yield of the land did not notably increase. This discrepancy between population growth and agricultural production explains the constant land hunger of the Russian peasant and the revolutionary force of appeals for a redistribution of land, much of which was technically still in the hands of the crown, the nobility, and the church.

Revolutionary Ferment

The relaxation of government censorship during the early part of Alexander II's reign resulted in a dramatic increase in the spread of revolutionary progaganda. The result was that after a few years government authorities imposed new restrictions, which were made especially stringent after an attempt on the tsar's life in April, 1866. But despite repression and censorship, new intellectual and revolutionary movements continued to flourish. Especially influential were the radical writings of Alexander Herzen (1812–1870), which were published abroad and smuggled into Russia on a remarkably wide scale. Herzen sounded the battle cry "land and freedom" and urged intellectuals to go "to the people" to spread their ideas. His mystic faith in the Russian peasant as the vehicle of social reform was to have a profound effect on the subsequent course of the Russian revolutionary movement. Herzen's ideas provided the intellectual foundation of populism, a peculiarly Russian form of socialism that advocated revolution and a reorganization of society on the basis of such specifically Russian institutions as communal land tenure and popular associations of peasants and artisans. The peasants were to be the core of the movement, for they were already "communists by instinct and tradition." Yet the peasant masses, around whom everything was to be built, were almost completely apathetic to the populist ideology.

Populist ideas were to be challenged by Marxism toward the end of the century. Meanwhile, extremist doctrines such as anarchism, terrorism, and nihilism claimed large numbers of adherents among intellectuals of the upper and middle classes who despaired of accomplishing significant reform within the existing framework of society.

As government repression increased, so did the appeal of terrorist methods of opposing the regime. In the 1870's the number of political assassinations mounted rapidly; high-ranking police and other officials fell victim to terrorist activities, and several attempts were made on the life of Alexander II. Government officials were divided on how to deal with the situation. The heir to the throne called for police dictatorship, but Mikhail Loris-Melikov (c. 1825–1888), the official entrusted with enforcement of the new security regulations, did not think that police methods alone were enough. He believed that the government should make a determined effort to win over the moderate advocates of social and constitutional reforms, the social classes that had a stake in the existing social order and were the government's natural allies against revolution. As minister of the interior, Loris-Melikov somewhat relaxed government censorship, and dismissed the foremost advocates of repressive measures. In an obvious bid for liberal support, he proposed to set up a commission composed of representatives of the zemstvos and the dumas to cooperate with the imperial council of state in the discussion of new laws. Innocuous as this measure was, it would have created a legal channel for the expression of opinion by a large and important section of the population. But on the day the tsar gave his approval to the proposal, March 13, 1881, he was assassinated by a bomb thrown by a member of a revolutionary terrorist organzation.

Alexander III

Alexander III (ruled 1881–1894), brought to the throne through the assassination of Alexander II, the Tsar Liberator and reformer, drew the moral from his father's life and violent death that reform and change of any kind were a mistake. To save Russia and the monarchy, he believed he would have to revert to the procedures of his more autocratic ancestors, and throughout his reign he pursued reactionary policies with stubborn tenacity.

A dominant figure in the court was his former tutor, Konstantin Pobedonostsev (1827–1907), who developed an entire philosophical and theological system to support the concepts of autocratic government. Pobedonostsev distrusted and condemned "western" ideas concerning freedom of thought, civil liberties, and constitutions, which were corrupting the morality of Holy Russia. Like the revolutionary populists, Pobedonostsev saw a mystic quality in the Russian people, but in his eyes they were the font of autocracy and Christian orthodoxy. As Procurator of the Holy Synod and thus, after the tsar, head of the Russian Orthodox Church, he proposed to use religion to restore the spiritual communion between the Russian people and their tsar, making religious unity the framework and support of political unity. Dissenters of every kind were persecuted and deprived of legal status. Partial exceptions were made for Roman Catholics and Lutherans because of the protection they received from Russia's allies, Austria and Germany, but even they were subject to numerous restrictions. An almost racial concept of Russianism played a strong role in Pobedonostsev's thinking. He believed that Muscovite Russia was the core of the Russian state and that the Muscovite Russians were the bearers of the true Russian spirit. Poles, Germans, Turks, Mongols, Jews, were treated as inferior peoples, a fact which explains the responsiveness of many of these minorities to revolutionary doctrines proclaiming racial and national equality.

Pobedonostsev's influence on imperial policies was soon manifest. Almost immediately after Alexander III's accession, the Loris-Melikov reform program was abandoned and Loris-Melikov himself was replaced as minister of the interior by the Russian nationalist Nikolai Ignatiev (1832–1908), who was soon succeeded by the notorious absolutist Count Dmitri Tolstoi (1823–1889). The secret police were given new powers, and a ruthless campaign of persecution was directed against advocates of constitutional government and social reform as well as against revolutionary societies. "Exceptional measures," enacted in August, 1881, gave provincial governors and police officials extraordinary powers to proceed against suspected enemies of the state and permitted them to place entire districts under martial law. There was a notable increase in censorship, in passport regulations limiting both movement within Russia and travel abroad, in

Tsar Alexander III, his wife, and three of their five children. *The tsarina was the Danish princess Sophie Frederica Dagmar, known in Russia as Maria Fedorovna. Unlike many monarchs, Alexander was a devoted family man and is reputed to have been faithful to his wife.*

government supervision of all phases of education. A statute of July 12, 1889, put rural districts under the control of so-called land captains appointed by the minister of the interior. Justices of the peace were eliminated in rural areas and their functions transferred to the land captains, who thus exercised both administrative and judicial authority. Because the land captains were selected for the most part from among the local landowners and hereditary nobility, the new law, in effect, restored many of the powers the nobility had lost through the reforms of the 1860's. A law of June 12, 1890, modified election procedures to make the zemstvos even less representative than before and imposed restrictions on their powers. Approval of the provincial governor was henceforth required for all personnel engaged by the zemstvos—teachers, doctors, veterinarians—and all zemstvo decisions were subject to review by the provincial governor or by the minister of the interior. Similar restrictions were imposed on municipal governments in 1892.

Every autocrat is dependent on the agents who carry out his policies. Alexander III relied less than his predecessor on the professional bureaucracy composed primarily of middle-class civil servants, reverting instead to dependence on members of the nobility, who were given greater authority in local administration and were consistently preferred over middle-class candidates in official appointments. This policy did not result in more effective or even more loyal administrators. As many of Alexander's ancestors had discovered, the nobles tended to be more independent than middle-class administrators, who relied on the government for their livelihood. The Russian autocracy was, indeed, ludicrously inefficient and slovenly, a fact which explains how despite the many repressive measures so much revolutionary agitation could flourish on so wide a scale.

Territorial Expansion

In the long run, perhaps the most significant feature of Russian history during the second half of the nineteenth century was the continuation of expansion along almost every frontier of the already enormous empire. Russia was the most important and the most successful imperialist power in Europe during this era, and unlike Britain, France, or Germany, has since succeeded in holding on to most of the conquered land.

The Russian drive to Constantinople and to the Mediterranean was stopped temporarily by the Crimean War, but scarcely fifteen years later Russia resumed its push southwest, repudiating the Black Sea clauses of the Treaty of Paris and restoring its naval bases in the Black Sea area. Revolts by the Slavic peoples in the Balkans against Turkish rule in 1875 gave Russia an excuse to resume pressure on the Ottoman Empire. This pressure was now strongly reinforced by the doctrine of Pan-Slavism, a nationalist-racist belief that all Slavs were members of the same race. According to the

Russian version of Pan-Slavism, it was Russia's mission to bring all Slavs together. In the 1870's the Pan-Slav movement became a driving force in Russian foreign policy, exploited but not always controlled by the government. In 1877 Russia again went to war with Turkey, but the presence of the British fleet in the Dardanelles prevented the capture of Constantinople, and in the months that followed, the Russians were compelled by diplomatic pressure to give up most of their gains in the Balkans. They nevertheless acquired Bessarabia, strategically located at the mouth of the Danube; a sphere of influence in Bulgaria, north of the Balkan Mountains; and an extension of territory on the east coast of the Black Sea. To the dismay of Russian Pan-Slavists, the Balkan Slavs failed to show any strong desire to replace Turkish with Russian domination. The Bulgarians, for example, resented Russian interference in their country and turned to Britain and Austria for protection. The Russians expanded no more in the Balkans in the nineteenth century, but their rivalry with Austria in this area was to be one of the major causes of the First World War.

Russian expansion in central and eastern Asia was on a far greater scale and met with far less resistance. On the whole, acquisition of territory there appears to have been the work of ambitious and enterprising local administrators rather than a matter of policy of the central government. A striking feature of these eastern conquests was the small size of the Russian forces involved. The Russians owed their success to the superiority of their weapons and of their military and political organization.

In the Caucasus region, conquered earlier in the nineteenth century, the last resistance to Russian dominion was crushed in the 1860's. Following Russia's victory over Turkey in 1878, Russia acquired still more territory in the Caucasus area, including the strategic cities of Batum, Kars, and Ardahan.

The subjugation of the greater part of Kazakhstan, the region east of the Ural River in central Asia, was followed in 1865 by the capture of Tashkent, which became the capital of the new province of Turkestan, a vast area stretching from the Aral Sea to the borders of India, Tibet, and the Chinese province of Sinkiang. In the 1870's the Russians began the conquest of the eastern littoral of the Caspian Sea, and by 1884 they had reached the borders of Afghanistan.

Not until Russia had pushed to the Caucasus and the Himalayas, and touched the frontiers or spheres of influence of other great powers, did the expansion in central Asia come to a halt. In 1881 Russia concluded a treaty with China settling the boundary between Russia and Chinese Turkestan (Sinkiang); and in 1885, after a dispute that almost led to war, an agreement was reached with Britain concerning the boundaries of Afghanistan, which the British regarded as a buffer state for India.

Meanwhile, in the Far East, the Russians had expanded in Siberia, taking

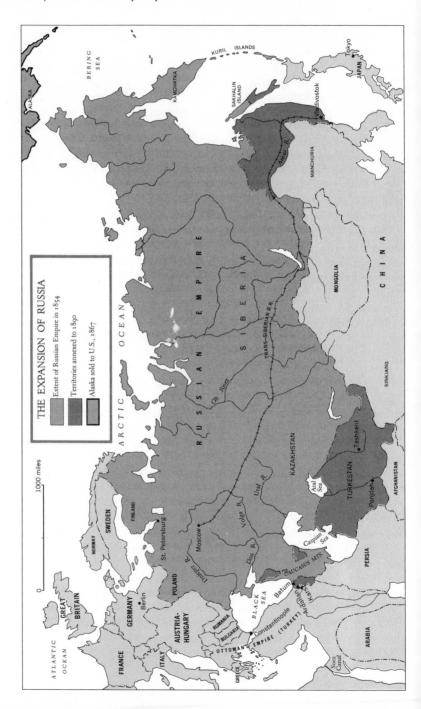

THE EXPANSION OF RUSSIA

Extent of Russian Empire in 1854

Territories annexed to 1890

Alaska sold to U.S., 1867

1000 miles

Kamchatka and the Kuril Islands, but their further movement south was blocked by Japan. By the Treaty of St. Petersburg (1875) Russia ceded the Kuril Islands to Japan, receiving in return clear possession of the entire island of Sakhalin, which lies off the Siberian coast and dominates the mouth of the Amur River.

In the eighteenth century the Russians had crossed into Alaska from northern Siberia and had set up trading stations and forts along the Pacific coast, reaching almost as far south as San Francisco. Eventually they realized that they were overextended in North America. The activity of British and French warships along the Alaskan coast during the Crimean War showed the Russian government how tenuous was its hold over the region, and in 1867 it sold Alaska to the United States for just over seven million dollars—a purchase strongly opposed by many economy-minded American congressmen.

Elsewhere in the Far East the Russians were expanding at the expense of China. Taking advantage of China's wars with Britain and France in the 1850's, Russia succeeded in forcing China's formal renunciation of the entire region north of the Amur River in 1858, and acquired another great block of territory, south of the Amur, in 1860. At the southern end of this area the Russians founded the city of Vladivostok ("Lord of the East") in 1860. The beginning of construction on the trans-Siberian railway in 1891 was to give this region greatly increased significance.

Russia's expansion gave the Russian empire a territorial base that was to be of inestimable strategic importance in the First and Second World Wars, but it also involved Russia in new and ever more dangerous conflicts with other states—and was an important factor in bringing about those wars. As opponents of Russian expansion in the west, Sweden and Poland were now replaced by Austria and by Austria's ally (after 1879), Germany. Russia's perennial opponent in the southwest, the Ottoman empire, had become the sick man of Europe in the nineteenth century, but there was not a single European great power which was not concerned about preventing further Russian seizures of strategic Ottoman territory. Along Russia's enormously long southern frontier, from the Black Sea to the Pacific, there was scarcely any sector where Russian interests did not clash with those of Britain. In East Asia, Russia was soon to encounter a new and even more formidable rival in Japan, which through a vigorous Europeanization of its army and administration was about to win a place among the world's great powers. Finally there was the potential danger of China, where Russia's encroachments aroused a hostility that might erupt in vengeance when China should at last mobilize its own vast resources effectively.

CHAPTER 7

The New Governments

THE NATIONAL revolutions of the mid-nineteenth century brought about fundamental changes in the governments of four of the six major powers of Europe. The states of the Italian peninsula, including Sicily, were absorbed by Sardinia to form the kingdom of Italy, while the majority of the German states were absorbed or "mediatized" by Prussia to form the German empire. The Habsburg empire, excluded from Italy and Germany, was transformed into the Austro-Hungarian empire as the result of a bargain with the Hungarians, and separate governments were set up for each section of what came to be known as the Dual Monarchy. In France the empire of Napoleon III, that ardent champion of the cause of nationalities, was defeated by a German national army and ousted by a national revolution at home that led to the establishment of the Third Republic. In each of these states, the leaders of the new governments were to find that the problems of consolidating power and actually running the country were complex and persistent, and that popular enthusiasm for the new national governments soon gave way to the humdrum conflict of domestic interests.

FRANCE, 1870–1890

The Beginnings of the Third Republic

With the French defeat in the Franco-Prussian War at Sedan on September 2, 1870, and the capture of Napoleon III, the Second Empire collapsed. Two days after Sedan the republican deputies in the imperial parliament proclaimed the establishment of a republic and set up an emergency government of national defense. The head of the new government was General Louis Jules Trochu (1815–1896), the governor of Paris,

The flight of Léon Gambetta from the siege of Paris, October 7, 1870. *The balloon L'Armand Barbès carried Gambetta over the German troops, who with cannons and small-arms fire tried to shoot it down.*

but the real leadership was provided by the fiery radical Léon Gambetta (1838–1882), who took the post of minister of the interior. While German troops besieged Paris, Gambetta escaped dramatically from the capital in a balloon on October 7 and began large-scale organization of French resistance in the provinces. Spurred by memories of 1793, when the armies of the French Revolution had hurled back the foreign foe, and with unshakable faith in the French nation, Gambetta succeeded in putting new French armies into the field. Despite their lack of training and equipment the new soldiers fought well. Guerrilla forces harassed the German supply lines, and to the amazement and annoyance of the Germans, the war which had seemed to be over dragged on. Finally, the surrender of General Bazaine at Metz on October 27, which released a veteran German army for action elsewhere, the successful siege of Paris, and the failure of French diplomats to secure foreign intervention, ended Gambetta's chances of achieving a military stalemate. With Paris in a state of starvation, the provisional

French government signed an armistice on January 28, 1871.

Before Bismarck would proceed with final peace negotiations, he demanded that the French establish a government that represented all of France. At his insistence elections on the basis of universal manhood suffrage were held for a National Assembly that was to make peace with Germany in the name of the French people.

The elections of February, 1871, showed that a large majority of the French people wanted peace. They gave an overwhelming endorsement to monarchist candidates, who promised the restoration of peace and political stability, and repudiated the republicans, whose foremost spokesmen advocated continuation of the war against Germany at any cost. The veteran Orleanist statesman Adolphe Thiers was made "chief of the executive power of the French Republic" by the new National Assembly, and under his leadership the final peace terms with Germany were arranged. France agreed to surrender the greater part of Alsace and Lorraine, to pay an indemnity of five billion francs, and to support a German army of occupation until the debt was paid. The final Peace of Frankfurt was signed on May 10, 1871.

After the conclusion of peace, the National Assembly could concentrate on the question of providing France with a permanent government. With a large monarchist majority in the assembly, it seemed certain that a monarchy would soon be restored. Early in March the delegates gave a strong indication of this intention by voting to move the seat of the government from Bordeaux, where it had been located since the last months of the war, to Versailles, the traditional royalist capital of France. Restoration was prevented at this time only by the fact that the support of the monarchists in the assembly was almost equally divided between the Legitimist Bourbon pretender, the count of Chambord, grandson of Charles X, and the Orleanist candidate, the count of Paris, grandson of Louis Philippe—the Bonapartists were still discredited by defeat. While the monarchists wrangled, the republic continued.

The activity of the National Assembly was viewed with hostility and alarm by the radical and militant citizens of Paris, embittered by the grueling four-month siege by the Germans and the subsequent humiliation of a German triumphal march through their city. Parisians resented the terms of the peace treaty with Germany; they resented the transfer of the government to Versailles; they resented the leadership of the conservative National Assembly, and its legislation on behalf of property owners.

Shortly after the end of the war the assembly ended the moratorium on promissory notes, through which much of the business of Paris was still being conducted, and required the immediate payment of rents which had not been paid during the war. These decisions seemed reasonable to the landed gentry of the assembly and to the financiers who had speculated in papers and rents, but they meant ruin for the lower middle classes of Paris. Further, the assembly canceled the pay of the National Guard, thereby depriving many workers of their only means of subsistence. It was in the National Guard of Paris that resistance to the National Assembly began to crystallize. Under the direction of a central committee of the guard, the chief arsenals of Paris were secured, and cannon belonging to the regular army were seized. Thiers saw the danger. On March 18 he sent troops of the regular army into Paris to capture the guns and bring the city under control. But the soldiers of the regular army, when confronted with the resistance of the Parisians, refused to fire on their fellow citizens. Instead, they fraternized with the mob and allowed the people of Paris to kill two of their generals. Government forces withdrew, the Parisians repudiated the authority of the National Assembly, and on March 26 they elected their own government, the Commune of Paris.

Marxists have customarily acclaimed the Paris Commune of 1871 as the first proletarian socialist revolution, the first uprising to bear out Karl Marx's prophecies. In fact, the government of the Commune was far more influenced by the precedents of 1793 than by Marxist ideology, and its leaders were a mixed group of old-style Jacobins, anticlericals, socialists of various persuasions (including a few genuine Marxists), and political adventurers. The legislation of the Commune reflected these several influences, and the passions and exigencies of the moment, rather than any distinct ideological pattern. It called for decentralization of the French government, an increase in the powers of the municipalities, the separation of church and state, the abolition of the regular army and its replacement by the citizen-controlled National Guard. None of these provisions could be carried out because the authority of the Commune was confined to Paris. The only practical legislation enacted by the Commune was the renewal of the wartime moratorium on rents and debts, which had been canceled by the assembly, and the abolition of night work in bakeries. No steps were taken to seize the resources of the Bank of France or to crush the weak forces of the National Assembly at Versailles before they could be reinforced, and very little was done to strengthen the defenses of the city of Paris.

While the leaders of Paris did nothing, Thiers steadily built up the military strength of the Versailles government. Aided by the premature release of large numbers of prisoners of war by Germany, he had a sufficiently strong force to lay siege to Paris at the beginning of April. In the final week of May, Paris was stormed in a battle more brutal and bloody than any waged in the recent war against the Germans. In the last days of the struggle the soldiers of the Commune, seeing that their cause was lost, shot their prisoners and hostages, including the archbishop of Paris, and set fire to the public buildings of the city—the Louvre and Notre Dame were barely saved. The troops of the National Assembly exacted a grim revenge. On May 28, 1871, the last organized defenders of the Commune were rounded up and massacred in the cemetery of Père-Lachaise, and in every part of the city men suspected of having fought for the Commune were arrested and shot without trial. In all, some twenty thousand were killed during that bloody week in May, and about half that number were deported to the penal colony of New Caledonia. The horrors of the suppression of the Commune left a legacy of hatred in French political life that has never been fully obliterated, and for many years it was successfully exploited by rival political parties. To conservatives the Commune represented anarchy and disorder, a horrible example to be avoided in the future; to radicals and socialists it was a landmark in the struggle for social justice, and its suppression epitomized the ruthlessness of the propertied classes in defending their unjust privileges.

The determination displayed by the Thiers government in quashing political disorder and civil war convinced French property owners that the new regime could be trusted. Because of the confidence he inspired in French financial circles, Thiers was able to secure the funds necessary to place the French currency on a sound basis and to prime the national economy. By September, 1873, two years ahead of schedule, the entire French war debt to Germany had been paid and the last German troops were withdrawn from French soil. In July, 1872, Thiers had secured legislation reorganizing the French military system and making all Frenchmen liable to five years of military service. So effective was this reorganization that by 1875 France's standing army was almost as large as Germany's, and it was equipped with the most modern weapons.

Within France, Thiers worked to heal the wounds of civil war and to prevent new political rifts among his countrymen. Although an Orleanist, he became convinced of the desirability of continuing the republican form of government "as the system that divides us least." As time went on he became so frank in expressing republican opinions that monarchists began to regard him as a menace to their cause. A crisis came in May, 1873, when one of Thiers' lieutenants submitted to the assembly the draft of a republican constitution. A motion condemning Thiers for not being sufficiently conservative was carried by a narrow margin. Confident of his own indispensability, and meaning to strengthen his position by forcing the assembly to recall him, Thiers resigned on May 24. He underestimated the hostility of his opponents, who at once accepted his resignation. At the same session they elected Marshal MacMahon, the hero against the Austrians at Magenta in 1859 (and the loser at Sedan) to succeed him.

Leader of the Third Republic, Adolphe Thiers (hand outstretched), and his Council of Ministers, 1872.

A staunch monarchist, conscientious and well meaning. MacMahon was a political nullity, clearly chosen to keep the throne warm until the monarchists had finally selected a royal candidate.

In August, 1873, it seemed that MacMahon's tenure would soon be over, for the monarchists at last reached agreement on a candidate for the throne—the Bourbon, Henry, count of Chambord (1820–1883). As he was without heirs, he was to be succeeded by the Orleanist, the count of Paris (1838–1894). It was a sensible arrangement, but the count of Chambord was not a sensible man. He insisted on the restoration of the white fleur-de-lis flag of the Bourbons as the emblem of France in place of the tricolor, which had been the national flag since the revolution. "Henry V cannot abandon the flag of Henry IV," said the high-minded candidate, referring to his ancestor who had changed his religion three times in the process of becoming king. The flag issue proved to be insurmountable. The French nation would not give up the banner that had flown at Austerlitz and Jena, at Sevastopol and Solferino. Even the loyal MacMahon admitted that if the white flag of the Bourbons were run up, the *chassepots* would go off of their own accord. In November, 1873, the monarchists in the assembly voted to give MacMahon the "executive power" in France for seven years, in the hope that by that time the count of Chambord would be dead and the candidate succeeding him would be more reasonable. But the monarchists had missed their opportunity. Their election victory in 1871 had been a mandate for peace rather than for a royal restoration; ever since, the tide had been running strongly against them in by-elections, and practical politicians in the assembly were beginning to shift their public attitudes in accordance with the changing mood of public opinion. It was in an atmosphere of uncertain political loyalties and values that the assembly finally completed the drafting of a constitution for France.

The Constitution of 1875

The Constitution of 1875 reflected the political dissension surrounding its creation. It was a patchwork affair, the result of much compromise and haggling, as each faction in the assembly tried to reserve for itself the greatest possible leeway for future maneuvering. It contained no statement of general principles, no bill of rights. The proposition designating the new government a republic was passed by only a one-vote margin.

The choice of the president, who had a seven-year term, was left to the two houses of the legislature because it was feared that direct election by popular vote might bring a potential dictator into office. The experience with Louis Napoleon had not been forgotten. Nominally the president's powers were extensive. He could initiate legislation, he was head of the armed forces, and he appointed the top civil and military officials. With the consent of the upper house, the Senate, he could dissolve the lower house, the Chamber of Deputies, and call for new elections. However, despite the apparently substantial authority of the executive, the legislature retained firm control over affairs of state. Every act of the president had to be countersigned by a minister, who in turn was responsible to the legislature. In practice this restriction came to mean that the real power of government was vested in the legislature.

In the bicameral legislature, the Senate consisted of seventy-five life members, chosen in the first instance by the National Assembly, and of three hundred members elected for nine-year terms, one third of them every three years, by the representatives of the municipal governments of France. In the beginning the smallest town had the same vote as the biggest city, but in 1884 the procedure was changed to give the towns representation according to size and the appointment of life senators was abandoned.

Members of the Chamber of Deputies were elected for four-year terms by universal manhood suffrage. Both the Senate and the Chamber of Deputies had the right to initiate legislation, but all laws had to be passed in the lower house before they were sent to the Senate for a final vote. Moreover, the lower house had the special right to initiate all financial legislation. As a result of these powers, and because the great majority of government ministers tended to be selected from the lower house, the Chamber of Deputies came to be the center of political power in the new French government. The prime minister, although appointed by the president, had to be a political leader who could organize a majority in the Chamber of Deputies, and it was he who appointed all the other ministers, usually with a view to getting the necessary support in the Chamber for his government.

There was no plebiscite to ratify the new constitution, but the fact that a majority of Frenchmen went to the polls in February, 1876, showed that they accepted the system. The republicans won an overwhelming victory in the Chamber of Deputies, and they would have carried the Senate as well had not more than two thirds of the senators been holdovers from the conservative period.

The Triumph of Parliamentarianism

MacMahon was still president—his seven-year term had another four years to run—and it was he who instigated the first important conflict of power under the new constitution. Influenced by his monarchist and clerical supporters, who were alarmed by the strength of republicanism, the president on May 16, 1877, dismissed the ministry of Jules Simon (1814–1896), which represented a majority in the Chamber of Deputies, and appointed a new ministry headed by the Orleanist duke of Broglie (1821–1901). This crisis of May 16 set the stage for a struggle between the advocates of authoritarian and of representative government which was similar to the conflict in Prussia in the 1860's. In France the issue was never seriously in doubt. Neither MacMahon nor Broglie was willing to risk a *coup d'état* and base an authoritarian regime squarely on the monarchist-dominated army. Instead, Broglie tried to secure a popular mandate for his government by employing methods similar to those of Napoleon III for influencing the vote. On July 19 MacMahon, with the consent of the monarchist-controlled Senate, dissolved the Chamber of Deputies and called for new elections. During the ensuing election campaign Broglie put all the machinery of the central government to work. To secure expert assistance, he put a Bonapartist in charge of "making" the elections. He made unabashed use of the government's power to appoint reliable men in key administrative positions. Seventy-seven of eighty-seven prefects were changed, the republican press was persecuted, republican clubs were closed, freedom of assembly was severely restricted. Meanwhile the official press deluged the country with propaganda. The government received strong support from the church, which feared, with good reason, the anticlerical attitude of many republican candidates.

The Broglie campaign was a failure. His exploitation of the machinery of government annoyed the French voters, but did not intimidate them. In the elections of October, 1877, the republicans lost only thirty-six seats, and in November, Broglie was greeted by a vote of no confidence in the new Chamber of Deputies. Broglie resigned, as did MacMahon's next appointee, and on December 13 the president at last named a prime minister who enjoyed the Chamber's confidence. The cause of representative government had won a crucial test. In the elections of January, 1879, the republicans won a majority in the Senate for the first time, and at the end of that month MacMahon himself resigned. As a result of the crisis of May 16 the president was relegated to the role of a figurehead in the French government, and ministers became responsible solely to the Chamber of Deputies. After 1879 the president could no longer even exert his right to dissolve that body.

Symbolic of the republican triumph was the transfer of the seat of the French government from Versailles to Paris in 1879. The fourteenth of July, the anniversary of the fall of the Bastille, was made a national holiday, and the "Marseillaise," the battle hymn of the revolution, became the national anthem.

The Republic of the Republicans

Having survived the threat of an authoritarian reaction, the republican majority in the Chamber of Deputies showed a pathological fear of strong leadership of any kind. The outstanding figure among the republican deputies was Léon Gambetta, the gallant organizer of French national defense in 1870 and the chief engineer of the republican election victory of 1877. Influenced by the example of parliamentary government in Britain, Gambetta saw that a political party had to be able to count on a certain voting strength in the Chamber if it was to carry through a vigorous legislative program. He proposed to unite the moderate republicans in a single party with sufficient power to govern France effectively and provide the country with strong and stable leadership. He wanted greater party discipline and advocated changing the electoral system along British lines to encourage the development of fewer but stronger parties.

Gambetta's ideas on party organization and election reform alienated republican deputies who feared the loss of their seats or their political independence. Jealous colleagues had no desire to concede authority to him. His old radical supporters disliked his new moderation and his abandonment of programs dear to the French left, such as the immediate separation of church and state and the abolition of the regular army in favor of a citizens' militia. Conservatives, clericals, the great industrialists, and financiers looked upon him as a dangerous radical and were only too happy to join forces with his republican enemies. Because of the strength of the parliamentary forces ranged against him, Gambetta had only one opportunity to form a ministry, and his government lasted a bare three months. His death on December 31, 1882, removed the one statesman who might have transformed the government of the Third Republic into a stable parliamentary system capable of giving the country strong and purposeful leadership.

Under the republican administration, laws restricting freedom of the press, public assembly, and the sale of printed material were relaxed. The control of the central government over provincial and municipal governments was eased. Amnesty was granted to all men sentenced to prison or exile for participation in the Paris Commune. Trade unions were given greater freedom to organize and conduct their own affairs.

However, the only major program upon which the republican deputies could agree was anticlericalism. The Jesuits were expelled from France, and restrictive measures against the church and religious organizations were enacted, though subsequently not always enforced. The central feature of the anticlerical program was the campaign against church control of education. The struggle over education was bitter, for both sides believed the issue at stake was the control of the minds and loyalties of future generations of Frenchmen. The aim of republican legislators was to bring the youth of France into a state-controlled, republican educational system that would be free, universal, and compulsory. The accomplishment of this program, which would ensure equality of educational opportunity for all citizens, would be not only a great social reform but a great patriotic reform as well: it would enable France to rival Prussia in the schoolroom, where, many republican educators confidently believed, the war of 1870 had been won. A law of March 29, 1882, made primary education in some kind of school, whether state, church, or private, compulsory for all children between the ages of six and thirteen. To implement the program of state education, the government founded teacher-training schools, including training schools for women teachers which hardly existed as yet. Less was done in the field of higher education, although the state took steps to improve the educational standards in secondary schools and laid the foundation for the great reforms of the French university system that took place toward the end of the century.

Because state schools were free, they had the advantage in attracting students, for even among good Catholics the temptation was great to avoid the payment of fees to church schools. Officially, the state schools were neutral, which meant that they gave no religious instruction. Politically, however, they were far from neutral, for they systematically sought to indoctrinate students with republican, nationalist, and anticlerical sentiments. The state imposed severe restrictions on teachers trained by the church and on church schools. No one was permitted to teach in a state school without a state teacher's certificate, and no religious teaching order could maintain a school not authorized by the state. These regulations provoked a bitter struggle with the church, and their implementation frequently involved the use of force.

In the early 1880's the French government was obliged to deal with pressing economic problems arising from the general European economic depression that had begun in 1873. The peasants, faced with the competition of grain from eastern Europe and America, and of wine from Italy and Spain, were protected by an agricultural tariff enacted in 1881. Taxes on agricultural land were reduced and a program of farm subsidies was inaugurated. Agricultural schools and model farms were set up to introduce modern methods of production, and the government subsidized research for the improvement of farm products. In the same year, new industrial tariffs gave French industry added protection from foreign competition, and the tax schedule was revised to aid French business.

Encouragement of business was a prominent feature of the third Republic, as it had been of the July Monarchy and the Second Empire. The government recognized the political advantages of securing the support of this immensely powerful section of French society and the desirability of maintaining a healthy national economy, which flourishing business enterprises seemed to foster. Under the republic the expansion of France's network of railroads and waterways and the development of its natural resources was continued, and France remained one of the strongest financial powers in the world.

But despite the encouragement given to business by the state—the lucrative construction contracts and concessions, the favorable taxation system, and the protective tariffs—French industry did not experience the boom that occurred in Germany in response to similar government stimuli. After 1880 France began to fall behind Great Britain and Germany as an industrial power. One reason for this lag in industrial development was France's comparative poverty in raw materials, especially coal. Another was the absence of the kind of government leadership and coordination of financial and industrial enterprises which had been prominent during the Second Empire and was now playing a major role in German economic development. Moreover, between a third and a half of France's available capital was invested abroad, an unhealthy situation in view of the underdeveloped condition of the French domestic economy.

The magnitude of French overseas investments had other important results. A good part of these funds went into countries with weak or unstable governments, where the interest rates were high but the risks great. When political or economic chaos in these areas threatened the security of their investments, French financiers called upon their government for protection. State intervention in response to such appeals was part of the process of financial, or economic, imperialism of the era, and resulted in a considerable extension of the French colonial empire.

But overseas expansion failed to release France from the grip of economic depression. Phylloxera ruined the French wine industry in many districts, and despite government tariffs, subsidies, and tax reductions both agriculture and industry had difficulty meeting foreign competition. The economic depression, along with setbacks in colonial policy in Indochina, was probably the major reason for the defeat of the republicans in the general elections of 1885. The monarchists more than doubled their strength in the new Chamber of Deputies. A serious split between moderates and radicals divided what was left of the republican majority.

The moderate republicans, called "opportunists" because they thought new laws should be introduced only when they were expedient, wanted to avoid disruptive issues, to limit the scope of reform, and to deal with one problem at a time. "Nothing must be put in the republican program that the majority of the nation cannot be induced to accept immediately," Gambetta had said, as spokesman of the opportunist point of view. The radicals, on the other hand, wanted to carry through sweeping reforms at once. They demanded a revision of the constitution to make it more democratic, the election of judges, a graded income tax, greater local self-government, and the immediate separation of church and state. The radicals were also among the most vociferous champions of a war of revenge against Germany; indeed, many of them were so intensely obsessed with this idea that they were willing to subordinate their reform program to the cause of patriotism—thus evincing the attitude that has been called the original sin of the French left.

The election setback of the republicans and the gains of the monarchists came just when the monarchists were in a particularly strong position. For the first time in many years their ranks seemed united. The deaths of the son of Napoleon III in 1879 and of the count of Chambord in 1883 had left the Orleanist candidate, the count of Paris, as the only serious pretender to the French throne. The peasants and businessmen who had suffered in the economic depression, the propertied classes alarmed at demands of the radical republicans for social reform, and the church, angered by the anticlerical legislation of the republicans, all rallied to support the monarchists. They were joined by the most rabid nationalists, including many radicals, who believed that a monarchy or some other form of authoritarian government would be more capable of leading France to victory against Germany than a weak and divided republic. The republic was threatened. Cynics noted that since 1789 no government in France had lasted more than twenty years.

The Boulanger Crisis

Contrary to general expectation, the danger to the republic that actually materialized came not from the monarchists directly, but from an avowed republican, General Georges Boulanger (1837–1891), appointed minister of war in January, 1886, because he was thought to be the only republican

General Georges Boulanger. *During the 1880's Boulanger was regarded as a man of destiny by many French patriots, who hoped he would lead their country to a new era of national greatness.*

general in the monarchist-dominated army. As minister he caught the public attention through his measures to improve living conditions in the army, which won him great popularity with the troops, while his mild efforts to republicanize the army won the applause of the radicals. His remarkable flair for publicity soon made him a national figure. The real basis of his appeal, however, and the quality that united so many diverse segments of French society in his support, was his embodiment of French hopes for a successful war of revenge against Germany. Here, at last, was the strong man the nation had been seeking, the French answer to Bismarck. As if to confirm French patriots in their opinion, Bismarck in a speech of January, 1887, named Boulanger as the greatest obstacle to good relations between France and Germany.

In May, 1887, moderate republicans, alarmed by Boulanger's popularity, dismissed him from the cabinet and assigned him to a military command in the provinces. Boulanger's dismissal and exile made him a martyr and only increased his popularity. Enthusiasm for him reached new heights when his supporters were able to exploit a scandal involving the son-in-law of the president of the republic, who had been selling national honors and decorations, including medals of the Legion of Honor. Although President Jules Grévy (1807–1891) was not directly implicated in the scandal, he was obliged to resign, while Boulanger gained new luster as a man of integrity among sordid politicians.

The rise of Boulangism in France coincided with a period of serious tension between Russia and Germany in the Balkans. The prospect of a collapse of the old diplomatic partnership between Germany and Russia aroused new hopes in France. Only the most myopic French patriot believed that France alone could defeat the German empire in war, but a France allied with Russia—especially a France under the inspired guidance of Boulanger—might well be a match for the Kaiser's legions. It was well known in France that a major obstacle to a Franco-Russian alliance was the tsar's aversion to the republican form of government. Restoration of the monarchy now began to appear to many Frenchmen as a national necessity and a patriotic duty. Republicans began to speak in terms of a constitutional monarchy under Boulangist auspices, and many monarchists seemed willing to concede to Boulanger a large measure of authority in a restoration government.

At the same time, the ministers of the republican government played into Boulanger's hands. In March, 1888, they committed the blunder of dismissing him from the army for engaging illegally in politics while in military service. As a result, Boulanger was no longer a soldier under government orders, and was free to stand for election to the Chamber of Deputies. In the following weeks he entered one by-election after another, as the French electoral system made it possible for him to do, and in each case he was triumphantly elected. The crucial test of Boulanger's popularity came on January 27, 1889, when he stood as a candidate in radical, skeptical Paris. The government threw all its resources into the campaign to defeat him, but again he won a tremendous victory. It was now generally expected that he would seize the opportunity offered by this popular mandate to overthrow the government. Plans for a *coup d'état* were made by his supporters; the commanders of the key regiments in Paris waited for his orders. But instead of leading the troops against the government, he spent the night of January 27 with his mistress. Afterward, alarmed by the news of the government's intention to arrest him for treason, he fled abroad. With his flight, the Boulanger myth and Boulangism collapsed.

The elections of September 1889 following the flight of Boulanger resulted in a rout of the Boulangist candidates, a severe defeat for the monarchists, and a surprisingly great triumph for the moderate republicans. The republic had survived another in a long series of severe political crises.

The Boulanger episode had important consequences for French politics. It reinforced the fear among republican legislators of strong men and strong governments. Realistic monarchist politicians recognized, once the monarchists' dubious dealings with Boulanger had been exposed, that to exert any influence at all they would have to join the republican ranks. Realistic statesmen in the Church, too, saw that they would have to reckon with the republic for some time to come. The year after the collapse of Boulangism,

Pope Leo XIII inaugurated the *ralliement*—the "rally" to the republic—in the belief that more could be achieved for the Church by working through republican parliamentary institutions than by adamantly opposing them. On the left, radicals had also been discredited by their association with Boulanger; their major reform proposal, a revision of the constitution, had been rendered suspect because Boulanger had supported it.

The republic of the moderates seemed to have won a new lease on life, but its position remained precarious. There was the constant threat of a *coup d'état* on the part of monarchists, clericals, and army officers, who refused to be reconciled to the republic. Meanwhile the mass of the French people remained indifferent to the republic or were becoming increasingly radicalized as a result of the government's resistance to programs designed to improve the lot of industrial and agricultural workers. The republic was therefore still extremely vulnerable when faced with new and even more severe political crises which erupted in the following decade: the Panama Canal scandals and the Dreyfus affair.

ITALY TO 1890

The Problems of Unification

Difficult as were the problems confronting the leaders of France, they at least were dealing with a state with ancient political traditions, and they had at their disposal the most centralized and effective administrative apparatus in Europe. In contrast, the new Italian national government faced the problem of ruling a country that had not been under one administration for over fifteen centuries, a country in which local loyalties and local political traditions were strongly entrenched.

In Rome, Pope Pius IX refused to accept the loss of his temporal power and maintained an uncompromising hostility toward the new national state. When in 1871 the Italian government tried to regulate its relations with the papacy by offering the pope and the Church certain guarantees, the pope denounced these proposals and refused to abandon his self-imposed imprisonment in the Vatican. He called upon the Catholic powers of the world to help him regain his territories, and ordered Italian Catholics to refrain from all participation in the affairs of the secular state. The pope received no direct support from abroad, and politically minded Italian Catholics for the most part disregarded the prohibition on political activity, but the hostility of the papacy was nevertheless a constant danger and embarrassment to the government.

Challenging the new government, too, was the omnipresent fact of poverty, aggravated by the heavy taxes levied to achieve a balanced budget—at the expense of the poor.

Nowhere were economic hardships more severe than in the south. A

Victor Emmanuel II. *The first king of Italy, he ruled from 1861 to 1878.*

large-scale civil war developed in southern Italy even before the process of Italian unification had been completed. The southerners resented the rule of the Sardinian "foreigners," with their centralized administration, higher taxes, and military conscription. The Bourbons now became the popular party and began to stir up rebellion against the Sardinians. Neopolitan royalist leaders became the new Garibaldis. They were joined by the unemployed, by hungry peasants who felt cheated by unfulfilled promises of land reform, by brigands who took advantage of the general turmoil to harass the countryside. In some areas the revolt against the national government assumed the character of a religious war in response to government measures directed against the Church. Shortly after the proclamation of the kingdom of Italy in 1861, the new state found it necessary to concentrate almost half the national army in the south. It has been estimated that more men died in the campaign to subdue the south than in all the wars of Italian unification. The struggle raged until 1866. Even after the worst fighting was over, the scars of civil war remained and the problems of the south continued to foment unrest.

Italian superpatriots were another source of danger and embarrassment to the government. The major work of Italian unification had hardly been completed when clamor began for the return of Nice and Savoy from France, and for the cession by Austria of Trent, Trieste, the Dalmatian coast, and other areas regarded as *Italia irredenta,* or unredeemed territory. Imperialism was to involve Italy in awkward and costly international complications, which would reach their climax in the twentieth century under Benito Mussolini. More immediately, efforts to establish Italy as a great power involved the state in ruinous military expenditures.

Italy's political institutions were not sufficiently developed to cope with the problems facing the nation. Although the constitution made the king supreme head of the state, with sole executive authority, the lower house of the Italian parliament, the Chamber of Deputies, was the real center of political power. The king's actual position was not strong. Republicanism was a constant threat; he faced the steady and uncompromising hostility of the Church; he was opposed by the regional nobility, many of whom remained loyal to the dynasts he had displaced and resented Sardinian restrictions on their traditional privileges. Lacking the support of the Church and a large section of the aristocracy, the bulwarks of monarchical government in other countries, the king of Italy was forced to rely heavily on the army and on the support or sufferance of the vested interests represented in the Chamber of Deputies.

The political foundations of the Chamber of Deputies itself, however, were unsteady. In Italy, as in France, no clear-cut party system developed. Since the time of Cavour, Italian governments had been based largely on political alliances rather than on a single party with a consistent political program. The system encouraged political moderation, but it prevented the formation of a strong government—and of a strong and responsible opposition. Election rigging, the political indifference of an uneducated populace, and the Church's prohibition on participation in politics helped to sustain the system and to impede the formation of a vigorous parliamentary tradition in Italy. The enthusiasm and generous impulses kindled in the period of unification were stifled by narrow-minded calculations of political or economic expediency. Patriots who had devoted their lives to the Italian national cause and now came forward with programs for political and social reform were shunted aside as dangerous revolutionaries. Garibaldi went into self-imposed exile. The disillusionment of the idealists was expressed by the greatest idealist of them all, Giuseppe Mazzini. "I had hoped to evoke the soul of Italy," he said shortly before his death in 1872, "but all I can see is its corpse."

The Politics of Trasformismo

Agostino Depretis (1813–1887), the leading figure in the Italian government from 1876 until his death was a natural product of Italian politics. Depretis's method of "transforming" opposition parties and interest groups into allies by political and economic bribery was used so consistently and so successfully that the word *trasformismo* came to describe an entire system of government. Ministries rose and fell with disconcerting rapidity after 1876, but Depretis generally managed to remain in control. The measures concerning education, franchise reform, and public health which were enacted while he was in power were never adequately implemented, and the net effect of his government was a further deterioration of the tone and prestige of Italian parliamentary life.

Depretis's most significant successor in Italian politics was Francesco Crispi (1819–1901). A former Garibaldian radical, Crispi was seduced by the prospect of power into adopting Depretis's system of *trasformismo*, but he nevertheless retained a good deal of radical idealism. Like his hero Garibaldi, he believed in the efficacy of dictatorial methods to accomplish his goals. And accomplish them he did—to the later admiration of Mussolini. In 1888 his government enacted measures concerning public health, prison reform, and franchise reform in municipal elections. In 1889 the criminal code was amended, special tribunals were set up for the redress of administrative abuses, and workers were granted a limited right to strike. Salutary as some of Crispi's reforms were, his dictatorial tactics further stifled the development of genuine parliamentary government in Italy. He sharply raised taxes to pay for increased armaments required for the support of his ambitious foreign policy. He ruthlessly suppressed revolts in his native Sicily. And he permitted a notable amount of political and financial corruption. His high-tariff policy and his abrogation of Italy's trade treaty with France in 1887 helped bring about a serious economic depression.

An economic crisis had been developing for some time. The construction of railroads, the opening of new routes to Italy through the Mont Cenis and Brenner passes in the Alps, and the reduction of charges for transporting freight by ships encouraged the large-scale importation of cheap agricultural and industrial products from America and from other parts of Europe. The resulting drop in prices in Italy provoked a demand for tariff protection. But Crispi's protectionism went to extremes; it dealt a crippling blow to Italy's economic relations with France, and the consequent heavy withdrawal of French capital from Italy was partly responsible for the collapse of several important banks, followed by a serious inflation. The high cost of food, a consequence of high agricultural tariffs, caused actual starvation in some areas and was a principal reason for serious revolts in Sicily in the late 1880's.

In 1890 the Italian government was still confronted with many of the problems it had faced in 1861. The cleavage between north and south was, if anything, worse than before unification. The national economy was still unstable. Taxes were high and the taxation system was unfairly administered. The budget had finally been balanced in 1876, but soon after the state was again heavily in debt. Inflationary policies had reduced Italian credit abroad and caused the flight of hard currency from the country.

Almost nothing had been done to aid Italian agriculture, the source of livelihood for the majority of the population, and Italian farmers were unable to meet foreign competition. Crispi's high tariffs helped the Italian peasants to some extent, but they also raised the price of food for all members of the population.

The picture was not entirely bleak. In the late 1870's great progress had been made in the textile, silk, and rubber industries, and above all in the production of armaments, which was generously subsidized by the state. Industry, like agriculture, was aided by Crispi's protectionist policies, but again at immense cost to the country. Prices remained abnormally high, and outmoded and inefficient methods of production prevailed.

Italian political life was dominated by the pursuit of special interests. No respected tradition of parliamentary or democratic government had been established. The system worked well enough to carry on the routine business of government, but it proved incapable of dealing purposefully or effectively with the fundamental evils besetting the nation.

THE HABSBURG EMPIRE TO 1890

The Creation of Austria-Hungary

In the wake of the Italian war of 1859, fundamental changes were introduced in the government and structure of the Habsburg empire. The war had revealed the dubious loyalty of many of the empire's non-German troops, especially the Magyars, who had deserted in large numbers and had proved unreliable in battle. The nationalities problem thus stood exposed as one of the empire's gravest difficulties.

Following the defeats in Italy, Emperor Francis Joseph dismissed Bach and other ministers who had favored a policy of bureaucratic centralization dominated by the German element in the empire, and inaugurated his first personal experiment aimed at solving the nationalities problem. Under the influence of the Polish nobleman Count Agenor von Goluchowski (1812–1875), the emperor in 1860 issued a new constitution, the so-called October Diploma, which gave the major share of power to the provincial assemblies dominated by the local nobility. In theory it ended the policy of centralization that had favored the German population, and it represented an effort to win over the feudal nobility of every national group, and especially to regain the support of the Hungarians.

The October Diploma satisfied certain feudal elements among the Slavs, to whom it gave considerable local autonomy, but the Hungarians objected that it did not give them enough independence, and the Germans resented the diminution of their power and importance. The combined opposition of the Germans and the Hungarians made government under the October Diploma impossible, and it was never really put into effect.

The emperor now entrusted domestic policy to a new minister of the interior, Anton von Schmerling (1805–1893), who in 1861 proposed another experiment intended to take care of the nationalities problem. His February Patent, supposed to reinterpret and supplement the October Diploma, actually changed it altogether. Instead of conceding power to the provincial assemblies, the February Patent provided for an imperial parliament in which all the nationalities of the empire were to be represented. The idea was sound, but the election procedures were arranged to give the Germans the dominant share of the votes. So little representation was accorded to the non-German elements that most of them boycotted the new parliament, dubbing it Schmerling's Theater. In operation, Schmerling's system proved very similar to Bach's, for the real power was concentrated in a centralized bureaucracy and the German element in the empire was again ascendant.

Schmerling's government, like that of Bach, fell as a result of mistakes in foreign policy. To conciliate their own Polish population and to establish closer diplomatic ties with the western powers, the Austrians joined Great Britain and France in expressing sympathy for the Poles who revolted against Russia in 1863. It was a futile gesture, for it did not help the Poles and further alienated Russia. In 1864 Austria antagonized Britain and France by joining Prussia in the war against Denmark over Schleswig and Holstein. Thus in 1866 Austria was without allies among the great powers in its contest with Prussia for hegemony in central Europe.

As tension between Prussia and Austria mounted after the Danish war in 1864, Emperor Francis Joseph of Austria became alarmed at the efforts of German liberals to increase the powers of the Austrian parliament at the expense of the crown, and at their apparent willingness to cooperate with disaffected groups in Hungary to achieve this aim.

The most fiercely nationalistic group in Hungary consisted of the Magyars, a Finno-Ugrian people who had settled there in the ninth century, and who predominated over the numerous other nationalities inhabiting the country. To undercut German parliamentarians and to win Hungarian support, the emperor encouraged Magyar leaders to draw up a program that would satisfy their national aspirations and enable them to cooperate with the imperial government.

This offer was accepted with some eagerness by the more realistic Hungarian politicians, who disliked the aims of the Independence party, which wanted to sever all ties with the Habsburg empire. They realized that an independent Hungary could never be a great power, and that all alone, and opposed by the Habsburgs, Hungary might not be able to control its many subject nationalities. In response to the emperor's conciliatory approach, the Hungarian statesmen Ferencz Deák (1803–1876) and Count Gyula Andrássy (1823–1890) worked out a program that would allow Hungary to enjoy a large measure of national autonomy while retaining the

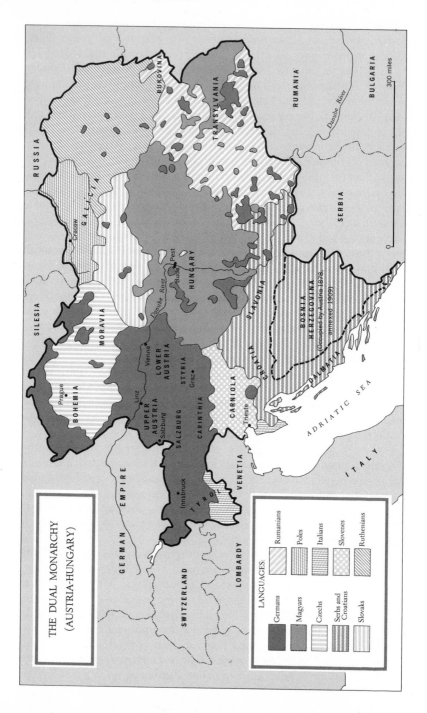

THE DUAL MONARCHY
(AUSTRIA-HUNGARY)

LANGUAGES:

Germans
Magyars
Czechs
Serbs and
Croatians
Slovaks

Rumanians
Poles
Italians
Slovenes
Ruthenians

RUSSIA

GALICIA

Cracow

SILESIA

MORAVIA

BOHEMIA

Prague

Danube River

BUKOVINA

TRANSYLVANIA

RUMANIA

BULGARIA

300 miles

Danube River

SERBIA

Pest
Buda

HUNGARY

SLAVONIA

CROATIA

BOSNIA
HERZEGOVINA
(Occupied by Austria 1878,
annexed 1909)

DALMATIA

ADRIATIC SEA

Vienna
LOWER
AUSTRIA

STYRIA

Graz

CARNIOLA

Trieste

UPPER
AUSTRIA

Linz

Salzburg

SALZBURG

CARINTHIA

VENETIA

GERMAN EMPIRE

Innsbruck

TYROL

LOMBARDY

SWITZERLAND

ITALY

advantages of affiliation with a great power. The emperor expressed his willingness to negotiate along these lines, but the war with Prussia broke out before anything definite had been arranged.

After Austria's defeat in 1866 an *Ausgleich*, or settlement, with the Hungarians was negotiated by Count Ferdinand von Beust (1809–1886), who became Austrian foreign minister in October, 1866. Beust's primary object was to prepare Austria politically and diplomatically for a war of revenge against Prussia. His main motive in sponsoring the *Ausgleich* was to regain Magyar loyalty, for Hungarian support was an essential precondition for a renewal of the contest with Prussia.

But he failed to recognize that the Magyars were the people least likely to support a war of revenge. To them, Austrian victory in such a war would mean the restoration of Habsburg influence in Germany and the consequent reestablishment of German influence in the empire. The *Ausgleich* was to mark the permanent defeat of the Germanizers in the empire, which from now on had to be governed to a far greater extent with and through the non-German elements. The settlement with Hungary of 1867 was to be the one lasting constitutional reform of Francis Joseph's reign.

By the terms of the *Ausgleich*, the Habsburg empire remained under a single ruler, who now presided over a newly formed Dual Monarchy as emperor of Austria and king of Hungary. The emperor was still the supreme authority; he personally continued to make major policy decisions affecting the empire as a whole. The unity of the empire was maintained in the three crucial fields of foreign policy, war, and finance, each under the jurisdiction of an imperial ministry whose head was appointed by the emperor. There was a common postal system, common currency, and after 1878, a common bank.

In all other respects the two parts of the empire were separate. Each had its own constitution, its own parliament, its own ministry for domestic affairs. The administrative language in the Austrian section of the empire was German, in the Hungarian, Magyar. Common problems were discussed by representatives of the parliaments of both states. In economic affairs agreement was reached through direct negotiation between the two parliaments. The Hungarians had the right to renegotiate tariff policies and the amount of their financial contribution to the empire every ten years.

So far as their domestic affairs were concerned, the Magyars had achieved the status of an independent nation.

Austria after the Ausgleich

After 1867, the non-Hungarian part of the Habsburg empire was known officially as the "kingdoms and lands represented in the Reichsrat" (the Austrian parliament), but for the sake of convenience was generally called Austria. Following the *Ausgleich*, attempts to deal through constitutional experiments with the problems of government, especially the nationalities question, were confined to the Austrian part of the empire.

In 1867 a new constitution was prepared for Austria. It recognized the equality of all nationalities, and the right of each to preserve its own language and culture; it contained an extensive bill of rights, which guaranteed equality before the law, and freedom of speech, press, and assembly; it provided for the independence of judges; and it recognized the principle of ministerial responsibility to parliament. This constitution remained in force until 1918, the only important change being the gradual extension of the franchise, culminating in universal manhood suffrage in 1907.

In theory the Austrian constitution seemed to provide every necessary guarantee of national and personal liberty, but its provisions were not always put into practice. The principle of equality among the nationalities was violated by an electoral system giving the Germans a disproportionate share of the seats in parliament. The principle of ministerial responsibility to parliament was ignored by the emperor, who assumed the power to appoint and dismiss ministers. Moreover, the constitution gave the emperor the right to rule by decree when parliament was not in session, and his signature was necessary to validate all legislation. Thus the emperor could legislate without parliamentary consent and could veto parliamentary action.

The policies of the first Austrian ministries under the new constitution reflected the views of German liberals, the largest group in the new parliament. Laws providing for compulsory military service and compulsory elementary education were enacted, along with some anticlerical measures. The 1855 Concordat with the Vatican was abrogated in 1870 in protest against the proclamation of papal infallibility, the right of civil marriage was restored, the education system was removed from Church control, and all Christian creeds were given equal legal status. The liberal regime also introduced a number of humanitarian reforms in the penal code, and abolished religious and legal discrimination against Jews.

The Prussian victory over France in 1871 ended all immediate hope of a successful Austrian war of revenge against Prussia. The danger now was that Prussia would try to complete the process of German unification by absorbing the German-speaking parts of the Habsburg realm. The enthusiasm with which Austrian Germans greeted Bismarck's achievements seemed to indicate that many of them would not be opposed to a closer political union with Prussia. Apprehensive about the loyalty of his German subjects and alienated by the liberalizing policies of his German-dominated government, the emperor early in 1871 appointed a new ministry led by Count Karl Sigismund von Hohenwart, who advocated greater autonomy for Austria's national minorities and believed that conciliation of the large Slavic population was essential to the preservation of the monarchy.

The dominant influence in the new cabinet was the minister of com-

merce, Professor Albert Schäffle (1831–1903), a German Protestant econmist who had been a radical in 1848. Dismayed by the human misery in the
industrial slums, Schäffle rejected the liberal concept of economic freedom,
which he regarded as merely freedom for the entrepreneur to exploit the
worker. In place of the *laissez-faire* capitalist system, he recommended
reforms that amounted to a program of state socialism. Schäffle also
resented the German assumption of racial superiority over the Slavs. To
break the power of the Germans and of the capitalist entrepreneurs at the
same time, he proposed the introduction of universal manhood suffrage.
This, he felt, would give each individual and each nationality in Austria
proper representation and end the artificial German-capitalist domination of
the Austrian parliament.

The new ministry granted numerous privileges to the Poles, who were
confirmed as the dominant element in Galicia. Henceforth, they were
comparatively loyal supporters of the Habsburg government. But the most
important part of Schäffle's nationalities program concerned the Czechs.
With the emperor's approval, he began negotiations with Czech leaders
aimed at granting the Czechs of Bohemia a status in the empire similar to
that of the Magyars. These efforts were opposed by the Germans in Austria,
who feared the dilution of their own influence. At the same time, objections
were voiced by the Hungarians, who saw a threat to their unique position.
Schäffle's purpose might still have been carried out with imperial support
had not the Czechs insisted on being given jurisdiction over the "historic"
kingdom of Bohemia, an area far larger than the one actually occupied by
Czech-speaking peoples. The Czechs would thus have gained control over
non-Czech national groups, including many Germans. The extent of the
Czech demands, the threat of revolution by the Germans in Vienna, the
adamant opposition of the Hungarians (who protested that granting the
Czechs a status similar to their own would destroy the "unity" of the
empire), persuaded the emperor not to grant the Czechs autonomy. On
October 28, 1871, the Hohenwart ministry resigned.

There followed another era of German-liberal domination of Austrian
politics, under Prince Adolf Auersperg (1821–1885). Changes in the electoral law gave townspeople—and thus Germans—greater representation,
and hence aroused bitter Slavic opposition, above all from the Poles and
Czechs. The latter boycotted the elections to parliament in protest against
the new electoral legislation.

Economic problems were the most pressing concern of the Auersperg
ministry. Austria's economic boom of the early 1870's ended in the great
financial crash of 1873, which was followed by a severe depression. The
government attempted to pump new life into the economy by financing
public-works projects. To ease the hardship of the workers and create more
jobs, it restricted employment of women and children and passed laws

requiring safer working conditions. These laws were not strictly enforced, however, and there was little real improvement in the lot of the working classes. The depression spurred the growth of labor organizations, which had been developing rapidly in the previous decade. Government legislation to curb trade unions and socialist political parties was ineffective; instead of hindering their expansion, it only made them more radical.

The depression and the steady opposition of non-German national groups weakened the Auersperg ministry. Church opposition had been aroused by anticlerical measures giving the government the power to tax Church property and *de facto* control over clerical education and the appointment of priests. The ministry was further weakened by revelations that many of its supporters in parliament had been involved in financial scandals during the economic boom. The emperor was disillusioned by the failures of the government in domestic affairs, and as usual, he resented the efforts of liberal legislators to increase their power at his expense. In August, 1879, he dismissed Auersperg. German liberals never again occupied a dominant position in the Austrian government. The collapse of their domestic influence coincided with the conclusion of a military alliance with Germany and the establishment of a close alignment between Germany and Austria-Hungary in foreign affairs.

Count Eduard von Taaffe (1833–1895), the man appointed to succeed Auersperg, was a childhood friend of the emperor. A conservative bureaucrat of wide experience, he professed to stand above party and nationality (he was of Irish descent), and to owe allegiance only to the crown. Like the emperor himself, Taaffe was suspicious of theorists and preferred to govern by expedients and by conciliation. Long before it became fashionable in England, he used the term "muddling through" (*fortwursteln*) to describe his method of operation.

Although his government made many concessions to the various nationalities, Taaffe never worked out a comprehensive program to deal with the minority question, nor did he develop any programs to resolve the financial, labor, and other major problems affecting Austria. His method of keeping rival forces in the country "in a balanced state of mild dissatisfaction" allowed him to govern Austria for fourteen years without major upheavals. But beneath the surface, Austria's national and social problems continued to fester.

To gain support for his government and break the power of the German liberals, Taaffe persuaded the Czechs and other Slavic groups to abandon their boycott of the Austrian parliament; he also secured the backing of the clericals, who represented the Catholic peasants of the empire, and of conservatives of every class and nationality who had disliked the liberalizing policies of the Auersperg government. Taaffe's coalition of Slavs, clericals, and conservatives gave him a comfortable majority in parliament that came

Count Taaffe at his desk.

to be known as Taaffe's Iron Ring. In 1882 he further strengthened his position by obtaining passage of an electoral law which increased the representation of the Slavic minorities at the expense of the Germans.

To retain the support of the non-Germans, Taaffe made a series of concessions to the national minorities. In Bohemia, Galicia, and Slovenia, for example, the Slavic languages as well as German might be used in education and administration.

Instead of conciliating the Slavs, however, such measures only increased their self-confidence and belligerence. The Czech leaders of the older generation were pushed to the background by nationalist extremists, who demanded the complete exclusion of German influence from Bohemia and national independence within the boundaries of the "historic" kingdom, an attitude that rendered an *Ausgleich* with the Czechs virtually impossible. Unlike the Hungarian leaders in the 1860's, the Czech nationalists failed to see the advantages to themselves in the existing imperial system. As an older Czech leader pointed out, Bohemia was too small to stand alone. If the Habsburg empire collapsed, the Czechs were bound to fall under German or Russian control—a prophecy that was tragically fulfilled.

Despite the Czech nationalists' complaints about political oppression and the economic impositions of the Vienna government, Bohemia enjoyed considerable prosperity under Habsburg rule. It became the most highly industrialized part of the empire and one of the major manufacturing centers of Europe. Czech textiles, leather goods, porcelain, and lace became world famous, as did the Skoda machine and armaments works.

Taaffe's concessions not only failed to conciliate the Slavs but infuriated the Germans, who saw their influence steadily eroded in the parts of the empire where they were in a minority. In 1890 militant German and Slavic nationalists combined to prevent the passage of government-sponsored legislation aimed at securing some kind of compromise on the nationalities question. In 1891 both Czech and German moderates were routed in the parliamentary elections.

Taaffe's failure to solve the minority problems was accompanied by failure to solve the serious financial problems of the empire. Expenditures for the army, bureaucracy, and public services were constantly increasing. The existing tax revenues were inadequate and the means of collecting taxes difficult and complex. Indirect taxes on consumer goods, documents, and newspapers were the principal sources of state funds. Instead of meeting the problem with a large-scale program of tax and financial reform, Taaffe simply increased the rate of state borrowing, thereby raising the cost of servicing the national debt.

Government efforts at social reform were also ineffective. New laws were passed regulating working conditions in mines and factories; the working day was limited to eleven hours in factories and to ten hours in mines; child and female labor was more strictly controlled; provisions were made for sickness and accident insurance. The enactment of these laws, most of them modeled on German examples, was a step toward the improvement of working conditions. Like so many laws in Austria, however, they lacked adequate means of enforcement. They failed to satisfy labor or to stem the growth of the socialist and trade-union movements.

Taaffe's government fell in 1893 as a result of his effort to introduce universal manhood suffrage. He had hoped by extending the franchise to undercut nationalist opposition, which he—by then mistakenly—believed to be a middle-class phenomenon, and to draw on the support of the conservative and loyal peasantry. He had also hoped to win over the workers, by introducing a new, large-scale labor-reform program. But Taaffe's proposals for universal suffrage and labor reform offended every vested interest in the country. His new policies were opposed not only by his old enemies—the German liberals and nationalists—but by conservatives and businessmen of every nationality, and by the Church. Most important of all, Taaffe's radical program alarmed the emperor. With the loss of the emperor's support, Taaffe was obliged to resign.

The threat of Taaffe's legislation to the position of the Germans in Austria gave rise to a new and virulent form of German nationalism, particularly in areas where Germans felt themselves most under pressure from the non-German nationalities. This was the case in Vienna, which attracted enterprising persons from every part of the Habsburg realm and was the scene of more direct confrontations between the nationalities than any other part of the empire. Here the Germans felt the hot breath of competition from new Slavic neighbors, who were generally willing to work

A court ball in Vienna during the reign of Emperor Francis Joseph. *This gay Vienna of Strauss waltzes, delightful cafés with their "chambres séparées," and seemingly lighthearted atmosphere, was also a city rent by social, racial, and religious antagonisms, the city of the anti-Semitic Mayor Lueger and of the great pioneer in the study of mental illness, Sigmund Freud.*

for lower wages and frequently proved to be disconcertingly able. Here Germans and Slavs came into contact with Jews, many of whom had risen to positions of prominence in financial, commerical, and cultural circles.

The political response to this situation was the spectacular growth in Vienna of the Christian Socialist movement, a product of German national-ism and labor distress. Dr. Karl Lueger (1844–1910), the outstanding leader of the movement, championed the rights of the worker, peasant, and small businessman against big business and "Jewish" capitalism. He advocated a socialist welfare state, but it was to be a peculiarly German and Catholic state, where Slavs, Jews, and Protestants would not be welcome. Lueger was enormously popular and was repeatedly elected mayor of Vienna.

The wealth of talent that poured into Vienna, the crosscurrents of culture, the competition among the nationalities, made the Habsburg

Emperor Francis Joseph and Dr. Karl Lueger, the long-time mayor of Vienna.

capital a lively and exciting place, a rival to Paris as an intellectual and artistic center. At the same time it was a place where Germans felt threatened, where Slavs and Jews sought assimilation while struggling to preserve a sense of identity, where incompetents and mediocrities of all nationalities had every reason to feel a sense of inferiority. Lueger's Vienna was the city of Bruckner and Mahler, of Johann Strauss and Arthur Schnitzler. It was also the city of Sigmund Freud—and of Adolf Hitler.

Hungary after 1867

The real winners in the *Ausgleich* of 1867 were the Hungarian nobles. They not only gained a large measure of independence in domestic matters, and control over their own national minorities, but also retained an important and often decisive voice in the affairs of the empire as a whole.

The Hungarian constitution adopted after the 1867 settlement was based on the constitution drawn up in 1848. It declared the Habsburg monarch to be king of Hungary, with the right to summon and dissolve parliament, to initiate legislation, to appoint ministers of state and other high officials. But although the Hungarian constitution seemed to give the monarch greater powers than the constitution of Austria, his actual authority was more limited. All royal acts and appointments had to be approved by the ministers concerned, and Hungarian ministers of state were responsible to the lower house of the Hungarian parliament, not to the crown. To a great extent the real power in Hungary lay in the lower house, and ministers able to secure majority support from that body could generally exercise decisive authority in Hungarian domestic affairs. This lower house, like the British

House of Commons in the eighteenth century, in no way represented the majority of the inhabitants of Hungary. It was an oligarchic body elected by oral vote by the Hungarian propertied classes. The lower house shared with the king the right to initiate legislation, and because there existed almost unlimited freedom of debate, the opposition of a few members could block the passage of any legislation. The power of the upper house, composed of great nobles, high officials of Church and state, and crown appointees, was slight. It could veto but not initiate legislation, and it exercised no legal control over the appointment of ministers.

As in Austria, the nationalities question was one of the great problems facing the government. In 1880 the population of Hungary, classified according to language, consisted mainly of Magyars (47 per cent), Germans (14 per cent), Slovaks (14 per cent), and Rumanians (18 per cent), with Ruthenians, Croatians, and Serbs forming 7 per cent. Unlike the Austrians, the Hungarians met the problem not by concessions but by suppression and a systematic program of Magyarization. An act of 1879 made the Magyar language obligatory in all state-supported elementary schools, and in 1883 this act was extended to include all state secondary schools. Magyar was the only language authorized for use by government administrators, the postal and telegraph services, the army, and even the workers on the railroads. The one important region which was spared Magyarization was Croatia, which was allowed to preserve its separate existence, its parliament, and its language.

The Hungarian policy of suppressing national minority movements prevented some of the chronic manifestations of national hostility evident in Austria, but in the long run suppression was no more successful than conciliation in quelling the spirit of nationalism.

During the latter part of the nineteenth century, the Industrial Revolution reached Hungary along with the other countries of central Europe, but Hungary remained primarily an agricultural state and the chief granary of the Habsburg empire. Some of the big landowners bought farm machinery and introduced scientific methods of agricultural production, but the mass of the peasantry adhered to traditional methods, and Hungary therefore had difficulty in meeting competition from abroad. Through their influence in the imperial government, however, the Magyars succeeded in imposing high agricultural tariffs on the entire empire, which protected antiquated agricultural techniques and raised food prices for all the peoples of the realm. These tariffs permitted some big landowners to realize large profits and enabled the peasants to maintain themselves at least at a subsistence level.

But tariffs did not save the Magyar petty nobles, who had been in economic difficulties since the abolition of forced peasant labor in 1848. They did not own enough land to run their estates profitably without forced labor, and they had not received enough compensation for the loss of their peasant labor to become agricultural entrepreneurs. Between 1867 and 1900 some 100,000 independent landlords were forced to sell their estates. Their lands were taken over by the great nobles, who by 1900 owned about a third of the land of the country. Most of the petty nobles entered government service to gain a livelihood. Their consequent dependence on the government does much to explain their loyalty to the settlement of 1867 and their jealous defense of the privileged status of their nation. In 1900 about 95 per cent of the state officials, 92 per cent of the county officials, and 90 per cent of the judges in Hungary were Magyar.

Industrial and financial affairs in Hungary were to a large extent in the hands of Germans and Jews. The Magyar gentry considered trade and commerce beneath their dignity. Jews were accorded full civil rights in 1867 and on the whole became enthusiastic and patriotic citizens.

The majority of industrial laborers in Hungary were landless peasants who had come to the city in search of work. Unlike the peasant migrants of other countries, the Magyar laborers had difficulty adapting to city life; the great ambition of most of them was to earn enough money to buy land and return to the soil. This sense of transiency prevented the growth of a strong class consciousness among the workers and obstructed the formation of powerful trade unions or labor parties. In 1872 trade unions were declared legal provided they were nonpolitical. Toward the end of the century they became closely but illegally associated with Marxian socialism.

The government did little to improve working conditions. A factory act of 1872 fixed the maximum working day at sixteen hours and placed certain restrictions on the employment of children. An act passed in 1884 regulated the hours and conditions of female workers and prescribed safety measures in factories and mines. Neither act was conscientiously enforced.

The most important figure in Hungarian politics in the last part of the nineteenth century was Kálmán Tisza (1830–1902). As head of the Liberal party, he was prime minister from 1875 to 1890. A fervent advocate of Hungarian independence in his early years, he became one of the staunchest supporters of the settlement of 1867, although he worked constantly to change it to Hungary's benefit. In pursuing this policy he represented the interests of the petty nobility, the dominant influence in the lower house of the Hungarian parliament. He consistently opposed agrarian and labor reforms, as well as the extension of the suffrage, and he ruthlessly defended the political supremacy of the Magyar nobility against encroachment by other classes and nationalities.

Tisza devoted his chief attention to financial problems. The Hungarian national debt had risen sharply after 1867 because of financial mismanagement, large-scale spending on the construction of railroads, and the costs of a growing bureaucracy and army. In 1875 about a third of the national revenue was being used to finance the national debt, and the government

Count Kálmán Tisza.

was having trouble finding money to meet current operating expenses. Tisza's major step toward solvency was to refund the national debt at lower interest rates; he also introduced more efficient methods of collecting taxes. During negotiations between Austria and Hungary in 1877 over their shares of the running expenses of the empire, he refused to increase Hungary's contribution, despite the growing costs of the imperial government and army. At the same time he persuaded the Austrians to agree to the reorganization of the Austrian National Bank as the Austro-Hungarian National Bank, thereby obtaining for Hungarians a greater voice in imperial financial affairs.

Tisza's administration fell in 1890 over the issue of the Magyarization of the army. Hungarian patriots demanded that Magyar be made the official language of regiments raised in their half of the empire, and that the Hungarian army leadership be given greater independence. Although Tisza had pursued a firm policy of Magyarization in domestic affairs, he saw that these demands were a threat to the security of the empire. His refusal to yield on the army issue furnished ammunition to the extreme nationalists. In 1890 Tisza's Liberal party gave way to the revived Independence party under the leadership of Francis Kossuth (1841–1914), son of the Hungarian nationalist leader of 1848, Louis Kossuth. As was to be expected, the

Independence party pursued policies which exacerbated relations with Austria and further weakened the empire as a whole.

In 1890 the problems in both Austrian and Hungarian sectors of the Habsburg empire and their relations with each other remained formidable —so formidable, in fact, that some students of Habsburg history have concluded they were insoluble: in an era that recognized the principle of nationalism, the multinational empire of the Habsburgs was doomed. Again, however, one should beware of abusing the wisdom of hindsight. All the governments of Europe were facing formidable problems, many of which have proved to be insoluble, but this did not necessarily mean that those governments would collapse. As for the Habsburg empire, it endured for over another quarter century, and was finally pulled asunder only after suffering defeat in what was until then the most terrible war in history.

THE GERMAN EMPIRE, 1871–1890

In contrast to the Habsburg empire, the new German empire consisted largely of people of one nationality, but here too centrifugal forces seemed to threaten the stability of the state. Unlike France, the empire was not tightly centralized; it was a federal union based on treaties between Prussia and the other states of Germany which permitted the individual states to preserve their separate identities and a large measure of local autonomy. Most of them maintained a good deal of financial independence; some of the larger states kept nominal control of their armies in peacetime; Bavaria and Württemberg retained their own postal systems. So great were the concessions to particularism and so numerous the powers held by local governments that many statesmen in Berlin seriously believed that the empire could not survive a severe crisis, a fear that often loomed large in their political calculations. Their apprehension was not altogether unjustified, for particularism remained a strong force in German politics.

The constitution of the empire was very similar to the constitution of the North German Confederation of 1867, and like the earlier document, it was largely the work of Bismarck. The supreme authority in the empire was vested in the emperor (kaiser), who, as king of Prussia, had the largest and most powerful state in Germany behind him. He had the right to appoint all imperial officials; he was the director of imperial foreign policy, the commander of all German armies in time of war; he had the authority to convoke and adjourn the imperial legislature, and through the chancellor, to initiate domestic legislation.

The representative of the emperor in all affairs of the empire as a whole was the imperial chancellor, who was responsible to the emperor alone. This position Bismarck created for himself, and during the reign of William I, who generally accepted his political guidance, the office gave Bismarck supreme authority in the state.

The individual states of the empire were represented according to size and population in the Bundesrat, the upper house of the imperial parliament, whose members were nominated by the governments of the states. The Bundesrat had the power to initiate legislation, and government measures affecting the entire empire were, as a rule, launched through this body. Because the Bundesrat was dominated by Prussia, which controlled enough votes to veto constitutional amendments, legislation was rarely introduced before the approval of the Prussian government had been secured. Only by uniting could the smaller states block Prussian measures, and thus preserve a certain balance of power in the Bundesrat.

The national and popular will was represented in the Reichstag, the lower house of the imperial parliament, whose members were elected from constituencies throughout the empire by universal manhood suffrage. The Reichstag, too, had the power to initiate legislation, but since measures passed by this body had to be approved by the Bundesrat, the governments of the federal states could block any proposal. The legislative initiative of the lower house was therefore severely limited. The Reichstag for its part, however, could veto all legislation passed by the Bundesrat, and by

Emperor William I and his sister, the Grand Duchess Alexandrine von Mecklenburg-Schwerin, at the spa of Ems.

threatening to exercise this right it could force through amendments to Bundesrat enactments or bargain for the passage of its own legislation. Moreover, the Reichstag controlled financial appropriations not already fixed by the constitution, and its approval was necessary for new or extraordinary expenditures, including those for the army and navy. Thus the Reichstag was in no sense a meaningless body or a mere facade for Prussian autocracy. The importance of the Reichstag is reflected in the strenuous efforts of successive imperial chancellors to secure majorities in this body to ensure the passage of their legislation.

The actual administration of the German empire was complicated by its federal nature. The administration of each of the individual states, including Prussia, was carried on by the government and bureaucracy of that state, and legislation for a particular German state did not apply to the empire as a whole. The empire itself, on the other hand, did not have a complete bureaucratic apparatus of its own, but was obliged to rely on the civil servants of the individual German states to carry out imperial legislation. In fact, certain key departments of the empire, notably the army and the foreign office, were merely extensions of those departments in the Prussian government. There was no imperial cabinet, and only one imperial minister, the chancellor. Imperial administrative departments were headed not by ministers, but by civil servants with the title of state secretaries, who might also be ministers of the Prussian government for the same departments. Thus the imperial and Prussian governments were closely intertwined, yet separate, a situation that allowed Bismarck, who except for two years was both imperial chancellor and prime minister of Prussia, to work through either administration as circumstances required and thus to keep the threads of authority in his own hands.

The lack of distinct spheres of authority was to create serious complications in the final years of the Bismarck regime and was subsequently to be a major source of conflict. It was unclear, for example, whether the Prussian ministers of state were responsible in the first instance to the prime minister of Prussia or to the monarch in his role as king of Prussia, and whether the imperial state secretaries were responsible to the imperial chancellor or to the monarch in his role as emperor. Only one thing was certain: the ministers and state secretaries were not responsible to any parliament or to public opinion.

Perhaps the greatest weakness of the Bismarck government, and of Bismarck himself as an administrator, was the lack of opportunity for other men to gain experience in the actual process of governing. Bismarck's refusal to delegate any real power to his subordinates and to allow others to make major policy decisions meant that a whole generation of German civil servants and politicians passed decisions along to a higher authority as a matter of course. As one official expressed it, no sturdy second growth was allowed

"Bismarck As Wild Animal Trainer." *This Hungarian cartoon shows a typical foreign view of the chancellor's relationship with the Reichstag. Bismarck himself frequently regretted that the Reichstag deputies were neither so muzzled nor so firmly under his control as the cartoon made it appear.*

to flourish under the Bismarck oak. The lack of politicians trained in leadership and having confidence in their capacity—and right—to rule was to be sorely felt after Bismarck's dismissal and was one of the chancellor's more unfortunate political legacies.

During the first years of the German Empire, Bismarck devoted his energies to consolidating the new state and providing it with an effective administration. Until 1878 a coalition of National Liberals (pro-Bismarck liberals) and members of the Reich party (pro-Bismarck conservatives) gave the chancellor a working majority in the Reichstag. Although these parties withheld support for a number of significant pieces of legislation, they did ensure the passage of many constructive measures that contributed to greater national unity. A system of uniform coinage, a commercial code for trade and industry, uniform methods of procedure for the civil and criminal courts, a national bank, an imperial bureau of railroads, were all products of Bismarck's alliance with national-minded members of the Reichstag.

The Kulturkampf

Bismarck's most important campaign conducted in alliance with the National Liberals was an attack on the power of the Roman Catholic Church in Germany, aimed at overcoming what he regarded as an antinational and potentially disruptive force in the new empire. To Bismarck and many other German nationalists, it appeared that the Roman Catholics owed spiritual allegiance to a foreign power which might support and encourage their opposition to Prussian rule in the areas they inhabited—in Prussian Poland, in Alsace and Lorraine, and in the German states so recently united. A further danger in Bismarck's view was the possible formation of an anti-Prussian alliance between the two vengeful Catholic powers, Austria and France, which might call upon Catholics within Germany to aid them by throwing off the yoke of Protestant Prussia.

In his campaign against the Catholic Church, Bismarck appears to have sought to bring it under government control and thereby to make it a unifying rather than a divisive force in the empire. He was encouraged in his policy by the conflict within the Church itself over the recent proclamation of the dogma of papal infallibility. A number of prominent German clerics, the Old Catholics, had seceded from the Church in protest, and Bismarck saw reason to hope that he could exploit this division in forming the national church he desired.

Bismarck's attack on the Catholic Church, called the *Kulturkampf* ("cultural struggle," or "struggle for civilization") by his liberal followers, resulted almost immediately in a consolidation of Catholic political forces in Germany in the Center party. This party, previously a minor factor in German politics, was to become one of the most powerful and stable influences in German party politics, a role it would continue to play until the Nazi era. The opposition of the Center party in the Reichstag made it almost impossible for the government to secure the passage of anti-Catholic legislation for the empire as a whole. The Jesuits were expelled from the empire in 1872, and in 1875 civil marriage was made compulsory, but there were no other moves of this sort on a national scale. Significant laws against the Church were passed only in Prussia. Of these the most noteworthy were the so-called May Laws of 1873, which were a patent attempt to place the Catholic Church under state control. The Church fought back with grim tenacity; all the bishops and over half the parish priests in Prussia preferred prison or deposition to acceptance of the state laws, and they were loyally supported by their congregations.

The *Kulturkampf* was a failure. The Center party won strength in the Reichstag elections of 1874, gaining even in Prussia, despite government hostility. Bismarck recognized his mistake and attempted to rectify it. In 1878 Pope Pius IX was succeeded by the more conciliatory and diplomatic Leo XIII, and shortly afterward Bismarck opened negotiations with the Vatican to put an end to the *Kulturkampf*. He had strong political reasons for doing so. In the course of the *Kulturkampf* he had gained a healthy respect for the strength and organization of the Catholic Church and for the political power represented by the Center party. By striking a bargain with the Church about the *Kulturkampf* legislation, he hoped to gain the support of the Center party for his own political purposes.

New Conflicts with the Liberals and the Antisocialist Campaign

By 1878 Bismarck was definitely on the lookout for new political allies, for he was finding it increasingly difficult to work with the National Liberals. In 1874 he had clashed with them over the familiar question of the military budget. The chancellor had wanted a long-term budget so that the army leaders could plan far ahead, but the liberals in the Reichstag had insisted on retaining parliamentary control over military expenditures, for this was their greatest source of political power. A government bill providing for a seven-year military budget (the "septennate") was finally passed with the support of the National Liberal leadership, but the issue had caused a rift in liberal ranks and weakened the effectiveness of the National Liberals as a progovernment party.

Bismarck had failed altogether to win liberal support for certain economic measures designed to make the government less dependent financially on the Reichstag. He had asked for direct taxes on beer and sugar, and for a government monopoly on tobacco, which would have yielded a large and steady revenue independent of Reichstag or state-government appropriations. But the liberals refused, realizing that the passage of such measures would result in a serious diminution of their control over imperial finances and hence in a serious loss of power. Moreover, many of them adhered to the doctrine of free competition and objected on principle to a government monopoly. The most serious split between Bismarck and the liberals, however, followed dissension over the policy to be adopted toward the socialists.

Since 1870, following their refusal to vote for war appropriations, Bismarck had carried on a campaign against the socialists, who like the Catholics appeared to sustain loyalties extending beyond the national state. With the union of all German socialist groups in the Social Democratic party at the Gotha Congress of 1875, and their gains in local and state elections in 1876, Bismarck intensified his opposition, on the grounds that the socialists' international revolutionary programs threatened national security and the existing political and social order. In 1876 he introduced legislation that would have made it a criminal offense to attack in print "family, property, universal military service, or other foundations of public order, in such manner as to undermine morality, respect for law, or love of the fatherland." This measure was ostensibly aimed against the socialists, but the liberals saw that it might easily be turned against any critics of the government, and much to Bismarck's annoyance, they voted against it.

Bismarck returned to the attack in 1878 after an attempt was made to assassinate the emperor. Although the would-be assassin was not a socialist, the chancellor tried to exploit the indignation aroused by the incident to obtain passage by the Reichstag of a new antisocialist proposal. The liberals on the whole disliked and feared socialism, but they regarded Bismarck's bill as an infringement of political freedom, and again they rejected it. Unfortunately for the liberals, a month later another attempt was made to kill the emperor, and this time the aged ruler was seriously wounded. Again the assassin was not a socialist, but Bismarck used the occasion to launch a fierce attack on the opponents of his antisocialist law. Accusing the liberals of indifference to the life of the emperor, he dissolved the Reichstag, and fought the ensuing election campaign on the issues of public order and patriotism. His propaganda was effective; the liberals were defeated and the conservatives made gains.

By this time Bismarck had clearly resolved to form new political combinations to support his domestic programs. The National Liberals had failed to become the obedient government party he had hoped to fashion, and their political usefulness was declining because of splits in their ranks. But Bismarck's main reason for turning away from the liberals at this time may have been his fear that they would become the political allies of the German crown prince, who professed to be a liberal himself. Since the emperor was already eighty-one, the succession of the crown prince could be expected at any moment. If the new sovereign should prove serious about wanting genuine representative government, he might wish to appoint a chancellor who had the backing of a majority in the Reichstag. It would therefore be desirable that he should find not a strong liberal group in parliament, but a majority that would support Bismarck, along with a public thoroughly alarmed by the socialist threat and hence hostile to any drastic changes in government leadership.

The antisocialist law over which the election campaign had been fought was passed in October, 1878, this time supported even by many of the National Liberals, under pressure from their constituents or convinced by Bismarck's arguments. The Social Democratic party was declared illegal, its meetings and publications prohibited; socialists found guilty of breaking the law could be expelled from certain key cities of the empire and exiled to other parts of the country. Bismarck's antisocialist law horrified genuine liberals in Germany and abroad, but in some respects it was so lenient as to raise the question of whether the chancellor was really serious about suppressing socialism, or was merely using it as a political bogey to frighten property owners and make himself appear indispensable as a bulwark against the "democratic" tendencies of the heir to the throne. Socialist candidates were still allowed to stand for election to the Reichstag and to sit if elected; socialist literature poured over the German border from Switzerland; the Social Democratic party formed a highly effective underground organization, and socialist agitators expelled from their homes went into the countryside and carried on their propaganda from there. Socialism throve on persecution. Between 1878 and 1890 the socialists increased their popular vote from 300,000 to 1,500,000, and increased their seats in the Reichstag from nine to thirty-five. As a measure to combat socialism, the antisocialist law was a failure. As a means of dramatizing the desirability of keeping Bismarck in power, however, the antisocialist campaign was most effective.

New Political Combinations; Protectionism and Economic Expansion

Bismarck next made a direct bid for the political support of the Center party. In 1878 he began his negotiations with the Vatican to end the *Kulturkampf*, and in June, 1879, he forced the resignation of Adalbert Falk (1827–1900), the Prussian minister whose name was most closely associated with the May Laws. By the summer of 1879 the chancellor had brought together an uneasy parliamentary coalition of Center-party members and progovernment conservatives, along with a number of National Liberals. With this support he embarked on a political course that differed radically from the one he had pursued during the preceding nine years.

He abandoned the policy of free trade and introduced protective tariffs for German agriculture and industry. Germany had been suffering from a serious depression since 1873, when the speculative boom that had accompanied the creation of the empire had suddenly come to an end in a catastrophic series of bank and business failures. German industry, faced with powerful competition from Great Britain, was slow to recover. German agriculture did not recover at all, but continued in a steady decline because of the influx of cheap grain from America and Russia. A German tariff law of July 13, 1879, gave protection to both agriculture and industry. It was supported by the Center party, with its large peasant constituency, by the many conservative landowners whose economic interests were primarily agrarian, and by both conservative and liberal representatives of business interests. It was opposed by those liberals to whom free trade was still an article of faith.

The tariffs brought about a notable economic recovery and marked the beginning of a period of industrial expansion that was to make Germany the most powerful industrial country in Europe. Germany soon passed both France and Great Britain as a producer of iron and steel; railway mileage was trebled between 1870 and 1914; its merchant marine came to be second only to that of Britain.

The Germans had the advantage of rich natural resources—coal, iron ore, lignite, potash—and they used these resources skillfully and efficiently. They made an intensive study of the production methods of other industrial countries, especially Britain, and profited from the lessons and mistakes of others. They purchased or manufactured the best and most modern machinery. With the creation of a national bank (the Reichsbank) in 1875 there began the kind of cooperation between government and industry that had brought such prosperity to France during the Second Empire. The government supplied long-term loans at reasonable rates to launch new industrial enterprises, and provided financial and political backing for the German drive to break Britain's domination of foreign markets. At the same time, the formation of great trusts (cartels) that controlled the major German industries facilitated the introduction of increasingly efficient manufacturing methods, including mass-production techniques. Furthermore, only industry organized on this large scale could afford to set up laboratories and engage research scientists from the universities to experiment in the creation of new and better products. German industrialists were the first to establish a close working relationship with scientists and technologists. The most spectacular result was the rise of the chemical industry, which pioneered in the development of drugs, synthetic dyes, and photography, and revolutionized German agriculture by making available cheap supplies of chemical fertilizers that enormously increased the yields per acre and brought new prosperity to the German landowner. The great trusts thus contributed substantially to Germany's rise as a major industrial power, but like the giant British and American corporations, these quasi-monopolistic institutions made a mockery of the idea of free enterprise.

The rapid industrialization of Germany during the 1880's was accompanied by all the familiar miseries of the Industrial Revolution. Hence it was chiefly after Bismarck's tariff law had set off the new German industrial boom that socialism in Germany became a serious political force. For socialist propaganda was primarily directed at the new urban proletariat, swelled by immigrants from rural areas, and the steady rise in the socialist vote showed that this propaganda was taking effect.

State Socialism

Bismarck met the socialist threat by continuing his repressive legislation—the antisocialist law was periodically renewed until 1890—but he also sought to correct some of the abuses on which socialism was thriving. In his social legislation, as in his economic measures, he rejected the *laissez-faire* theories of liberalism. By his government-sponsored tariff law and by government encouragement of German industry and agriculture he had succeeded in gaining the sympathy of powerful business and agricultural interests. Accordingly, perhaps a government-sponsored welfare program could win the allegiance of the working classes. Revolutionary socialism was to be undercut by state socialism.

The government's intention of inaugurating a social-welfare program was announced in an imperial message to the Reichstag in November, 1881. "A remedy cannot be sought merely in the repression of socialist excesses," the emperor said. "There must be at the same time a positive advancement of the welfare of the working classes." Between 1883 and 1889 the Reichstag passed government-sponsored laws establishing health, accident, old-age, and invalidism insurance which provided the most comprehensive protection of the working man yet introduced in any country. Bismarck resisted efforts to introduce legislation that would regulate the hours and conditions of work. His ideas on labor had been formed by his observations in the countryside, where women and children worked with men in the fields as long as there was daylight, and he disliked the idea of fixing maximum hours or forbidding the employment of women and children.

Bismarck's welfare program was continued and extended under his successors, but it never achieved the political results the government had expected. Socialism was not killed with kindness. The workers accepted the benefits conferred by the state, but they continued to agitate for more. The socialist vote, and socialist representation in the Reichstag, continued to rise steadily despite the welfare program and the antisocialist law. One important purpose of the program, however, was achieved. Although the socialist political party continued to thrive, revolutionary socialism was undermined as more and more workers were given a stake in the existing system.

The Succession Crisis and the Fall of Bismarck

Revival of prosperity in the 1880's and the general success of German foreign policy made it possible for Bismarck to govern with a coalition of conservatives, members of the Center party, and liberal protectionists. But in December, 1886, he again found himself in conflict with the Reichstag over the familiar issue of army appropriations. Once again Bismarck wanted enactment of a long-term military-appropriations bill, and once again the Reichstag rejected his bill in order to retain strategic control over military expenditures. His position was difficult. The old emperor's death was expected at any moment. The succession of Crown Prince Frederick William during a conflict with the Reichstag might provide the prince's liberal advisers with the long-awaited opportunity to bring about Bismarck's dismissal. During this same period the chancellor was faced with a serious crisis in international affairs. Anti-German sentiment was rampant in both Russia and France, and there was a strong possibility that these powers would form an alliance against Germany.

Upon the rejection of his military-appropriations bill, the chancellor dissolved the Reichstag and called for new elections. To carry on the election campaign, he succeeded in patching together the old patriotic alliance of moderate conservatives and National Liberals, which became known as the Bismarck Cartel. Patriotism was his keynote. The fatherland was in danger; opponents of the military-appropriations bill were betraying their country; it was the duty of all good Germans to vote for pro-Bismarck candidates who would support the bill.

The elections of 1887 resulted in a clear-cut victory for the Bismarck candidates. For the first time since the formation of the empire the

"Blown Up, But Not Blown Out." *This 1884 cartoon from the German satirical magazine* Kladderadatsch *comments on the ineffectiveness of the anti-socialist law.*

chancellor seemed to have secured a loyal parliamentary majority which would guarantee the passage of his domestic legislation. If, upon becoming emperor, Frederick William were bent on selecting a chancellor who enjoyed the support of a majority in parliament, he would find that the head of this majority was none other than Bismarck. But Bismarck's election success proved to be a hollow victory, for it was won against a dying man. In the spring of 1887 it was learned that the crown prince was mortally ill with cancer. It was doubtful whether he would outlive his aged father.

Emperor William I died on March 9, 1888. The crown prince took the title of Emperor Frederick III, but his illness rendered him incapable of exercising any real authority. During his brief reign of ninety-nine days Frederick III was not able to carry out the liberal program that he had dreamed of during his seventeen years of waiting for the imperial crown. He died on June 15, 1888, and was succeeded by his son, William II, who was destined to be the last German emperor.

William II (ruled 1888–1918) was twenty-nine when he came to the throne, but was still immature in his conduct and thought. The great tragedy for Germany was that he never grew up. An arm crippled at birth may have contributed to a feeling of inadequacy or inferiority, which he attempted to offset by bombastic self-assertion. Disliking opposition, he surrounded himself with sycophants and mediocrities, yet he could be won over to almost any policy by a person able and willing to handle him in the right way.

With his sense of self-importance and his dislike of contradiction, William II was not the man to submit indefinitely to the authority of a Bismarck, despite a professed admiration for the chancellor. It was only a matter of time before he would use the power Bismarck himself had given the emperor in the German constitution to exercise supreme authority in the state. Bismarck's only means of retaining his influence was to use the utmost tact in dealing with the young man, or to engineer a *coup d'état* that would give him an excuse to introduce changes in the constitution granting the chancellor greater power at the expense of the throne.

Bismarck tried both courses during his final months in office, and in both he failed. The chancellor's fine political touch deserted him at several critical moments, and he made the crucial error of spending too much time at his estates in the country in the mistaken belief that his son Herbert, state secretary of the German foreign office since 1886, had the new emperor safely under control.

The final clash between the emperor and the chancellor ostensibly concerned labor policy. Actually, it was a clash over power. William II had been warned from many quarters that Bismarck was preparing to foment a domestic crisis so that he could prove himself indispensable to the inexperienced young ruler and then dictate his terms. In March, 1890, the emperor demanded that Bismarck submit his resignation. On March 20, 1890, the fateful document was signed. The Bismarck era had come to an end. It was replaced by the personal rule of William II, who sought to exercise supreme power in the state but who possessed none of that awareness of the limitations of power which was the essential feature of the old chancellor's *Realpolitik*.

CHAPTER 8

The Search for a New International Stability, 1871–1890

SHORTLY AFTER PRUSSIA's victory over France in 1871 and the formation of the German empire, the British statesman Benjamin Disraeli declared:

> This war represents the German revolution, a greater political event than the French Revolution of the last century. ... . Not a single principle in the management of our foreign affairs, accepted by statesmen for guidance up to six months ago, any longer exists. There is not a diplomatic tradition which has not been swept away. You have a new world, new influences at work, new and unknown objects and dangers with which to cope. . . . The balance of power has been entirely destroyed, and the country which suffers most, and feels the effect of the change most, is England.

Disraeli's statements were somewhat extravagant. As leader of Her Majesty's loyal opposition, he was criticizing the foreign policy of his rival Gladstone, who was in power when the final unification of Germany took place. But he was nevertheless expressing a concern felt by many European statesmen. Prussia now stood at the head of an empire which was unquestionably the greatest military power on the Continent. How would Prussia use that power? Would the objective of German unification now be extended to the Netherlands, Belgium, or Switzerland? What was to be the fate of the Germans in the Habsburg empire, in Russia's Baltic provinces, in Scandinavia?

Bismarck was well aware of Europe's apprehensions, and he also saw the dangers they implied for the new German empire. In their dread of

Germany, all the states anxious to restore the European balance of power might join forces with the recently defeated foes of Prussia in a great anti-German coalition. Bismarck's first concern, therefore, was to reassure Europe. The new German empire, he said, was a satiated state whose principal foreign-policy objective henceforth would be the preservation of peace and the *status quo.*

Bismarck meant what he said. The operation of the European balance of power would make further German conquests impossible, at least in the foreseeable future, and he did not believe there was any area where expansion for Germany would be profitable in relation to the costs and risks involved. By far the most important reason for his pacific policy, however, was his conviction that the preservation of peace was the most certain and least costly means of safeguarding the state he had created. Bismarck's conception of the future course of German policy was of fundamental importance. As leader of the most powerful state in Europe, and as one of the most talented diplomats of his age, he was to dominate the European international scene until his dismissal in 1890. And because he saw his country's best interests in the preservation of the peace of Europe, he was one of the few political leaders before 1914 to pursue a European as opposed to a narrowly national or dynastic foreign policy.

THE SEARCH FOR STABILITY IN EASTERN EUROPE

The First Three Emperors' League

Bismarck's first move to stabilize the European states system established in 1871 was an attempt to revive the Metternichian Concert among the conservative powers of Europe. He looked upon Russia and Austria as natural allies in working toward this goal. In both states the threat of revolution was constant, and both might be expected to join Germany in a policy of preserving the international as well as the domestic *status quo,* for a major war, with all the risks it entailed, could only benefit the forces of revolution.

In the course of 1873, several treaties concluded among the three imperial powers resulted in the formation of what came to be known as the first Three Emperors' League. Germany, Austria, and Russia agreed to combat subversive activities in their respective countries and to consult in case other powers threatened the peace of Europe. Thus the league, which was joined by Italy in September, 1873, was based on little more than a mutual interest in suppressing revolution at home and preventing the formation of a coalition against any one of its members. It worked as long as the interests of the conservative powers were in harmony; it cracked the moment their interests began to diverge.

The Balkan Crisis, 1875–1878

As an instrument of international stability, the Three Emperors' League proved useless when in 1875 and 1876 revolts against Turkish rule erupted throughout the Balkan peninsula. All the great powers of Europe, but especially Russia and Austria, had interests in this area. For Russia, the Balkans represented the shortest overland route to Constantinople and the Straits; for Austria, now excluded from Germany and Italy, they were the last available avenue for an extension of influence. Great Britain and France, as at the time of the Crimean War, were concerned lest Russia use the Balkans as a stepping stone toward establishing influence in the Mediterranean and the Middle East, a possibility all the more threatening for both powers because of the opening in 1869 of the Suez Canal.

Germany had no vital interests in the Balkans themselves. Its concern, as conceived by Bismarck, lay in preventing a war between the great powers over the spoils of the Balkans in which Germany might be compelled to participate to prevent a serious disruption of the balance of power in eastern Europe. Because he believed Germany had little to gain and much to lose from such a conflict, Bismarck put the strongest kind of diplomatic pressure on Russia and Austria to arrange a peaceful partition of the Balkans, and warned that if they did go to war he would intervene to prevent either power from gaining a decisive victory.

Bismarck's diplomacy temporarily restrained Russia and Austria, but in the summer of 1876 the Balkan states of Serbia and Montenegro declared war on Turkey. Despite the aid of Russian volunteers and supplies, Serbia and Montenegro were soundly beaten. The Russians now took Bismarck's advice, made a treaty with Austria defining their respective spheres of influence in the Balkans, and in April, 1877, went to war against the Turks to ensure their final expulsion from the peninsula. After being held in check throughout the summer of 1877 before the fortress of Plevna in the Balkan Mountains, the Russians overcame Turkish resistance by the end of the year and on March 8, 1878, imposed the Treaty of San Stefano on Turkey.

The most important provision of the Treaty of San Stefano was the creation of a large Bulgarian state stretching from the Black Sea to the mountains of Albania on the west, and from the Danube to the Aegean Sea. As the new Bulgaria was clearly intended to be a Russian satellite, the treaty in effect gave the Russians the outlet to the Mediterranean they had so long desired. The treaty was thus a blow to both Britain and France, who wanted to keep Russia out of the Mediterranean; but it also violated Russia's prewar agreement with Austria concerning the Balkans.

By concluding a treaty with Turkey which impinged on the interests of three great powers, the Russians made a serious blunder. Only three days after the treaty was signed the Austrian foreign minister issued an invitation to the European powers to attend a conference in Berlin to discuss its revision. The Russians, their resources exhausted by the conflict with Turkey, were obliged to accept the invitation or face a war against a European coalition.

To salvage as many as possible of their gains in the Turkish war, the Russians tried to buy the support of a majority of the great powers before the conference convened. They first tried Austria, but the Austrians were wary about another betrayal and posed too many conditions. They had better luck with Great Britain. The British could never be sure that the three imperial powers might not join forces at the expense of British interests and hence seized the opportunity to safeguard those interests. On May 30, 1878, they concluded a secret treaty with the Russians that pushed the frontier of the new Bulgaria away from the Aegean Sea, thus preventing the establishment of a Russian naval base on the Mediterranean.

British diplomatic activity did not end with the Russian treaty. The British had consented to Russia's retention of its Turkish conquests east of Black Sea, which meant a decided extension of Russian power into the Middle East and augmented the threat to British interests in that area. To bolster their own position in the Middle East, the British concluded a secret treaty with Turkey on June 4, 1878, in which they guaranteed Turkey's Asiatic possessions and thereby obtained an excuse to send troops into Turkey at any time they felt their own interests threatened. To enable them to implement this guarantee, the British persuaded the Turks to give them the strategic island of Cyprus. Britain therewith acquired a splendid naval base in the eastern Mediterranean, within striking distance of Constantinople, Asiatic Turkey, the Balkans, and the Suez Canal.

Britain made yet a third preconference agreement. The Austrians had learned from Bismack of the secret Anglo-Russian negotiations and feared that Russia would indeed gain the support of the majority at the forthcoming conference. They therefore hastened to strike a bargain of their own with Britain. The Austrians wanted above all to keep open an avenue for their economic and political influence in southeastern Europe and to prevent the formation of any large state in the Balkans that would close this avenue or threaten Austrian security. On June 6, 1878, they concluded a treaty with Britain which gave them the assurances they needed.

Thus before the Congress of Berlin even met, agreement had been reached among the great powers on the most important revisions of the Treaty of San Stefano. It remained for the congress to set the seal on these preconference decisions and to work out the details.

The Congress of Berlin

The Congress of Berlin (June 13–July 13, 1878) was one of the most brilliant diplomatic assemblies of the nineteenth century. Great Britain was represented by its prime minister, Benjamin Disraeli, and his foreign secretary, Lord Salisbury; Russia by its chancellor, Prince Gorchakov, and his ambassador to London, Count Peter Shuvalov; the Habsburg monarchy, France, and Italy by their foreign ministers—Count Andrássy, William Henry Waddington, and Count Corti. All the plenipotentiaries were supported by their ambassadors to Berlin and by distinguished staffs. The location of the conference in Berlin was an indication of the importance of the new German empire in the European states system. Bismarck, the head of the government playing host to the congress, was elected its president, in accordance with diplomatic custom. But Bismarck was head of the congress in more than name. He dominated the meetings and set the pace and tone of the negotiations.

By the terms of the final Treaty of Berlin, the large Bulgarian state created by the Treaty of San Stefano was divided into three parts. The largest of these parts was Bulgaria proper, bounded on the north by the Danube, on the west by the mountains of Albania, and on the south by the Balkan Mountains. Nominally, Bulgaria became a separate principality under Turkish suzerainty; in fact, it was tacitly conceded to Russia as a satellite. The second part, the area south of the Balkan Mountains, was to be called Eastern Rumelia, so that even in name it would be distinct from Russia's Bulgaria. Eastern Rumelia was placed under the administration of a Turkish governor-general, but a reform of the government was to be carried out by a European commission. The rest of Bulgaria, including the territory bordering the Aegean Sea, was left directly under Turkish rule.

The three Balkan states of Serbia, Montenegro, and Rumania, hitherto still nominally part of the Turkish empire, were recognized as completely independent, but they lost some of the territory assigned to them at San Stefano. Rumania, which had been Russia's ally in the recent war against Turkey, was forced to cede to Russia the fertile province of Bessarabia and control of the mouth of the Danube, receiving in exchange the arid Dobruja, which was detached from Turkey.

Among the great powers, Austria was given the right to occupy (but not to annex) Bosnia and Herzegovina, and to garrison the Turkish administrative district (sanjak) of Novi Pazar, a strategic area lying between Serbia and Montenegro. Thus Austria pushed a military wedge between Serbia and Montenegro, frustrated Serbian ambitions to form and dominate a large Balkan state, and kept its own routes to the south open. Russia received Batum, Kars, and Ardahan, at the eastern end of the Black Sea, and control of what was left of Bulgaria. Britain received Cyprus. France was secretly given permission to take Tunis, also nominally part of the Turkish empire. The Italian delegates came home with clean but empty hands, and were stoned in the streets by compatriots who would have preferred a few stains. Germany received no territory, but was relieved of the necessity of choosing between Russia and Austria in eastern Europe or of engaging in a costly and dangerous conflict where vital German interests were not at stake. The preservation of peace was in itself a major gain for Germany.

The German-Austrian Alliance of 1879

By refusing to allow the balance of power in eastern Europe to be upset by either Russia or Austria, by playing midwife to many of the individual agreements modifying the Treaty of San Stefano, and by assuming the role of "honest broker" at the Congress of Berlin, Bismarck contributed much to the prevention of a general European war during the Near Eastern crisis. But he paid a heavy price for his success. The Russians had expected to receive German support at the congress and bitterly resented the fact that Germany allowed them to sustain what they regarded as a severe diplomatic setback. The wrath of the Russians after the congress was turned not against Austria or Britain, their real opponents in the recent crisis, but against Germany, the false friend. Russia was swept by a wave of anti-German sentiment, with the result that Germany now faced the hostility of Russia in addition to that of France. If these powers were to form an anti-German alliance, they might be joined by an Austria anxious to regain its lost supremacy in central Europe.

Bismarck's reply to Russian hostility was a defensive alliance with Austria against attack by Russia or by a power supported by Russia. Concluded on October 7, 1879, this alliance served a multiplicity of purposes. It assured both powers of support in case of Russian aggression. For Austria it reduced the danger of an agreement between Germany, Russia, and Italy to partition the Habsburg empire, while for Germany it lessened the possibility of an Austrian alliance with Russia and France. For Bismarck another advantage of the treaty was the control it gave him over Austrian foreign policy. Any aggressive move by Austria in eastern Europe involved the danger of war with Russia, and Austria did not dare risk a clash with Russia without the certainty of German support. As long as Germany remained in a position to withhold that support, it would be able to exercise a strong if not decisive check on Austrian aggression in eastern Europe.

The Second Three Emperors' League

In view of the alliances subsequently concluded by Bismarck, it is safe to assume that he did not intend to restrict his treaty making at this time to Austria, but hoped to return to some kind of treaty relationship with Russia as well, in order to avoid driving Russia into the arms of France. But he evidently realized that this could not be achieved immediately, for the hysterical anti-German attitude then prevalent in Russia meant that any German effort to establish closer relations would almost certainly be

TREATY OF BERLIN • 1878

——— Ottoman boundary in 1800

– – – Boundary proposed by Treaty of San Stefano, 1878

Ottoman Empire after 1878

Independent after 1878

* (Garrisoned by Austria, 1878)

interpreted by the Russians as a sign of fear. A German agreement with Russia, if it could be arranged at all, would have to be purchased at an extremely high price. It seems likely that Bismarck therefore decided on an indirect approach in dealing with the Russians. The German-Austrian alliance was supposed to be secret, but the secret was badly kept and the Russians learned of its existence even before the treaty was signed. They now found themselves in an awkward position, for the two great central-European powers were forming an alliance, with a friendly Britain in the wings.

The next turn of events in Russia may well have been what Bismarck had been counting on. News of the Austrian alliance had a chastening effect on the anti-German agitation. The Russian leaders began to realize that their anti-German attitude had been not only pointless but extremely dangerous. Consequently, while negotiations for the German-Austrian treaty were still in progress, the Russians were at Bismarck's door as suppliants for a renewal of the Three Emperors' League in some form. Thus Bismarck's bargaining position was far better than it would have been if he had approached Russia directly.

The request to revive the Three Emperors' League was well received in Berlin. Bismarck assured the Russian ambassador that his main purpose in making the Austrian alliance was "to dig a ditch between [Austria] and the western powers," and that he would be glad to reestablish the Three Emperors' League "as the only system offering the maximum stability for the peace of Europe."

The representatives of the second Three Emperors' League meeting in Skierniewice in 1884. *From left to right: Count Giers, the Russian foreign minister; Bismarck; and Count Kálnoky, the Austro-Hungarian foreign minister.*

Bismarck's chief difficulty in reviving the Three Emperors' League lay in persuading the Austrians to admit Russia into the German-Austrian partnership, which many Austrian statesmen had hoped to exploit against Russia. In his efforts to persuade Austria to accept the Russian alliance, Bismarck was aided by the victory of Gladstone in the British elections of March, 1880. Gladstone had violently denounced Austria during the election campaign, and his victory temporarily ended Austrian hopes of gaining British support against Russia in eastern Europe. Even so, it was not until Bismarck ostentatiously threw his diplomatic support on the side of Russia and against Austria on every current issue concerning eastern Europe that the Austrians finally yielded.

The second Three Emperors' League, in contrast to the first, was based on an agreement that contained definite, clear-cut terms. The treaty, which was secret, was signed on June 18, 1881, and was to be in force for three years. Most significant was the stipulation that if one member of the league found itself at war with a fourth power (except Turkey) the other two were to remain neutral, a provision that safeguarded all members from the danger of hostile coalitions. The other articles of the treaty were primarily aimed at removing the major possibilities for friction between the signatory powers: the western Balkans were recognized as an Austrian and the eastern Balkans as a Russian sphere of influence.

The treaty by no means ended tensions between Russia and Austria, nor did it settle all the problems of eastern Europe. It simply eased the tensions and provided a basis for negotiation among the imperial powers in the event of a crisis. The second Three Emperors' League, for all its weaknesses, was considerably better than no league at all.

Austria's Balkan Policy

To reduce further the danger of international friction in the Balkans, Bismarck made several efforts to secure an agreement for a definite partition of the Balkans between Austria and Russia. He reasoned that both powers would then be fully occupied for several years in assimilating their respective spheres. But the partition scheme never materialized. Austrian leaders feared any permanent extension of Russian power in the Balkans, and the Hungarians disliked the project because the inclusion of more Slavs in the Habsburg empire would diminish their own importance.

In the meantime, Austrian interests were being advanced successfully without territorial annexations. The rapid construction of railroads in the Balkans permitted Austria to extend its economic influence in southeastern Europe to areas which were not readily accessible to the sea and hence were relatively untouched by British and French economic influence. Austria also succeeded in extending its political influence. By bribing the prince of Serbia with loans and dangling before him the prospect of recognition as king of Serbia, Austria was able to gain agreement in 1881 to political and economic treaties with Serbia which reduced that nation to the status of an Austrian dependency. In 1883 Austria and Rumania concluded a defensive alliance, which was later expanded to include Germany.

The Problem of Bulgaria

Austria's most spectacular success in the Balkans—or more properly, Russia's most spectacular failure—came in Bulgaria. The Russians used their influence in Bulgaria tactlessly in dealing with a people experiencing an awakening of national self-consciousness and highly sensitive about honor and prestige. The Russian choice of Alexander of Battenberg (1857–1893) as prince of Bulgaria was also unfortunate. Prince Alexander disliked playing the part of a Russian puppet, and wanted to establish himself as the independent ruler of an independent state. Although Bismarck warned the prince in the strongest possible terms that he could expect no help from Germany, Alexander was encouraged to pursue his quest for independence by the Austrians and by Queen Victoria of Great Britain.

In 1883 the prince's ambitions received a further powerful stimulus when he was allowed to become engaged to Princess Victoria of Prussia, the daughter of the heir to the German throne and the granddaughter of Queen Victoria. From a political standpoint the marriage would have been most welcome to the British, who were anxious to push Russian influence out of Bulgaria and must have seen in this union a means of using Germany to help them do so. Even if Germany refused to back up Prince Alexander against Russia, his marriage to a Prussian princess would arouse serious doubts in Russia about the honesty of German's policy in the Balkans, and would shake Russia's confidence in the German government, which Bismarck was trying to regain with so much effort.

These dangers were only too evident to Bismarck, who did everything in his power to prevent the so-called Battenberg marriage from taking place. He pointed out to the Austrian foreign minister that by opposing the establishment of Russian influence in Bulgaria, Austria was disregarding its treaties with Russia and creating a situation of extreme danger in the Balkans. To compensate for Austria's attitude, Bismarck made very effort to reassure Russia of Germany's good faith. He denounced Prince Alexander and applied heavy pressure to force Austria to desist from its Balkan policy.

Despite Bismarck's efforts, the Bulgarian problem came very close to involving the European powers in war. In September, 1885, a revolution broke out in Eastern Rumelia. The aim of the revolutionaries was to unite their province with Bulgaria, and Prince Alexander found himself compelled by Bulgarian national sentiment to assume leadership of the movement or to forfeit his throne.

The union of Bulgaria and Eastern Rumelia constituted a violation of the

Treaty of Berlin and affected the interests of all the great powers. To complicate matters, the Serbs, jealous of the potential enlargement of their neighbor, invaded Bulgaria with the intention of securing territorial compensation. Peace between Serbia and Bulgaria was finally restored on the basis of the prewar *status quo*, and in April, 1886, the powers recognized the union of Bulgaria and Eastern Rumelia. Even then international tension did not die down. The Russians, unable to tolerate the rule of Prince Alexander any longer, had him kidnapped, and finally secured his abdication in August, 1886. But their position in Bulgaria did not improve. The new Bulgarian government proved just as unwilling as Prince Alexander had been to submit to Russian overlordship.

The Russians seethed with frustration. They were indignant with Austria for violating both the spirit and the letter of the Three Emperors' agreement; many Russians were convinced that Austria would not have dared to act in that way without assurances of support from Germany. Russian Pan-Slavists, always hostile to the Teutonic empires of Germany and Austria, proclaimed that Russia could never hope to score solid gains in the Balkans while remaining committed to the Three Emperors' League, and should therefore look elsewhere for support.

THE SEARCH FOR STABILITY IN WESTERN EUROPE

Germany and France

The surge of anti-German feeling in Russia coincided with a powerful revival of anti-German feeling in France. Since the Congress of Berlin, Bismarck had been working to reduce French animosity toward Germany and to compensate France for the loss of Alsace-Lorraine by helping it to acquire an overseas colonial empire. He hoped in this way to divert French attention from Germany and embroil France with other colonial powers. French statesmen were aware of Bismarck's motives, but some of them thought France should nevertheless take advantage of German support and strengthen its colonial holdings. The colonialists were opposed in France by the politicians of the continental school, who feared that a colonial policy would lead to disputes with other European powers and delay the reestablishment of French supremacy in Europe.

In 1881, under the leadership of the colonialist Jules Ferry (1832–1893), the French made their bid for Tunis, which had been promised to them by Bismarck and Salisbury at the Congress of Berlin. They knew that the seizure of Tunis would involve them in a quarrel with the Italians, who had large investments in this area and regarded it as a natural sphere for Italian expansion. But the French, too, had large investments in Tunis. Spurred by signs that the Italians were about to take Tunis themselves, the French on

May 12 forced the Bey of Tunis to sign the Treaty of Bardo, which established a virtual protectorate over the country.

The Triple Alliance of 1882

Just as the French anticolonialists had feared, the seizure of Tunis involved France in a bitter dispute with Italy, and drove Italy into an alliance with Germany and Austria. The Tunis incident showed the Italians that their old policy of diplomatic independence, which had enabled them to sell their friendship to the highest bidder, was no longer profitable. Within Italy a strong element, primarily republican, advocated friendship with republican France despite Tunis, hoping with French aid to acquire the Italian-speaking territories still under Austrian control. But an even more influential political group favored collaboration with Germany, which because of its superior military power would be a more valuable ally than France, and better able to aid Italy in acquiring colonial territory. As a Protestant state, Germany would be of assistance against the papacy, which was still intent on recovering the Papal States. As a monarchy it would support the existing Italian government against republicanism and the forces of revolution.

Bismarck, for his part, was interested in preserving the Italian monarchy, which was less likely than an Italian republic to seek an alliance with France. Above all, he saw that an Italian alliance would be valuable for Austria. The Italian desire for the Austrian territories of Trent and Trieste was always a danger, and should Austria become involved in war with Russia it would be well to have some assurance of Italian neutrality.

In the negotiations leading to the alliance between Italy, Austria, and Germany, Bismarck forced the Italians to work through Vienna. He had no intention of acting as a buffer between these old enemies, although he was always available to help the negotiations along. The treaty of May 20, 1882, establishing the Triple Alliance, was a general agreement to support the monarchical principle and the existing political and social order. It also provided for a defensive alliance which would function against France or against "two or more great powers not members of the alliance"—in other words, any combination of France, Great Britain, and Russia. This treaty improved the prospects for stable government in Italy and assured Germany of Italian neutrality in the event of a German war with France. Austria secured Italian neutrality in the event of a war with Russia and the hope of a diminution of Italian nationalist agitation for "unredeemed" territory still under Austrian control. The Italian monarchy gained badly needed prestige, two powerful defensive allies, support against efforts of the Vatican to regain the Papal States, and support against revolution.

The newly created Triple Alliance was destined to become a fixture in the international politics of Europe. Intended originally to run for five years, it was renewed periodically until 1915, when the Italians deserted the Germans and Austrians in the First World War.

The British Occupation of Egypt

Shortly after the treaty establishing the Triple Alliance was signed, an international crisis erupted in Egypt. With the opening of the Suez Canal in 1869, Egypt had become an area of prime strategic importance, but even before the building of the canal it had been a target of European economic imperialism. The khedives of Egypt, nominally under the suzerainty of the sultan of Turkey, had for years behaved as independent rulers and had contracted huge debts with European banking houses, often at usurious rates. It was the need for money to pay the interest on his debts that forced the khedive to sell his Suez Canal stock to Great Britain in 1875. But this sale failed to stabilize Egyptian finances, and in November, 1876, the British and French governments established what amounted to joint control over the Egyptian government on behalf of the holders of Egyptian bonds. This move aroused deep animosity among the Egyptians, who found themselves heavily taxed simply to pay the interest on foreign debts. In January, 1882, a group of Egyptian army officers overthrew European control, and established an Egyptian national government.

The British responded in July by bombarding Alexandria and landing troops to protect the Suez Canal. In September, 1882, these British forces clashed with an Egyptian army at Tel el-Kebir. The Egyptians were routed, and somewhat to the embarrassment of the anticolonial Gladstone government, the British found themselves in sole control of Egypt.

Gladstone was against colonialism, but he was also a sound financier and a firm believer in law and order. He therefore resolved to use the opportunity afforded by Britain's occupation of Egypt to restore order and stabilize Egypt's finances. He assured the other European powers that the occupation was temporary and that the British forces would be withdrawn "as soon as the state of the country and the organization of proper means for the maintenance of khedival authority will admit of it." But to the fury of the French and the Italians, who also had important strategic and economic interests in Egypt, the British were never satisfied that a proper state of order had been established; they remained in control of Egypt until they were pushed out by a more successful Egyptian nationalist movement after the Second World War.

During the entire Egyptian crisis, Bismarck had urged agreement among the powers to prevent the problem from erupting in a general European war. As the crisis dragged on without any agreement being reached, he

The building of the Suez Canal. *The construction of a canal across one hundred miles of sand and swamp was not only a formidable engineering and technological problem but involved major financial and diplomatic manipulations as well. Manual laborers with shovels and palm-leaf baskets were eventually replaced by a fleet of steam excavators and mechanical dredgers capable of digging out the canal at the rate of six million cubic feet a month. Begun in 1859 and completed a decade later, the canal cut the length of the sea route to India by more than half and enormously increased the strategic importance of the eastern Mediterranean and the surrounding lands, especially Egypt.*

encouraged the British to act alone, and used his influence to prevent intervention by other states. The consequent tension between Britain, France, and Italy was not unwelcome to him. He feared an entente between the liberal government of Gladstone and republican France, which the volatile Italians might be tempted to join. The Egyptian affair temporarily put an end to these possibilities.

Bismarck's Colonial Policy

Bismarck was soon to use Britain's awkward diplomatic position for political purposes of his own. Early in 1884 he suggested to the British government that in return for Germany's continued diplomatic support in Egypt and elsewhere, Britain should cede Germany the island of Helgoland, a strategic base off the German coast in the North Sea, and agree to Germany's acquisition of a few overseas colonial territories. In making this bid for colonies, Bismarck was adopting a policy he had heretofore opposed because he did not believe overseas possessions would contribute in any way to Germany's national security or prosperity. Why then did his policy with respect to colonies change?

As usual, his motives were mixed. He was undoubtedly annoyed by the maneuvers of the allegedly anti-imperialist Gladstone government to extend British influence in Africa, but in this case he appears to have been motivated primarily by domestic political considerations. The problem of the imperial succession in Germany, a concern of many years, was looming ever larger. The octogenarian emperor William I was in poor health, and his liberal-minded son, Crown Prince Frederick William, made no secret of his dislike for Bismarck or of his desire to oust him when he came to the throne, a sentiment strongly supported by his English wife, the daughter of Queen Victoria. By acquiring colonies, Bismarck undoubtedly hoped to enhance his own popularity among the growing number of imperialists in Germany and among business leaders who stood to profit from them, and to strengthen his position in the Reichstag in preparation for the next reign. A colonial policy would have the further advantage of undercutting the position of the crown prince, whose English wife made no secret of her hostility to German colonial ambitions. As one of Bismarck's aides put it, "No other question is so liable to put the future empress, with her Anglophile tendencies, in a false position vis-à-vis the German nation. For it is precisely the liberals and democrats who want colonies."

Bismarck had no desire for serious tension with Britain, and under ordinary circumstances he would probably have dropped the entire colonial business when he found that the Gladstone government failed to respond favorably to his bid. But the circumstances in 1884 were far from ordinary. Germany was allied with all the great powers on the Continent with the exception of France, and the French, like the Germans, were smarting from British opposition to their attempts to acquire new colonies. Moreover, the government of France was at this time under the leadership of Jules Ferry, who was prepared to cooperate with Bismarck on the colonial issue. The German chancellor was therefore in an admirable position to bring pressure to bear on Britain, which he was all the more willing to do because Britain was currently under the leadership of Gladstone, whom he despised and would have been glad to bring down.

The British found that they were helpless against Bismarck's continental coalition. They were compelled to abandon a treaty with Portugal whereby they had sought to ensure their influence in the Congo area. The claims of the several European powers in the Congo were defined instead by an international conference on African matters that met in Berlin in 1884–1885 under the auspices of Bismarck and Ferry. At this conference too, the powers agreed to cooperate to suppress slavery and the slave trade in Africa, and the principle was laid down that an imperial state had to establish effective control over a colonial territory before it could claim ownership.

By 1885, largely as a result of diplomatic agreements imposed on Britain through Franco-German cooperation, Bismarck had succeeded in securing international recognition of Germany's claims to Southwest Africa, Togoland, the Cameroons, East Africa, and part of New Guinea. The French for their part were conceded French Guinea, part of the Red Sea coast, and predominant influence in southeast Asia.

In cooperating with France on colonial questions, Bismarck may also have had another purpose in view. He was disturbed by the uncompromising French hostility toward Germany and tried to allay this antagonism by supporting French policy in a variety of ways. "I want to persuade you to forgive Sedan as you have forgiven Waterloo," he told the French ambassador. There is no way of knowing whether Bismarck seriously believed he could change the French attitude toward Germany, but the situation in 1884–1885 gave him an excellent means of testing the possibility of doing so.

The attempt to conciliate France failed. At the end of March, 1885, Ferry's ministry fell as a result of a military setback in Indochina, and this change in government marked the end of Franco-German cooperation. For Bismarck the short-lived entente had served its purpose. He had proved to himself that a genuine reconciliation with France would be impossible for some time to come, he had taught the British that they could not ignore German requests with impunity, and he had acquired a colonial empire for Germany. Throughout the period of his cooperation with France, Bismarck had recognized the probable limitations of French friendship, and for this reason he had never gone so far in putting pressure on the British as to risk alienating them permanently.

A vigorous argument has recently been advanced that Bismarck's motives in pursuing a colonial policy were primarily economic and social, and thus political in a far more profound and fundamental sense than anything suggested in the preceding paragraphs. Through colonies, so this argument runs, Bismarck sought to ensure a steady growth rate for the expanding system of advanced capitalism, a source of cheap raw materials, and commercial outlets abroad; in social terms, he saw imperialism as a means of integrating a state torn by class differences, of diverting domestic grievances toward objectives abroad, and of defending the traditional social and power structures of the Prusso-German state. This argument places Bismarck's imperialism squarely in the pattern of Marxist theory, and in one respect it is absolutely correct: Bismarck never made any secret of the fact that after 1871 *all* his policies were directed toward preserving the existing political and social structure. There is no evidence of any kind, however, that Bismarck was ever converted to a colonial policy for its own sake, or that he thought the impoverished African territories he might acquire could make any substantial contribution to Germany's economic or social security. "All this colonial business is a sham," he is reported to have said, "but we need it for the elections." Once his colonial policy had served its purpose, he abandoned it entirely and concentrated (as indeed he had always done) on the problems of the continent, where he felt the real security of Germany was at stake. In response to the arguments of a German colonial enthusiast who pointed out further desirable territorial acquisitions on a map of Africa, Bismarck is supposed to have said: "Your map of Africa is very handsome, but my map of Africa lies in Europe. Here lies Russia and here lies France, and we are in between: that is my map of Africa."

THE CLIMAX OF BISMARCK'S ALLIANCE SYSTEM

With the fall of Ferry, there was a sharp reaction in France against his policies. Colonial affairs had involved France in costly conflicts overseas and had aroused a great deal of opposition. To many patriotic Frenchmen the whole colonial business appeared to be a German plot to divert French resources and French attention from the recovery of Alsace-Lorraine, and they regarded Ferry's cooperation with Bismarck as nothing less than treason. French defeats in Indochina, along with the agitation of French patriotic societies demanding the return of Alsace-Lorraine, brought about a powerful resurgence of anti-German feeling in France. It was largely this sentiment that thrust General Boulanger into prominence as the man who could lead a successful war of revenge against Germany.

The wave of anti-German feeling and the rise of Boulanger in France coincided with Russian frustration in Bulgaria and a similar wave of anti-German feeling in Russia. Bismarck again found himself in a dangerous diplomatic position. The Three Emperors' League was due to lapse in 1887, and the Russians had made it clear that they would not renew it. There was a strong possibility that Russia would now form an alliance with France, despite the tsar's dislike of France's republican government, and if such an alliance were concluded, hotheaded leaders in either country might decide that the time had come to settle accounts with Germany and Austria. Germany would then be faced with a war on two fronts which would threaten its very existence. Even a German victory in such a war could not possibly yield benefits that would in any way compensate for the costs and hazards it would involve. By far the best policy for Germany would be to keep the peace. How this was to be done posed one of the most difficult problems of Bismarck's career.

The problem was solved by Bismarck through the development of his most complicated and brilliant set of alliances. The Russians did indeed refuse to renew the Three Emperors' League when sounded on the subject in 1886, and it was clear that their present distrust of Austria made an agreement between Russia and Austria as impossible as an agreement between Germany and France. But an agreement between Germany and Russia was not impossible, and indeed seemed the simplest and most obvious way of preventing a Franco-Russian alliance and avoiding the danger for Germany of a two-front war. To secure an agreement with Russia, however, the Germans would have to remove all possible reasons for Russian suspicion of their policy and offer the Russians the prospect of gaining more concrete advantages from cooperation with Germany than they could hope to acquire in association with France.

At the same time, Bismarck had no intention of abandoning Austria or of allowing Russia to achieve a political domination in eastern Europe that would upset the balance of power. If Germany had to throw its weight on the side of Russia, Austria would have to be given additional support for its position in eastern Europe. Austria, in fact, would have to become the nucleus of an anti-Russian coalition, from which Germany would be rigidly excluded so that it could have a free hand to bargain with Russia.

The most obvious ally for Austria among the great powers was Great Britain, but if the isolationism of the British was to be overcome, they would have to be convinced that unless they assumed their share of the burden in containing Russia, Germany and Austria would allow Russian power to flow into the Mediterranean. Turkey could be counted on as an ally against Russia as long as outside support was assured. Austria already had defensive alliances with Serbia, Rumania, and Italy, and Bulgaria was still hostile to Russia. With the backing of Britain, Italy, Turkey, and the Balkan states, Austria would be in an excellent position. Germany could then make any necessary concessions to Russia, knowing that Russia would be blocked by the Austrian coalition. Such a grouping of alliances would have the further advantage for Germany of leaving France in isolation.

In the last weeks of 1886 and the early part of 1887, Bismarck was engaged in fostering four sets of negotiations: for the renewal of the Triple Alliance, to safeguard Austria from a stab in the back by Italy; for an agreement primarily involving Austria and Britain, to preserve the *status quo* in the Balkans and the Near East; for an agreement centering around Britain, Italy, and Austria, to preserve the *status quo* in the Mediterranean; and for an agreement between Germany and Russia.

The first tangible result of this complicated network of negotiations was the so-called First Mediterranean Agreement of 1887, which in form was not a full-dress treaty, but a confidential exchange of notes between the powers concerned. It provided for the maintenance of the *status quo* in the Mediterranean, Turkey, and the Balkans. Italy was to support British policy in Egypt; Britain was to support Italian policy in North Africa. The Anglo-Austrian note stressed the common interests of Britain and Austria in the Near East. The various notes were somewhat loosely worded and admitted differences of interpretation, but they did provide a basis for cooperation and a definition of the mutual interests of the powers involved.

On February 20, 1887, the Triple Alliance was renewed for another five years. The Italians saw clearly that anti-German agitation in France and Russia had enhanced their value as an ally, and they consequently raised the price of their partnership. The old Triple Alliance treaty was renewed without change, but it was supplemented by separate, secret Austro-Italian and German-Italian notes that met the added Italian demands. The Austro-Italian note provided for the maintenance of the *status quo* in the Near East, with the stipulation that if the *status quo* could not be preserved, Italy would participate in settling the affairs of that region. Thus Italy gained a diplomatic foothold in any future partition of the Balkans or of the Ottoman Empire. The German-Italian note provided for the maintenance of the *status quo* in North Africa, and Germany promised to aid Italy if French activity in that area threatened Italian interests. Britain had provided Italy with similar assurances, and Bismarck felt confident that Germany and Britain together could prevent any Italian abuse of these promises of support.

With the conclusion of the First Mediterranean Agreement and the renewal of the Triple Alliance, the decks were clear for Bismarck to make whatever arrangement he could with Russia. As Bismarck had hoped, the tsar, although he flatly refused to renew any kind of treaty relationship with Austria, was not averse to a treaty with Germany. Even so, the negotiations between Germany and Russia proved to be very difficult, for the Russians hesitated to give Bismarck the assurance he most needed, namely a promise of Russian neutrality in the event of a French attack on Germany.

Finally, on June 18, 1887, a three-year secret treaty between Russia and Germany was signed. In this Reinsurance Treaty, each agreed to remain neutral if the other became involved in war with a third power, but these terms did not apply to an aggressive war by Germany against France, or by Russia against Austria. Both powers promised to support the *status quo* in the Balkans; Germany specifically recognized Russia's interest in Bulgaria. The principle of the closure of the Straits in time of war was affirmed. The most important part of the treaty was contained in a top-secret protocol. Germany promised to support Russian efforts to regain influence in Bulgaria and to oppose the restoration of Prince Alexander of Battenberg. Germany also promised Russia moral and diplomatic support for any measures the tsar might find necessary to control the "key of his empire"—Constantinople and the Straits. Thus Bismarck offered Russia freedom of action and diplomatic support in areas where German interests were not directly affected, but only after he had helped Austria form a coalition of powers to preserve the *status quo* in these areas.

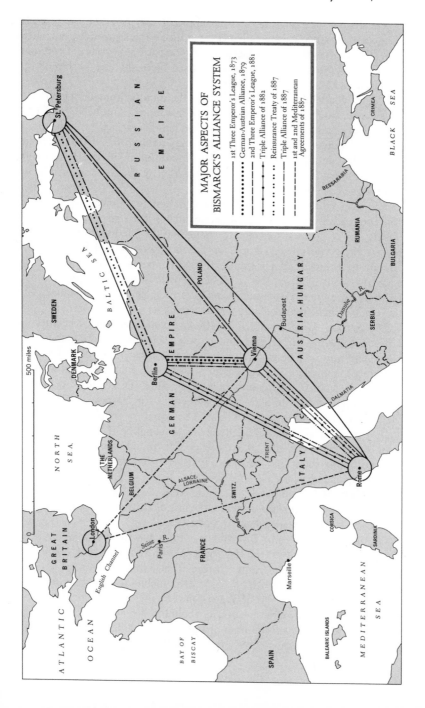

The main achievement of the Reinsurance Treaty was that it reduced the chances of a Franco-Russian alliance, or at least of an aggressive Franco-Russian alliance directed against Germany. As long as France was not certain of Russian support in an aggressive war against Germany, the likelihood of a French attack was greatly diminished.

The value of the treaty was evident in the months immediately after its ratification. Boulangism reached its peak in France in mid-1887 and 1888, and Russia's frustration in Bulgaria reached new heights with the election in 1887 of a German, Prince Ferdinand of Saxe-Coburg (1861–1948), as prince of Bulgaria, despite strenuous Russian opposition. Had the Reinsurance Treaty not existed, it is highly probable that a Franco-Russian alliance would have been formed.

The intensification of anti-German agitation in France and Russia in 1887 persuaded Bismarck not to place all his trust in the Reinsurance Treaty, but to do what he could to strengthen the Mediterranean coalition against these two powers. The cooperation of France and Russia against Britain in colonial affairs during this same period aided him in this endeavor, for it made British statesmen conscious of the dangerous potentialities of the Franco-Russian combination and receptive to arguments that they should make more definite commitments in the Near East.

The Second Mediterranean Agreement, concluded on December 12, 1887, took the form of an exchange of notes between Austria, Britain, and Italy. The principle of maintaining the *status quo* in the Near East was reaffirmed. Above all, the agreement stressed the importance of keeping Turkey free from foreign domination of any kind. Turkey was not to give up any of its rights or to allow occupation by a foreign power of Bulgaria, the Straits, or any part of Asia Minor. The signatory states agreed to help Turkey to resist all encroachments on its sovereignty; if Turkey failed to resist such encroachments, the three powers would consider themselves justified in provisionally occupying Turkish territory in order to safeguard Turkish independence.

The terms of the various 1887 treaties were secret, but to increase their effectiveness as instruments of peace, the gist of their contents was allowed to leak out—a warning to potential aggressors.

The alliances fostered by Bismarck, in contrast to those that would be in force before the outbreak of the First World War, did not divide the powers into two hostile camps. Instead, they brought them all into an interlocking network in which no single state, including Germany, could be assured of support in a war of aggression. On the contrary, an aggressive power would be confronted by an overwhelming defensive coalition, based either upon actual alliance treaties or upon natural alliances that could be expected to form. Because the system would come into operation against any effort to upset the *status quo,* it served as a deterrent to chauvinist agitators in every country.

The strength of Bismarck's treaties lay in the fact that the advantages they afforded to the powers concerned were great enough to give each participant a vested interest in maintaining them. Also, the formal treaties were sufficiently limited in time to prevent any power from growing restive in the toils of a particular agreement. When the time limit was up, the treaty would lapse; or it could be negotiated anew to accord with changes in the international situation, for no power liked to be left without the assurance of defensive support of some kind.

The greatest weakness of Bismarck's system was its Metternichian emphasis on preserving the territorial and political *status quo* in Europe. Most European powers were not satisfied with the *status quo.* Russia and Austria had ambitions in southeastern Europe; France sought the restoration of Alsace-Lorraine; Italy wanted Trent, Trieste, and the Dalmatian coast. Among Bismarck's own compatriots there was growing criticism of his conception of Germany as a satiated state and increasing speculation about the nation's future as a great power if it remained restricted to its narrow territorial base in central Europe. German nationalists wanted more territory, either overseas or in eastern Europe; army leaders and diplomats alike wished to stop diplomatic finessing and go to war with France and Russia to put an end to the menace of these powers once and for all.

While Bismarck held office he put a check on such agitation in his own country, and used all his influence and ability to preserve peace and the *status quo* in Europe. But in 1888 there came to the German throne a new

Bismarck. A *photograph taken shortly before his dismissal.*

emperor, receptive to the most irresponsible demands for national expansion. After the dismissal of Bismarck in 1890 his alliance system was allowed to collapse, and the formation began of new alliances, which were to divide Europe into two armed camps. In international affairs even more than in domestic, his dismissal marked the end of an era.

A GOLDEN AGE OF HOPE

The historian examining the last decades of the nineteenth century can readily identify the forces that were to explode so soon in war and revolution. Such forces exist in every society, however, and in the Europe of 1890 there seemed no cause for undue alarm. On the contrary, the preceding forty years had been a great age. The material achievements seemed to prove that evolution was synonymous with progress, and recent manifestations of the human spirit encouraged the belief that the quality of man was improving with each new generation. The selfless devotion of a Garibaldi in the cause of nationalism had been matched by the exploits of humanitarians in the cause of reform. As a result of the efforts of national leaders, new political units had been established throughout a large part of the Continent on the basis of the principle of nationalism, which many theorists and practical politicians had come to accept as the natural and hence the only sound foundation of a state. As a result of the efforts of reformers, the condition of the population of all countries was steadily being improved. The most obvious forms of serfdom and slavery had been abolished, great strides had been made in combating hunger and disease. Moreover, these reformers, at one time voices crying in the wilderness, could now count on broad support from enlightened public opinion in their struggles against illiteracy, social injustice, and all forms of human cruelty. Despite national hatreds and rivalries, international intercourse had never been more general. People could travel throughout western and central Europe easily and safely, without passports. Artists and scholars of all nationalities went to foreign cities and universities to study and exchange ideas.

Thoughtful Europeans were fully aware of the gravity of the many problems still besetting their society and there was no lack of prophets of disaster among them, but the prevailing mood in Europe as the nineteenth century drew to a close was one of optimism. Human reason seemed to have demonstrated its capacity to cope with human problems. After three quarters of a century without a general European war, people had begun to count on the future. In the light of later events this confidence may seem naïve, but it is easy to understand how those who grew up during these years could look back upon them after the First World War as a golden age, perhaps not a golden age of reality, but certainly a golden age of hope.

Suggestions for Further Reading

(Books marked * are available in paperback.)

GENERAL

Two volumes of the *New Cambridge Modern History* cover the later nineteenth century: Vol. X, *The Zenith of European Power, 1830–1870*, ed. J. P. T. Bury (Cambridge, Eng., 1960) and Vol. XI, *Material Progress and World-Wide Problems, 1870–1898*, ed. by F. H. Hinsley (Cambridge, Eng., 1962). They consist of separate essays of uneven quality on a variety of topics, including intellectual developments, armies and navies, art and literature, as well as political and economic history. *The Nineteenth Century: The Contradictions of Progress*, ed. Asa Briggs (London, 1970) is another collection of essays by specialists, and is especially valuable for its lavish illustrations. The immediate background of the period covered by the present volume is surveyed authoritatively and comprehensively by *William L. Langer, *Political and Social Upheaval, 1832–1852* (New York, 1969) (Harper and Row), which includes a magnificent bibliography.

*A. R. Vidler, *The Church in an Age of Revolution, 1789 to the Present Day* (London, 1961) (Penguin), and Josef L. Altholz, *The Churches in the Nineteenth Century* (New York, 1967) are two convenient surveys of church history.

For military history, *Theodore Ropp, *War in the Modern World* (Durham, N.C., 1959) (Collier) is a useful survey with excellent bibliographies. Also valuable are two works by Cyril Falls: *A Hundred Years of War, 1850–1950* (New York, 1953) (Collier); and *The Art of War from the Age of Napoleon to the Present Day* (New York, 1961) (Hesperides).

The immense and controversial literature on the subject of imperialism is competently introduced in the brief American Historical Association pamphlet by *David Healy, *Modern Imperialism: Changing Styles in Historical Interpretation* (Washington, D.C., 1967), a subject treated in greater detail in the excellent work of Richard Koebner and H. D. Schmidt, *Imperialism: The Story and Significance of a Political Word, 1840–1960* (Cambridge, Eng.,

1964), which exhaustively explores the origins and uses of the term. A number of excellent interpretive essays are reprinted in *Imperialism and Colonialism, ed. George H. Nadel and Perry Curtis (New York, 1964) (Collier-Macmillan). One of the best of these essays, "The New Imperialism: The Hobson-Lenin Thesis Revised," is by D. K. Fieldhouse, who has also written a survey of European and American imperialism *The Colonial Empires: A Comparative Survey from the Eighteenth Century (New York, 1966) (Delta), and the more specific Economics and Empire, 1830–1914 (Ithaca, New York, 1973).

ECONOMIC AND SOCIAL HISTORY

The most useful and authoritative work for all the countries of Europe is the Cambridge Economic History of Europe, ed. by M. M. Postan and H. J. Habakkuk, Vol. VI (in two parts), The Industrial Revolutions and After (Cambridge, Eng., 1965), which includes a splendid bibliography. A section of part 1 of Vol. VI of the Cambridge Economic History by David S. Landes has been expanded and reprinted as *The Unbound Prometheus: Technological Change and Industrial Development in Western Europe from 1750 to the Present (Cambridge, Eng., 1969) (Cambridge), a brilliant, informative, and beautifully written work. For the problems of agriculture, see J. D. Chambers and G. E. Mingay, The Agricultural Revolution, 1750–1880 (New York, 1966), which deals exclusively with England; and Agrarian Change and Economic Development, ed. E. L. Jones and S. J. Wolf (London, 1970).

Other valuable works on special aspects of economic history are A. P. Usher, A History of Mechanical Inventions (Cambridge, Mass., 1954); T. K. Derry and T. I. Williams, A Short History of Technology (London, 1961), a general introduction from earliest times to 1900; N. J. G. Pounds and W. N. Parker, Coal and Steel in Western Europe (Bloomington, Ind., 1957); G. R. Taylor, The Transportation Revolution, 1815–1860 (New York, 1951); L. F. Haber, The Chemical Industry during the Nineteenth Century (Oxford, 1958); W. Ashworth, A Short History of the International Economy, 1850–1950 (London, 1951); *Herbert Feis, Europe: The World's Banker, 1870–1914 (New Haven, 1930) (Norton); and Leland Jenks, The Migration of British Capital to 1875 (London, 1927), a readable and authoritative study on this important and difficult subject. R. N. Salaman's The History and Social Influence of the Potato, 2 vols. (Cambridge, Eng., 1949) unfortunately deals almost exclusively with Britain and Ireland.

Peter N. Stearns, European Society in Upheaval: Social History since 1800 (New York, 1967) is the first major synthesis on this subject, an excellent and valuable survey. For the transformation of Europe's cities, see *Asa Briggs, Victorian Cities (London, 1963) (Penguin); R. E. Dickenson, The West European City: A Geographical Interpretation (London, 1962); E. A. Gutkind, International History of City Development, 3 vols. (New York, 1964–67); and the classic study, first published in 1899, A. F. Weber, The Growth of Cities in the Nineteenth Century (New York, 1969).

The American Historical Association pamphlet by *Franklin D. Scott, Emigration and Immigration* (Washington, D.C., 1966) is a useful bibliographical guide on this important subject. *Population Movements in Modern European History*, ed. by Herbert Moller, (New York, 1964) (Collier-Macmillan) contains several suggestive articles, as does *Population in History: Essays in Historical Demography*, ed. by D. V. Glass and D. E. C. Eversley (London, 1965). *C. M. Cipolla, *The Economic History of World Population* (Harmondsworth, Eng., 1962) (Penguin) is an excellent brief survey. Still the best and fullest analysis is Walter F. Willcox, *International Migrations*, 2 vols. (New York, 1929–31); the first volume is devoted largely to statistics, the second is a country by country (or ethnic group) interpretation.

INTELLECTUAL AND CULTURAL HISTORY

J. T. Merz, *A History of European Thought in the Nineteenth Century*, 4 vols. (Edinburgh and London, 1896–1914) is a detailed, comprehensive survey with emphasis on science and philosophy.

W. C. D. Dampier, *A History of Science and its Relations with Philosophy and Religion* (New York, 1949) is useful, although not so comprehensive as its title suggests. W. P. D. Wightman, *The Growth of Scientific Ideas* (New Haven, 1951) provides a competent survey of nineteenth-century developments, as does Charles Singer, *A Short History of Scientific Ideas to 1900* (Oxford, Eng., 1959). See also the brilliant interpretation of C. C. Gillespie, *The Edge of Objectivity: An Essay in the History of Scientific Ideas* (Princeton, N.J., 1960). Two useful surveys are J. D. Bernal, *Science in History* (London, 1954) and S. F. Mason, *Main Currents in Scientific Thought* (New York, 1954). A. D. White, *A History of the Warfare of Science with Theology* (New York, 1896) remains of great value, especially as a reflection of the opinions of its time. There are many editions of Darwin's writings. Among the most interesting is his brief and revealing *Autobiography*, ed. by Nora Barlow (New York, 1958) (Norton). Of the many excellent works on the impact of Darwin's thought, one of the best is *Gertrude Himmelfarb, *Darwin and the Darwinian Revolution* (New York, 1959) (Norton). The fascinating work by *Stephen Toulmin and June Goodfield, *The Discovery of Time* (New York, 1965) (Harper Torchbooks) is a series of essays on time in history, with an excellent analysis of Darwin's contribution.

*John Bowle, *Politics and Opinion in the Nineteenth Century* (London, 1954) (Oxford Galaxy) is a stimulating survey of major ideas of the age. The American Historical Association pamphlet by *Boyd C. Shafer, *Nationalism: Interpretors and Interpretations* (Washington, D.C., 1959) is a good bibliographical guide on this important and controversial subject, and the same author's *Nationalism: Myth and Reality* (New York, 1955) (Harcourt Brace) provides a brief and lucid analysis of the problem. *Hans Kohn, *The Idea of Nationalism: A Study of its Origins and Background* (New York, 1944) (Collier) is a good introduction by a scholar who has written numerous other works on the subject; K. R. Minogue, *Nationalism* (New York, 1967) is brief and suggestive. H. M. Chadwick, *The Nationalities of Europe and the Growth of National Ideologies* (Cambridge, Eng., 1945) is a historical survey while *E. Kedourie, *Nationalism* (London, 1960) (Praeger) provides an analytical approach. For the other side of the picture, see F. S. L. Lyons, *Internationalism in Europe, 1815–1914* (Leyden, 1963).

Walter M. Simon, *European Positivism in the Nineteenth Century* (Ithaca, N.Y., 1963) is an excellent study of Comte and his influence.

On liberalism there are the works of Frederick M. Watkins, *The Political Tradition of the West: A Study in the Development of Modern Liberalism* (Cambridge, Mass., 1948) and *Guido de Ruggiero, *A History of European Liberalism* (London, 1927) (Beacon).

On socialism, see Carl Landauer, *European Socialism: A History of Ideas and Movements from the Industrial Revolution to Hitler's Seizure of Power*, 2 vols. (Berkeley, Calif., 1959); G. D. H. Cole, *Socialist Thought: Marxism and Anarchism, 1850–1880* (London, 1954); and *George Lichtheim, *The Origins of Socialism* (New York, 1969) (Praeger), which is brief, scholarly, and readable, and includes an excellent bibliography. There are many editions of Marx's major works. An excellent brief study of Marx is *Isaiah Berlin, *Karl Marx: His Life and Environment* (Oxford, 1939) (Galaxy), while one of the best analyses of his ideology is *George Lichtheim, *Marxism: An Historical and Critical Study* (London, 1961) (Praeger). For a study of the central thesis of the Marx-Engels doctrine of social evolution, see *M. M. Bober, *Karl Marx's Interpretation of History* (Cambridge, Mass., 1927) (Norton).

The best work in English on Nietzsche is *Walter A. Kaufmann, *Nietzsche: Philosopher, Psychologist, Anti-Christ* (Princeton, N.J., 1950) (Meridian), who has also done the best English editions and translations of Nietzsche's works.

The important problem of education is surveyed in William Boyd, *The History of Western Education* (London, 1966); Brian Simon, *Studies in the History of Education, 1780–1970* (London, 1960); and H. M. Pollard, *Pioneers of Popular Education, 1760–1850* (London, 1956). There is a recent survey of national education in England by John Hurt, *Education in Evolution: Church, State, Society, and Popular Education, 1800–1870* (London, 1971).

On art, a good analytical survey is E. P. Richardson, *The Way of Western Art, 1776–1914* (Cambridge, Mass., 1939). Fritz Novotny, *Painting and Sculpture in Europe, 1780–1880* (London, 1960) does not include the art of Great Britain, but is otherwise excellent. It contains a fine collection of illustrations, as does the Phaidon Press publication *The French Impressionists* (London, 1952), with an introduction by Clive Bell. *Herbert Read, *A Concise History of Modern Painting* (London, 1959) (Praeger) is a competent brief analysis. *Linda Nochlin's suggestive *Realism* (Harmondsworth, 1972) (Penguin) deals almost entirely with nineteenth century painting. John Rewald, *The History of Impressionism* (New York, 1973) is the best general survey, lavishly illustrated. For the impact of one of the most original and interesting artists of the period, see the fascinating work of *George H. Hamilton, *Manet and his Critics* (New York, 1969) (Norton).

The literature and music of the period should be read and heard. The works of the major writers are available in many editions, those of the major composers on records and tapes. For the literature, there are several interesting works analyzing the relationship of literature and society: W. E. Houghton, *The Victorian Frame of Mind, 1830–1870* (New Haven, Conn., 1957); Eda Sagarra, *Tradition and Revolution: German Literature and Society, 1830–1890* (New York, 1971); and F. W. J. Hemmings, *Culture and Society in France, 1848–1898: Dissidents and Philistines* (New York, 1971). Brilliant and beautifully written, but somewhat discursive, is Harry Levin, *The Gates of Horn: A Study of Five French Realists* (New York, 1963), which analyzes the work of Stendahl, Balzac, Flaubert, Zola, and Proust. The fourth volume of René Wellek, *A History of Modern Criticism, 1750–1950: The Later Nineteenth Century* (New Haven, Conn., 1965) contains a good analysis of symbolist literary criticism. See also A. G. Lehmann, *The Symbolist Aesthetic in France, 1885–1895* (Oxford, 1950). Among the general histories of music, Donald Jay Grout, *A History of Western Music* (New York, 1960) (Norton) is an intelligent and sensitive survey. *The Memoirs of Hector Berlioz* (New York, 1960) (Norton) is one of the great autobiographies of the nineteenth century, well translated.

NATIONAL HISTORY

For Great Britain, the American Historical Association pamphlet by *Robert K. Webb, *English History, 1815–1914,* (Washington, D.C. 1967) is a useful bibliographical guide. The same author has written a general history, *Modern England: From the Eighteenth Century to the Present* (New York, 1968) (Dodd, Mead), which embodies the most recent research, as do the excellent shorter volumes by *Derek Beales, *From Castlereagh to Gladstone, 1815–1885* (London, 1969) (Norton) and *Henry Pelling, *Modern Britain, 1885–1955* (London, 1960) (Norton). Two volumes in the Oxford History of England, Ernest L. Woodward, *The Age of Reform, 1815–1870* (Oxford, 1962) and R. C. K. Ensor, *England, 1870–1914* (Oxford, 1936), are well-written, comprehensive treatments. *David Thomson's brief *England in the Nineteenth Century, 1815–1914* (London, 1950) (Penguin) stresses social and economic trends, as does *Asa Briggs, *The Making of Modern England, 1783–1867: The Age of Improvement* (New York, 1959) (Harper Torchbook), an admirable work. Another outstanding analysis of British society is the intelligent and splendidly written book of *W. L. Burn, *The Age of Equipoise: A Study of the Mid-Victorian Generation* (London, 1964) (Norton). J. H. Clapham, *The Economic History of Modern Britain, 1815–1914,* 2 vols. (Cambridge, Eng., 1921) remains authoritative and is full of valuable information. Sir Ernest Barker, *Political Thought in England, 1848–1914* (Oxford, 1928) is brief and lucid. For the machinery of government, Emmeline Cohen, *The*

Growth of the British Civil Service, 1780–1939 (Hamden, Conn., 1965) provides a good introductory survey. The most authoritative biography of Queen Victoria is Elizabeth Longford, Queen Victoria: Born to Succeed (New York, 1965). See also the brilliant literary portrait by Lytton Strachey, *Queen Victoria (London, 1921) (Capricorn). For an appreciation of the queen, nothing can replace the reading of her letters, large selections of which have been published in many volumes. Lytton Strachey's *Eminent Victorians (London, 1918) (Capricorn) contains a group of delightful biographical sketches. More substantial biographies of Victorian notables include H. C. Bell, Lord Palmerston, 2 vols. (Hamden, Conn., 1936); John Morley, The Life of William Ewart Gladstone, 3 vols. (1903); *Philip Magnus, Gladstone: A Biography (New York, 1964) (Dutton); *Robert Blake, Disraeli (New York, 1967) (Doubleday Anchor); and Gwendolyn Cecil, Life of Robert, Marquis of Salisbury, 4 vols. (London, 1921–1931). On Irish politics, there are two interesting works: L. P. Curtis, Coercion and Conciliation in Ireland, 1880–1892 (Princeton, N.J., 1963) and C. C. O'Brien, Parnell and his Party, 1880–90, (Oxford, 1957).

For France, the American Historical Association pamphlet by *Jean T. Joughin, France in the Nineteenth Century: Selected Studies in English since 1956 (Washington, D.C., 1968) is a useful bibliographical essay. Among the excellent general histories of France, the following are brief and well written: Gordon Wright, France in Modern Times: 1760 to the Present (Chicago, 1960), with excellent bibliographies; *Alfred Cobban, A History of Modern France, vol. 2, 1799–1871; vol. 3, 1871–1962 (Harmondsworth, 1966) (Penguin); *John B. Wolf, France, 1814–1919 (New York, 1963) (Harper Torchbook). Lively but somewhat elliptical is *D. W. Brogan, The French Nation: From Napoleon to Pétain, 1814–1940 (London, 1961) (Colophon). A very different kind of general history is provided by Theodore Zeldin, France, 1848–1945: Ambition, Love, and Politics (London, 1973), the first of two volumes. On the controversial figure of Napoleon III, Albert Guérard, Napoleon III: A Great Life in Brief (New York, 1955) is sympathetic toward its subject, while *James M. Thompson, Louis Napoleon and the Second Empire (Oxford, 1954) (Norton) is somewhat more critical. *Roger L. Williams, The World of Napoleon III, 1815–1870 (New York, 1962) (Collier) is a delightful collection of essays originally published under the title Gaslight and Shadow. The best account of the war with Prussia is *Michael Howard, The Franco-Prussian War (New York, 1961) (Collier). On the Paris Commune the most recent work is *Roger L. Williams, The French Revolution of 1870–1871 (New York, 1969) (Norton). On the Third Republic, *Alexander Sedgwick, The Third French Republic, 1870–1914 (New York, 1968) (Crowell) is straightforward, brief, and lucid. Among the longer studies, there is the lively history by *D. W. Brogan, France under the Republic, 1870–1939 (New York, 1940) (Harper Torchbook, in two volumes), also published under the title The Development of Modern France, which assumes a good deal of background knowledge. *David Thomson, Democracy in France since 1870 (London, 1969) (Oxford) is an excellent analysis of the French political system and social structure. On more specialized aspects of French history, see R. H. Soltau, French Political Thought in the Nineteenth Century (London, 1931);

J. P. Mayer, *Political Thought in France from the Revolution to the Fourth Republic* (London, 1949); *J. H. Clapham, *The Economic Development of France and Germany, 1815–1914* (Cambridge, Eng., 1936) (Cambridge), old but full of valuable information; Shepard B. Clough, *France: A History of National Economics* (New York, 1964), which emphasizes the role of government in the economy; Rondo Cameron, *France and the Economic Development of Europe, 1800–1914* (Princeton, N.J., 1961) on the contribution of French capital and technical experts, and French legal and organizational influences; David H. Pinkney, *Napoleon III and the Reconstruction of Paris* (Princeton, N.J., 1958) describes how Paris was rebuilt and how the project was financed; J. M. and Brian Chapman, *The Life and Times of Baron Haussmann* (London, 1957), on the same subject, concentrates on the emperor's chief architect and city planner; Jean T. Joughin, *The Paris Commune in French Politics, 1871–1880*, 2 vols. (Baltimore, 1955) is a valuable study of this volatile problem; P. Campbell, *French Electoral System and Elections* (London, 1958) shows the importance of the complicated French systems of voting; Frederic H. Seager, *The Boulanger Affair: Political Crossroads of France, 1886–1889* (Ithaca, N.Y., 1969) deals with one of the most critical episodes of the period; on the problem of the military in general, David B. Ralston, *The Army of the Republic, 1871–1914* (Cambridge, Mass., 1967) is excellent.

For Germany, the American Historical Association pamphlet by *Norman Rich, *Germany, 1815–1914* (Washington, D.C., 1968) is a useful bibliographical guide. Walter Simon, *Germany: A Brief History* (New York, 1966) is an excellent short survey. *Golo Mann, *The History of Germany since 1789* (New York, 1968) (Praeger), by the son of the great German novelist, is balanced, scholarly, and eminently readable. More detailed are Koppel S. Pinson, *Modern Germany: Its History and Civilization*, second ed. (New York, 1966), which stresses cultural and social forces; W. H. Dawson, *The German Empire, 1867–1914, and the Unity Movement*, 2 vols. (New York, 1919), which emphasizes political history; and Hajo Holborn, *A History of Modern Germany*, Vol. III (New York, 1968), dealing with the years 1840–1945, which embodies the most recent research. *Otto Pflanze, *Bismarck and the Development of Germany: The Period of Unification, 1815–1871* (Princeton, N.J., 1963) is the most detailed recent biography in English. The excellent older work of Charles G. Robertson, *Bismarck* (New York, 1919) remains valuable. See also *Erich Eyck, *Bismarck and the German Empire* (London, 1950) (Norton). The brief biography by *A. J. P. Taylor, *Bismarck: The Man and the Statesman* (New York, 1955) (Vintage) is erratic but often penetrating and always lively and readable. The best available biography of William II is *Michael Balfour, *The Kaiser and his Times* (New York, 1964) (Norton). Among special studies on modern German history, *Leonard Krieger, *The German Idea of Freedom: The History of a Political Tradition* (Boston, 1957) (Beacon) is in effect a history of German political thought, difficult but rewarding. *Theodore S. Hamerow, *Restoration, Revolution, Reaction: Economics and Politics in Germany, 1815–1871* (Princeton, N.J., 1958) (Princeton) deals with the economic background of German politics, an emphasis which the same author has expanded in two other valuable works, *The Social and Economic Foundations of German Unification*, vol. 1, *Ideas and Institutions* (Princeton, N.J., 1969), and vol. 2, *Struggles and Accomplishments* (Princeton, N.J., 1972). The well written work of *Gordon Craig, *The Politics of the Prussian Army, 1640–1945* (New York, 1955) (Oxford Galaxy) analyzes the fateful impact of military thinking on politics. On the same subject, see the work by the eminent German scholar Gerhard Ritter, *The Sword and the Scepter: The Problem of Militarism in Germany*, vol. 1, *The Prussian Tradition, 1740–1890* (Coral Gables, Fla., 1969). Another branch of the Prussian government is examined in the excellent monograph of John R. Gillis, *The Prussian Bureaucracy in Crisis, 1840–1860: Origins of an Administrative Ethos* (Stanford, Calif., 1971). On the crucial constitutional crisis in Prussia, there is a detailed and reliable monograph by E. N. Anderson, *The Social and Political Conflict in Prussia, 1858–1864* (New York, 1954). Henry Cord Meyer, *Mitteleuropa in German Thought and Action, 1815–1945* (The Hague, 1955) examines the important subject of German policies and attitudes toward central Europe.

For the Habsburg lands, the recent work of C. A. Macartney, *The Habsburg Empire, 1790–1918* (London, 1969) is massively detailed and authoritative, but unfortunately avoids the subject of foreign policy. *A. J. May, *The Habsburg Monarchy, 1867–1914* (Cambridge, Mass., 1951) (Norton) is balanced, scholarly, and reliable. *Oscar Jaszi, *The Dissolution of the Habsburg Monarchy* (Chicago, 1929) (Phoenix) contains much valuable information. Robert Kann, *The Multinational Empire: Nationalism and National Reform in the Habsburg Monarchy, 1848–1918*, 2 vols. (New York, 1950) deal intelligently with the most difficult problem the empire faced in the nineteenth century. William M. Johnston, *The Austrian Mind: An Intellectual and Social History, 1848–1938* (Berkeley, Calif., 1972) is lively and readable.

For Italy, the American Historical Association pamphlet by *Charles F. Delzell, *Italy in Modern Times: An Introduction to the Historical Literature in English* (Washington, D.C., 1964) is a useful bibliographical guide. *Arthur J. Whyte, *The Evolution of Modern Italy* (New York, 1959) (Norton) is a brief and readable general history. Derek Beales, *The Risorgimento and the Unification of Italy* (London, 1971) deals intelligently with the most recent scholarly interpretations and includes a useful selection of documents. Far more detailed is the lively and well written work of George Martin, *The Red Shirt and the Cross of Savoy: The Story of Italy's Risorgimento, 1748–1871* (London, 1969). The older work of Bolton King, *A History of Italian Unity, Being a Political History of Italy from 1814 to 1871*, 2 vols. (London, 1912) remains outstanding. On the period since unification, Christopher Seton-Watson, *Italy from Liberalism to Fascism, 1870–1925* (London, 1967) is permeated with an optimism that should be balanced by the more somber analysis of Denis Mack Smith, *Italy: A Modern History* (Ann Arbor, Mich., 1959). Shepard B. Clough, *The Economic History of Modern Italy* (New York, 1964) is a competent survey. Still of great interest is the work of the eminent liberal philosopher-historian Benedetto Croce, *A History of Italy, 1871–1915* (Oxford, 1929). On Cavour, William R. Thayer, *The Life and*

Times of Cavour, 2 vols. (Boston, 1911) is detailed and reliable. Denis Mack Smith, *Cavour and Garibaldi, 1860: A Study in Political Conflict* (Cambridge, Eng., 1954) is an important monograph, critical of Cavour. The same author's *Garibaldi: A Great Life in Brief* (New York, 1956) is readable and reliable. Arthur C. Jemolo, *Church and State in Italy, 1850–1950* (Oxford, 1960) is a translated abridgment of a major Italian study on this important topic.

For Russia, *Hugh Seton-Watson, *The Decline of Imperial Russia, 1855–1914* (New York, 1952) (Praeger) is a competent brief survey. More detailed and somewhat more difficult for students unfamiliar with Russian history is the same author's *The Russian Empire, 1801–1917* (London, 1967), and Nicholas Riasanovsky, *A History of Russia* (New York, 1969). Also detailed and still valuable is the older work of M. T. Florinsky, *Russia: A History and an Interpretation*, 2 vols. (New York, 1953). The best brief survey of the reform era is *Werner E. Mosse, *Alexander II and the Modernization of Russia* (New York, 1958) (Collier). There are a number of excellent studies on special aspects of Russian history: P. I. Liashchenko, *History of the National Economy in Russia to the 1917 Revolution* (New York, 1949), and the section on Russian economic history by Alexander Gerschenkron in vol. VI of the *Cambridge Economic History* (see above); *G. T. Robinson, *Rural Russia under the Old Regime: A History of the Landlord-Peasant World and a Prologue to the Peasant Revolution of 1917* (New York, 1930) (Univ. of California); Terence Emmons, *The Russian Landed Gentry and the Peasant Emancipation of 1861* (Cambridge, Eng., 1968); Daniel Field, *The End of Serfdom: Gentry and Bureaucracy in Russia, 1855–1861* (Cambridge, Mass., 1975); S. Frederick Starr, *Decentralization and Self-Government in Russia, 1830–1870* (Princeton, N.J., 1972); Jacob Walkin, *The Rise of Democracy in Pre-Revolutionary Russia: Political and Social Institutions under the Last Three Tsars* (New York, 1962); *Franco Venturi, *The Roots of Revolution: A History of the Populist and Socialist Movements in Nineteenth Century Russia* (New York, 1960) (Universal Library); B. H. Sumner, *Russia and the Balkans, 1870–1880*, (Oxford, 1937); B. H. Sumner, *Tsardom and Imperialism in the Far and Middle East, 1880–1914* (London, 1942); Michael B. Petrovich, *The Emergence of Russian Panslavism, 1856–1870* (New York, 1956); Charles Jelavich, *Tsarist Russia and Balkan Nationalism: Russian Influence in the Internal Affairs of Bulgaria and Serbia 1879–1886* (Berkeley, Calif., 1958); Richard A. Pearce, *Russian Central Asia, 1867–1917: A Study in Colonial Rule* (Berkeley, Calif., 1960); and Donald W. Treadgold, *The Great Siberian Migration: Government and Peasant in Resettlement from Emancipation to the First World War* (Princeton, N.J., 1957).

INTERNATIONAL RELATIONS

A. J. P. Taylor, *The Struggle for Mastery in Europe, 1848–1914* (Oxford, 1954), although erratic and contradictory, is full of illuminating insights, with an excellent bibliography.

Brison D. Gooch, *The Origins of the Crimean War* (Lexington, Mass., 1969) is a collection of interpretations, with a useful bibliography. For the background of the problems of the Near East, see the brief and lucid work of M. S. Anderson, *The Eastern Question, 1774–1923* (London, 1966); Harold Temperley, *England and the Near East: The Crimea* (London, 1936), an analysis of the Eastern Question from 1839 to the Crimean War; and G. B. Henderson, *Crimean War Diplomacy* (Glasgow, 1947), a collection of valuable essays. Paul W. Schroeder, *Austria, Great Britain, and the Crimean War: The Destruction of the European Concert* (Ithaca, N.Y., 1972) emphasizes the much neglected role of Austria and is very critical of Britain; especially valuable is a brilliant final chapter on the impact of the war on the relations of the great powers. On the war itself there is Peter Gibbs, *Crimean Blunder: The Story of War with Russia a Hundred Years Ago* (New York, 1960), a straightforward popular history. Far more exciting and readable is *C. Woodham-Smith, *The Reason Why* (New York, 1954) (Dutton), which deals with Britain's military leadership in general and the background of the charge of the Light Brigade. W. E. Mosse, *The Rise and Fall of the Crimean System, 1855–1871* (New York, 1963) makes the point that a peace treaty which cannot be enforced is useless.

The most authoritative general work on the period after 1871 is *William L. Langer, *European Alliances and Alignments, 1871–1890* (New York, 1931) (Knopf), which includes a splendid bibliography brought up to date in 1950. The best brief study is R. J. Sontag, *European Diplomatic History, 1871–1932* (New York, 1933). The same author's *Germany and England: Background of Conflict, 1848–1894* (New York, 1938) (Norton) brilliantly explains why the "natural alliance" between these countries did not materialize. Robert Furneaux, *The Breakfast War* (New York, 1958) is a lively account of the Russo-Turkish war of 1878 about which Europeans read over their breakfasts, while *R. W. Seton-Watson, *Disraeli, Gladstone, and the Eastern Question* (London, 1935) (Norton) provides a clear, authoritative analysis of a problem that continued to plague European diplomatists.

Index

Affirmation Bill (1888; British), 163
Afghanistan, 165, 181
Africa, 242
  East, 243
  North, 30, 245
  South, 18, 165
  Southwest, 243
Agricultural Holdings Act (1875; British), 161
Agricultural tariff (1881; French), 194
Agriculture
  competition in international, 13
  farm laborers, 24–25
  French, 194
  German, 223
  Hungarian, 213
  Italian, 202
  population growth and, 4, 15
  revolution in, 1–4
  Russian, 177
  women in, 20
Alaska, 183
Alexander II (Tsar of Russia; Tsar Liberator), 88, 168–70
  industrialization under, 176
  reforms under, 168–69
  revolutionary ferment under, 178
  serfs emancipated under, 170
Alexander III (Tsar of Russia), 169, 178–80
Alexander of Battenberg (Prince of Bulgaria), 237–38, 246
Algeria, 70
Alsace-Lorraine, 143–44, 186, 238, 244, 249
Americas. See Latin America; North America
Andrássy, Count Gyula, 203, 232
Anglo-Austrian treaty (1878), 231
Anglo-Russian agreement (1885), 181
Anglo-Russian treaty (1878), 231
Anglo-Turkish treaty (1878), 231
Animal husbandry, growth of, 2
Antisocialist law (1878; Prussian), 222–23
Aquinas, St. Thomas, 28
Architecture and engineering, 52–53
  bridges, 7, 52–53
  British, 52–53, 145, 146
  French, 53, 93–95
  See also Public works
Armaments, xii
  changes in, 67–68
  in Crimean War, 88
  Czech, 209
  in Franco-Prussian War, 100
  French, 95–96, 142
  Prussian, 95–96, 133, 135, 142
  smokeless powder for, 7
Armed forces. See Armaments; Army; Navy
Army
  effect of railroads on mobility of, 67–68, 133, 135
  growth of modern, xii, 67–68

See also under specific nationalities: French army; Prussian army; etc.
Army Enlistment Bill (1870; British), 157
Artisan's Dwelling Act (1875; British), 161
Arts, the, realism in, 32–33. See also specific art forms
Ashley, Lord (Anthony Ashley Cooper; 7th Earl of Shaftesbury), 150
Auersperg, Prince Adolf, 207–8
Ausgleich, 205–12
Austen, Jane, 54
Austerlitz, battle of (1805), 80
Australia, 70, 74, 75
  agriculturally competitive, 13
  emigration to, 18
Austria, x, 27, 44
  after Ausgleich, 205–12
  Balkan policy of, 236–38
  and Crimean War, 91, 109, 110
  and France, 95, 98–99
    Austro-Prussian War and, 132–33, 136
    Franco-Prussian War and, 138, 140
  Habsburg empire. See Habsburg empire
  minorities problem in, 205–12
  and Polish Revolt, 129–30
  Prussia and, 123, 124, 220
    alliance, 233, 235
    Austro-French war, 98–99
    Franco-Prussian War, 138, 140
    and German alliance system, 244–50
    and Habsburg customs union, 109
    post–Franco-Prussian War, 206
    rivalry, 119–20
    Schleswig-Holstein question, 130–32
    war between, 132–37
  Roman Catholic Church in, 29, 102, 103, 108, 206, 208, 210
  Russia and, 82, 83, 110, 168, 179
    and Austro-Prussian War, 132, 136
    and Crimean War, 85, 88, 91
    and expansion of Russia, 181, 183
    and Habsburg customs union, 109
  Sardinian conflict with, 111–16
  in stabilization of Eastern Europe, 229–38
  in stabilization of Western Europe, 239
  and unification of Germany, 129
  and unification of Italy, 101, 111–17, 133, 199
Austria-Hungary
  creation of, 202–3, 205
  effects of education on, 69
  nationalism in, 45–46
Austrian army, 102, 135
Austrian National Bank (later Austro-Hungarian National Bank), 106, 215
Austro-British treaty (1878), 231
Austro-Hungarian Empire, x, 184. See also Austria; Austria-Hungary; Habsburg empire; Hungary
Austro-Prussian War (1866), 132–37, 205

Austro-Rumanian alliance (1883), 237
Authority, new principles of, 31–47
Autocracy. *See* Habsburg empire; Russia
Automobiles, 11

Bach, Alexander von, 108–9, 202, 203
Bach System, 108–10
Bacteriology, 16–17
Balkans, ix, x, 197
  Crimean War and Russian control of, 82.
    See also Crimean War
  crisis in (1875–1878), 230–31
  stability of region, 229–38
Ballot Act (1872; British), 158
Balzac, Honoré de, 54
Banks, founding of investment, 12
Bardo, Treaty of (1881), 239
Baudelaire, Charles, 57
Bazaine, Gen. Achille, 142–43, 185
Beaulieu, Pierre Leroy, 71
Beethoven, Ludwig van, 48, 49
Belgium, 71, 95, 99, 137, 142, 228
Benedetti, Count Vincent, 139–40
Berlin, Congress of (1878), 231–33, 238
Berlin, Treaty of (1878), 232, 238
Berlioz, Hector, 63, 65
Beust, Count Ferdinand von, 205
Birth rate, 15, 16
Bismarck, Herbert von, 227
Bismarck, Johanna von (Johanna von Putt-
    kamer), 126
Bismarck, Otto von, 119, 123–44, 158, 216–
    50
  alliance system of, 244–50
  Austro-Prussian War and, 132–33, 135–36
  becomes prime minister, 123, 125
  Boulanger compared with, 196
  Bulgarian problem and, 237–38
  colonial policy of, 241–44
  at Congress of Berlin, 232
  Egyptian crisis and, 240
  end of constitutional conflict under, 136–37
  European stability and, 228–31
  fall of, 225–27
  in Franco-Prussian War, 137–44, 185
  German-Austrian alliance of 1879 and,
    233, 235
  German empire and, 216, 218–19
    in conflict with liberals, 221–23
  economic policies of, 223–24
  Kulturkampf and, 29–30, 219–20
  state socialism and, 224–25
  nature of policies of, 77
  and Polish Revolt, 129–30
  popularity of, in Austria, 206
  Realpolitik of, 32, 126–28, 227
  relations with France, after Franco-Prus-
    sian War, 238
  in Schleswig-Holstein issue, 130–32
  and second Three Emperors' League, 235–
    36
  Triple Alliance and, 239
Bleak House (Dickens), 157–58
Boer War (1880), 165
Bonaparte, Louis Napoleon. *See* Napoleon
    III
Bonaparte, Napoleon. *See* Napoleon I
Bonaparte, Prince Napoleon (cousin to Na-
    poleon III), 113
Boris Godunov (Mussorgsky), 65
Borneo, 5
Boulanger, Gen. Georges, 195–98, 244
Boulangism, 196–98
Bourgeoisie in Second Empire, 91–92. *See
    also* Middle class

Boycott, Charles, 164
Bradlaugh, Charles, 162
Brahms, Johannes, 65
Breech-loading guns, 67, 68, 88
  in Austro-Prussian War, 133
  chassepot as, 96, 142
Bridges, 7, 52–53
Britain. *See* Great Britain
British army, 157
Broglie, Achille Duke of, 191–92
Brothers Karamazov, The (Dostoevsky), 56
Bruck, Karl Ludwig von, 109
Bruckner, Anton, 212
Brunel, Isambard Kingdom, 9, 53
Bulgaria, x, 181, 230–33, 237–38, 244, 245
Buol-Schauenstein, Count Karl Ferdinand
    von, 110
Burckhardt, Jacob, 76
Bureaucracy
  British, reform and, 157
  colonial, 75
  French, 81
  growth of, xii, 66–67
  Habsburg, 102, 108–10, 202, 203
  Prussian, 121, 122
  Russian, 168, 169, 173–74, 180
Burke, Thomas, 164
Business enterprises, new scale of, 12–13,
    224. *See also* Economy

Cameroons, 243
Canals, 8, 122
Canning, George, 148
Cape Colony, 70
Capital demand, 12
Capitalism. *See* Economy
Castlereagh, Viscount (Robert Stewart), 32
Catholic Church. *See* Roman Catholic
    Church
Cavendish, Lord Frederick Charles, 164
Cavour, Count Camillo Benso di, 32, 110,
    200
  and aftermath of Crimean War, 91, 112–13
  emergence of, 77
  Garibaldi and, 117–19
  and unification of Italy, 111–16
Cecil-Gascoyne, Robert Arthur Talbot (3rd
    Marquis Salisbury), 165–68, 232, 238
Cézanne, Paul, 61
Chamberlain, Joseph, 162, 166
Chambord, Henry Count of, 186, 189–90,
    195
Changarnier, Gen. Nicolas, 80
Charles X (King of France), 186
Chassepot (rifle), 96, 142
Chaucer, Geoffrey, 54
Chemical industry
  fertilizers from, 2–3, 7
  German, 224
  rise of, 3
Chemistry, 3
China, 181, 183
  British-French cooperation over, 97
  Christian missionaries in, 30
  European imperial expansion and, 74
  Marxist doctrine in, 43
Christian churches, 27–31
  Darwinism and, 36
  imperialism and, 72–73, 75–76
  See also Protestantism; Roman Catholic
    Church
City planning, 93–95
Class struggle, 40–42. *See also* Social classes
Coal

as energy and power source, 4, 5
French production of, 93, 194
Coal-mining machines, 4, 6
Cobden, Richard, 151
Cobden-Chevalier trade treaty (1860), 95
Colonies (colonialism). *See* Imperialism
Colonization, 71, 73
Commune (Paris; 1870), 186–88, 193
Communication, revolution in, 7, 11–12. *See also* News; Telegraph
Compulsory military service, xii, 68
Comte, Auguste, 34
Concert of Europe, disruption of, ix–x, 77–100, 229
Concordat of 1855, 108, 206
Concrete (building material), 7
Congo area, 242
Constitutional government. *See* Parliament; *and specific countries*
Construction, new era of, 7. *See also* Architecture and engineering; Public works
Convention of Gastein (1865), 132, 133
Corporations, 12, 224. *See also* Economy
Corti, Count, 232
Cottage industries, 19, 175
Council of Trent (1545), 28
Courbet, Gustave, 32, 58, 59, 61
Credit, expansion of, 12, 92–93
Crédit Foncier, 93
Crédit Mobilier, 93, 106
Crime and Punishment (Dostoevsky), 56
Crimean War (1854–1856), x, 81–91, 148, 151, 168, 180
aftermath of, 88, 90–91
Austria and, 91, 109, 110
background to, 81–83
Sardinia and, 91, 112, 113
serf-soldier in, 170
start of, 83–84
strategy in, 85–88
and west coast of North America, 183
Crispi, Francesco, 201
Cromwell, Oliver, 97
Crop rotation, 1–3
Cultural imperialism, 75–76. *See also* Imperialism
Cultural nationalism, 46
Customs union (*Zollverein*), 109, 120, 122, 123
Cyprus, 161, 231, 232
Czech nationalists, 207–9, 210

Danish War (1864), 130–32, 136, 149, 150, 203
Darwin, Charles, 33–36, 39–40
Das Kapital (Marx), 40
Deák, Ferenz, 203
Death rate, 16
Democracy. *See* Parliament; *and specific countries*
Demographic revolution, 14–19. *See also* Migrations; Population growth
Denmark, 120
in Schleswig-Holstein issue, 130–32, 136, 149, 150, 203
Depressions (economic), 13
in Austria, 109, 208
European, 161
in France, 194–95
in Germany, 223
in Great Britain, 161, 162
in Italy, 201
Depretis, Agostino, 200–202
Derby, 14th Earl (Edward George Stanley), 152, 154

Dickens, Charles, 52–54, 156–58
Disease, revolution in control of, 15–17
Disestablishment Act (1869; British), 155, 158
Diskonto-Gesellschaft (Austrian bank), 106
Disraeli, Benjamin (Earl of Beaconsfield), 148
at Congress of Berlin, 232
first ministry of, 152–54
on Franco-Prussian War, 228
on Gladstone, 158
second ministry of, 159–62
Dostoevsky, Fëdor, xiii, 56, 57
Dynamite, invented, 7

East Africa, 243
Economy
Austrian, 106, 207, 209
British, 146
contributions to economic nationalism, 13, 72
credit and, 12, 92–93
French, 92–96, 194–95
German, 120, 122–23, 223–24, 243
of Hungary, 213–15
Italian, 201, 202
new scale of enterprises, 12–13, 224
Sardinian, 112
See also Depressions; Imperialism; Industrialization; International trade; Mining; Railroads; Social classes
Edison, Thomas A., 6
Education
British, 23, 69, 156–57
compulsory, 68–69, 206
French, 69, 193
Hungarian, 213
nationalism and, 69
Russian, 179–80
spread of technical and agricultural schools, 3
of women, 23
Education Act (1870; British), 156
Egypt, 74, 165, 240–41, 245
Eiffel, Gustave, 53
Electricity, 5–6
Emancipation edict (1861; Russian), 171–72
Emigration, 18–19
misery resulting from, 23
Employers and Workmen Bill (1875; British), 160
Employers' Liability Act (1880; British), 163
Engels, Friedrich, 39
England. *See* Great Britain
Eugénie (Empress of the French; Eugénie de Montijo), 91, 140

Factories Act (1850; British), 151
Factory Act (1872; Hungarian), 214
Factory Act (1875; British), 160
Falk, Adalbert, 223
Faraday, Michael, 5
Farming implements, 2. *See also* Agriculture
Farm laborers, 24–25
Feminist movement, 22–23
Ferdinand of Saxe-Coburg (Prince of Bulgaria), 248
Ferry, Jules, 238, 242, 244
Fertilizers, 2–3, 7
Finland, 82, 84
First Mediterranean Agreement (1887), 245–46
First World War (1914–1918), 75, 181, 183

Flaubert, Gustave, 32–33, 55–56
Förster-Nietzsche, Elizabeth, 47
Fould, Achille, 95
France, ix, x, 44, 137
 Austria and, 95, 98–99
  and Austro-Prussian War, 132–33, 136
  and Franco-Prussian War, 138, 140
 Boulanger crisis in, 195–98
 Commune, 186–88, 193
 constitution of 1875 in, 190–91
 coup d'état in (1851), 80–81
 in Crimean War. *See* Crimean War
 education in, 69, 193
 franchise in, 22, 185–86
 Germany and. *See* Germany, France and
 Great Britain and, 95, 148, 149
  France compared as industrial power,
   194
  and Franco-Prussian War, 138, 140, 142
  improved relations, 97
  See also Crimean War
 imperial expansion of, 70–71, 74
 Italy and, 140, 201
  and unification of Italy, 112–17, 199
 nationalism in, 98
 Near East policy of, 83
 new ascendancy of, 77–81
 new government in (Third Republic
  period), 184–90
 parliamentarism in, 191–95. *See also*
  Parliament, French
 and Polish Revolt, 129–30, 203
 population growth in, 14, 15
 Roman Catholic Church in, 29, 79–80,
  193, 197–98
 Second Empire. *See* Napoleon III
 in stabilization of Eastern Europe, 231–33,
  236
 in stabilization of Western Europe, 238–
  44
 supports association of science and business, 12–13
 waning of power of, 72
 women fail to win suffrage in, 22
Franchise
 Austrian, 206, 207
 British, 150–54, 158
 French, 22, 185–86
 German, 150
Francis II (King of Naples and Sicily), 116–
  17
Francis Joseph I (Emperor of Austria),
  106–8, 202, 203, 205
Franco-British trade treaty (1860), 151
Franco-Italian trade treaty (1887), 201
Franco-Prussian War (1870–1871), 36, 68,
  100, 119, 137–44, 206
 armaments and defeat of France in, 96
 end of, 184–86, 188
Frankfurt, Peace of (1871), 143–44, 186
Frederick II (the Great; King of Prussia),
  101
Frederick William (later Frederick III, Em-
  peror of Germany), 125, 242
Frederick William IV (King of Prussia), 82,
  121–24
Free enterprise. *See* Economy
Free trade, imperialism of, 70–71. *See also*
  Imperialism; International trade
French army, 81, 95–96, 100, 142, 196
French Guinea, 243
French Revolution (1789), ix, 104
Freud, Sigmund, 48, 212
Furniture, Victorian, 51

Gambetta, Léon, 184–85, 192, 195
Gambia, 70
Garibaldi, Giuseppe, 104, 115–19, 250
Gatling guns, introduced, 67
Genesis, Book of, 27, 35
German-Italian alliance treaty (1866), 133
Germany, ix
 antisocialist campaign in, 221–23
 Austria and. *See* Austria, Prussia and
  climax of alliance system of, 244–50
 colonial policy of, 241–44
 France and, 220
  competing, 223
  France compared as industrial power,
   194
  and German alliance system, 244–50
  and Schleswig-Holstein question, 131
  and unification of Germany, 129
  and War of 1859, 114
  and war of revenge against Germany,
   195–97

  See also Franco-Prussian War
 imperial expansion of, 71, 74–75
 nationalism in, 44, 46, 47, 64, 144, 249–50
 new empire, x, xii
 parliaments. *See* Parliament, German Confederation; Parliament, German empire
 Prussian dominance of, 216–27. *See also*
  Prussia
 Roman Catholic Church in, 29–30, 219–20
 Russia and, 82, 83, 120, 168, 179
  and expansion of Russia, 183
  See also Poland
 social Darwinism and, 36
 and stability of Eastern Europe, 229–38
 and stability in Western Europe, 238–44
 state socialism in, 224–25
 supports association of science and business, 12–13
 trade with, 95
 unification of, x, 44, 98, 119–37, 184, 228
  anti-German coalition, 228–29
  Habsburgs and, 101
  Second Empire and, 99, 100
  waning of power of, 72
  and War of 1859, 114
Gladstone, William Ewart, 151, 154–68, 230
 Bismarck's colonial policy and, 242
 and British occupation of Egypt, 240–41
 as defender of imperialism, 147–48
 Disraeli and, 152, 160
 in election campaign of 1880, 161–62
 first ministry of, 154–59
 and Franco-Prussian War, 140, 142
 fourth ministry of, 167
 Salisbury vs., 165–68
 second ministry of, 162–65
 third ministry of, 166
Goethe, Johann Wolfgang von, 48, 49
Goluchowski, Count Agenor von, 202
Gorchakov, Prince (Aleksandr Mikhailo-
  vich), 90, 232
Gordon, Gen. Charles George (Gordon
  Pasha), 165
Government. *See* Parliament; State, the; *and
  specific countries*
Great Britain, ix–xii
 and Austro-Prussian War, 132
 competing with Germany, 223, 224
 education in, 23, 69, 156–57
 France and, 95, 148, 149
  France compared as industrial power,

194
and Franco-Prussian War, 138, 140, 142
improved relations, 97
and German alliance system, 244–50
imperial expansion of, 71, 74, 75
Ireland and. *See* Ireland
lack of state intervention in economy in, 13
Mexico and, 99
parliament of. *See* Parliament, French
and Polish Revolt, 129–30, 203
Protestants in, 30, 155, 156, 158
reform in, 145–68
Russia and, 149, 165
    Russia opposed by, 82–83
    Russian expansion and, 181, 183
    See also Crimean War
and Schleswig-Holstein issue, 131
in stabilization of Eastern Europe, 231–33, 236, 237
in stabilization of Western Europe, 238–44
women fail to win suffrage in, 22
Greece, x, 72, 148
Gramont, Antoine Alfred Duke of, 139–40
Gregory I (Pope|), 28
Grévy, Jules, 196
Grimm, Jacob, 46
Grimm, Wilhelm, 46
Grooved-bore rifles, introduced, 67
Guizot, François, 69

Habeas Corpus Act (British), 164
Habsburg army, 102
Habsburg empire, 101–10
    bureaucracy under, 102, 108–10, 202, 203
    creation of Austria-Hungary, 202–3, 205
    culture in, 102, 103
    disruptive forces in, 103–4
    emancipation of peasants and industrialization in, 105–6
    Francis Joseph I as ruler of, 106–8
    history of, 101–2
    industrialization in, 105–6
    legal reform in, 108–9
    nationalism in, 103–6
    Roman Catholic Church in, 29, 102, 103, 108, 120, 206, 208, 210
    Schwarzenberg government and Bach System in, 108–10
    and unification of Italy, 101, 110, 112, 116, 117, 133, 199
    unifying forces of, 102–3
    See also Austria; Austria-Hungary; Austro-Hungarian Empire; Hungary
Hall-Héroult electrolytic process, 7
Harbor development, French, 93, 100
Harrows, improved, 2
Hartington, Lord (Victor Christian William Cavendish; 9th Duke Hartington), 166
Haussmann, Baron Georges Eugène, 93
Helmholtz, Hermann von, 34
Herder, Johann Gottfried von, 46
Herzen, Alexander, 177
Hitler, Adolf, 212
Hohenwart, Count Karl Sigismund von, 206–7
Holland, ix, 94, 228
Home Rule bill (1886; Irish), 166, 167
Hong Kong, 70
Household gadgets, 7
Hugo, Victor, 78
Hungarian army, 214
Hungary, ix, x, 82, 168

after *Ausgleich,* 212–16
Austria-Hungary created, 202–3, 205. *See also* Austria-Hungary
and Franco-Prussian War, 140
Habsburg taxation resisted by, 109
nationalism in, 44
nationalities problem in, 213
parliament in, 212–13
revolt in, 104

Ignatiev, Nicholas, 179
Immunization, 17
Imperialism, 200
    cultural, 75–76
    German colonial policy, 241–44
    growth of, 70–76
    nationalism and, 71, 76
    popular press and, 52
    social Darwinism and, 36
    and stability of Eastern Europe, 229–38
    and stability of Western Europe, 238–44
Impressionism, 60–62
Incandescent light, 6
India, 70, 181
Indochina, 70, 243, 244
Industrialization, xi, 1–26
    development of machines and power sources for, 4–7
    European imperialism and world, 75
    French, 93
    in Habsburg empire, 105–6
    in Hungary, 213
    in Russia, 174–77
    social consequences of, 14–26
    sweep of, 4–7
Industrial Revolution. *See* Industrialization
Industrial workers. *See* Working class
Intellectual climate, 27–65
    arts, 49–65
    Christian churches, 27–31. *See also* Protestantism; Roman Catholic Church
    new principles of authority in, 31–47. *See also* State, the
    voices of protest in, 47–49
Internal combustion engines, 4–5
International conference on African matters (Berlin; 1884–1885), 242
International trade
    British, 151
    colonies and, 74–75
    flourishing, 13
    Habsburg, 109
    and imperialism, 70–71. *See also* Imperialism
    in Second Empire, 95
Inventions, spread of, xii, 4–12
Ireland, ix, x
    franchise reform for, 153–54
    home rule for, 166, 167
    industrialization and, 17
    nationalism in, 45
    potato and, 2
    resistance to British rule in, 155–56, 163–65
    Roman Catholic Church in, 29, 155
Irish Land Act (1870; British), 155, 163, 164
Irish Land Act (1881; British), 164
Iron
    ore-mining machines, 6
    production of, in Germany, 223
    in ship construction, 10
Italian army, 199
Italy, ix, x
    France and, 140, 201
        and unification of Italy, 112–17, 199

Italy (*continued*)
  and German alliance system, 245
  imperial expansion of, 71
  industrialization and, 17
  nationalism in, 28, 29, 44, 64, 110, 198–200
  parliament in, 200–202
  Roman Catholic Church in, 28, 29, 198–200
  and stability of Eastern Europe, 229, 230, 232
  and stability of Western Europe, 238, 241
  trade with, 95
  trasformismo in, 200–202
  unification of, x, 110–19, 133
    civil war, 199
    Habsburgs and, 101, 110, 112, 116, 117, 133, 199
    and Lombardy, 104
    problems of, 198–202
    Second Empire and, 98–100
    unified, 184

Japan, 30, 70, 183
Joseph II (Emperor of Austria), 105, 108
Juárez, Benito, 99–100
Judicature Act (1873; British), 157
Julius Caesar, 48
Junker (Prussian aristocracy), 121, 126, 128

Karl Anton of Hohenzollern-Sigmaringen (Prince), 139
Khartoum massacre (1885), 165
Kilmainham Treaty (1882), 164
Koch, Robert, 16, 17
Königgrätz (Sadowa), battle of (1866), 135, 137
Koestler, Arthur, 16
Kohn, Hans, 46
Kossuth, Francis, 215
Kossuth, Louis, 215
Krupp, Alfred, 135

Labor. *See* Peasants; Trade unions; Working class
Lagos, 70
Laissez-faire, 13, 38
Land use, new methods of, 2
Langensalza, battle of (1866), 135
Latin America, 18, 70, 74, 116
Lavoisier, Antoine, 34
Legislation. *See specific acts*
Leo XIII (Pope), 28, 29, 198, 220
Leopold of Hohenzollern-Sigmaringen (Prince), 138–39
Liberalism, 36–38
Liebig, Justus von, 3
Lincoln, Abraham, 171
Literature, 52–58
Local Government Act (1888; British), 167
London, treaty of (1852), 130
Loris-Melikov, Mikhail, 178, 179
Louis XIV (King of France), 144
Louis Philippe (King of France), 93, 186
Loves of a Harem, The (Reynolds), 52
Lueger, Karl, 211–12
Luxembourg, 99, 137

MacMahon, Marshal Marie Edmé de, 142, 189, 191–92
Madame Bovary (Flaubert), 55
Magenta, battle of (1859), 114, 189
Magne, Pierre, 95

Mahler, Gustav, 212
Mails, 11
Malay states, 70
Mallarmé, Stéphane, 58
Malthus, Thomas, 15
Manet, Édouard, 33, 59–61
Manufacturing, development of, 4–7. *See also* Industrialization
Marquesas Islands, 70
Married Women's Property Act (1870; British), 22
Marx, Karl, 34, 38–43, 48, 187
Marxism, 38–43
  Bismarck's policies compared with, 243
  in China, 43
  imperialism and, 76
  in Russia, 43, 177–78
Mass movements, cities and, 26
Mass production
  development of, 4, 7
  mass taste and, 50
  See also Industrialization
Materialism, 31–47
Maximilian (Archduke of Austria and Emperor of Mexico), 99–100
May Laws (1873; Prussian), 220, 223
Mazzini, Giuseppe, 46, 98, 116, 200
Medical revolution, 15–17
Meistersinger von Nürnberg, Die (Wagner), 64
Merchant Shipping Act (1875; British), 161
Metternich, Prince Klemens von, x, 32, 104
  Bach compared with, 108
  dissolution complex of, 104
Metz, siege of (1870), 142, 143, 185
Mexico, 70, 97, 99–100, 132, 137
Michelangelo Buonarroti, 48, 49
Middle class
  attitudes of, 31–32
  Austrian, 106, 109
  British, 150, 152–53
  German, 137
  Russian, 177–78
Migrations, 17–19
  nationalism and, 44–45
Military power, European, 74. *See also* Armaments; Army; Navy; *and under specific nationalities:* Hungarian army; Prussian army; etc.
Mill, John Stuart, 22, 153
Mines (armament), invented, 68
Minié breech-loading rifles, 88
Mining
  development of, 4–7
  French, 93, 194
  machinery for, 4, 6, 7
  Russian, 176
Mir (Russian village communes), 171–72
Missionaries, Christian, 30–31
Mitrailleuse
  in Franco-Prussian War, 142
  introduced, 67
Moltke, Gen. Helmuth von, 125, 134–35
Monet, Claude, 61
Monetary system, 13
Montenegro, x, 44, 232
Montijo, Eugénie de (Empress Eugénie), 91, 140
Music, 63–65
Mussolini, Benito, 200, 201
Mussorgsky, Modest, 64–65

Napoleon I (Emperor of the French), 77, 100
  abdicates, 91

Austerlitz victory of, 80
Bismarck compared with, 127, 128
bureaucracy perfected by, 81
Habsburgs defeated by, 101
Napoleon II (son of Napoleon I), 91
Napoleon III (Louis Napoleon Bonaparte;
    Emperor of the French), x, 91–101,
    190
  Bismarck and, 132–33
  court style under, 91–92
  Disraeli compared with, 159, 160
  economic policy of, 92–96
  Flaubert exiled by, 32–33
  foreign policy of, 97–101
    Palmerston and, 149
    War of 1859 and, 114–15
    See also Crimean War; Franco-Prussian
      War; Italy, unification of
  influence of, 152
  isolation of France under, 90
  liberalism and, 96–97
  MacMahon compared with, 191
  as president, 77–81
    coup of 1851, 80–81
  Roman Catholic Church and, 29, 79–80
National Bank (Austrian), 109
Nationalism, 43–47. *See also specific countries*
*Natural and Social History of a Family under
    the Second Empire, A* (Zola), 54
Natural gas, as energy source, 4
Navy
  effects of Crimean War on, 88
  growth of modern, 68
  ships. *See* Ships
Netherlands, 14, 95, 228
New Caledonia, 188
New Guinea, 243
News
  machinery and communication of, 11–12
  popular taste and, 51–52
Newton, Sir Isaac, 33
New Zealand, 18, 70
Nicholas I (Tsar of Russia), 88, 109, 170, 175
Nicholas Nickleby (Dickens), 156
Nietzsche, Friedrich, xiii, 47–49, 56
Nightingale, Florence, 22, 87
Nikolsburg, Peace of (1866), 136
Nobel, Alfred, 7
North Africa, 30, 245
North America
  emigration to, 18
  white settlers expand in, 70, 74

Offenbach, Jacques, 92
Official art, 49–54
Oil, discovery of, 4–6
Oil-drilling machines, 4, 6
Ollivier, Émile, 97, 140
Olmütz, Treaty of (1850; Humiliation of Ol-
    mütz), 123
"Olympia" (Manet), 59–60
*On the Origin of Species by Means of Natural
    Selection* (Darwin), 35
Orthodox Church, Russian, 30
O'Shea, Kitty, 167
Ottoman Empire. *See* Turkey
Overpopulation, 15. *See also* Population
  growth

Pacifico, Don, 148
Painting, 58–62
Palmerston, 3rd Viscount (Henry John Tem-
    ple), 84, 152

on Crimean War, 84
  ministry of, 148–50
  Salisbury compared with, 165
Panama Canal, 198
Paris (France), rebuilt, 93–95
Paris, Count of (Louis Philippe Albert d'Or-
    léans), 186
Paris, Treaty of (1856), 88, 90, 113, 142, 180
Paris Commune (1870), 186–88, 193
Parliament
  Austrian, following *Ausgleich,* 206, 207,
    209–10
  British, xi–xii, 145, 147
    Disraeli and, 159–61
    Gladstone and, 154–59, 162–64, 166–68
    Palmerston and, 148, 150
    Reform Bill of 1867 and, 151–54
    Salisbury and, 165
    See also Franchise
  French, 191–95
    Second Empire and, 96
    Second Republic and, 79–80
    Third Republic and, 186–87, 190–92, 195
  German Confederation
    Austro-Prussian War and, 133
    Schleswig-Holstein question and, 130, 132
  German empire, 217–18, 221–22, 224–26
  Hungarian, 212–13
  Italian, 200–202
  Prussian, 123–25
    Bismarck and, 128–29, 136–37
  Russian, Dumas, 174
  Sardinian, 113
Parnell, Charles Stewart, 163–64, 166, 167
Pasteur, Louis, 16, 17
Paxton, Joseph, 53
Peasants
  German, 137
  Hungarian, 213–14
  Italian, 117, 199
  serfs emancipated, 18, 19, 105–6, 170–76
Peel, Sir Robert, 147, 151
Peter the Great (Tsar of Russia), 82
Pius IX (Pope), 27, 28, 198, 220
Plevna, battle of (1877), 230
Plimsoll, Samuel, 161
Plombières agreement (1858), 113–15
Pneumatic tires, invented, 10
Pobedonostsev, Konstantin, 178–79
Poland, ix, 82, 84, 98, 168, 183
  independence for, 90
  Polish Revolt, 104, 129–30, 203
  Roman Catholic Church and, 29
  Second Empire and, 98
Political organization. *See* Parliament; State,
    the; *and specific countries*
Popular art, 49–54
Population growth, xi, 14–19
  agricultural revolution and, 4, 15
  Europe, 14
  of Habsburg Empire, 103
  Russian, 177
Portland cement, 7
Portugal, 70, 242
Possessed, The (Dostoevsky), 56
Prague, Peace of (1866), 136
Pretoria, Treaty of (1881), 165
Printing presses, 11
Proletariat. *See* Working class
Property rights for women, 22–23
Protestantism, 30–31, 103
  British, 30, 155, 156, 158
  German (Prussian), 120
Prussia
  Austria and. *See* Austria, Prussia and

Prussia (*continued*)
  under Bismarck. *See* Bismarck, Otto von
  bureaucracy in, 81
  constitutional problems in, 123–25, 128–29, 136–37
  and Crimean War, 90
  and Denmark, over question of Schleswig-Holstein, 130–32, 136, 149, 150, 203
  dominates Germany, 216–27. *See also* Germany
  parliament of. *See* Parliament, Prussian
  public works in, 122–23
  railroads of, 122–23, 133, 135
  rise of, 121–25
  Russia and, 82, 83, 120, 168, 179. *See also* Poland
Prussian army, 67, 124, 125, 133–36, 140
  general staff of, 134–35
Public Health Act (1875; British), 161
Public works, 7
  British, 52–53, 145, 146
  French, 53, 93–95
  Habsburg, 109
  Prussian, 122–23
  Sardinian, 112
  See also Architecture and engineering; Railroads
Puttkamer, Johanna von (Johanna von Bismarck), 126

Quanta cura (papal encyclical), 28

Racism, 36, 207
Raglan, 1st Baron (Fitzroy James Henry Somerset), 87
Railroads
  agriculture and, 13
  built by colonial powers, 75
  in Crimean War, 88
  development of, 8–11
  effects on armies' mobility, 67–68, 133, 135
  French, 93, 100
  German, 223
  Habsburg, 109
  Italian, 201
  Prussian, 122–23, 133, 135
  Russian, 175
Realism, 31–47
  of Bismarck, 32, 126–27, 227. *See also* Bismarck, Otto von
  in literature, 54–58
  in painting, 58–60
Reapers (threshing machines), 2
Redistribution bill (1885; British), 163
Reformation, 101
Reform Bill (1832; British), 148–49, 152
Reform Bill (1867; British), 147, 151–54
Reform Bill (1884; British), 163
Refrigeration, invented, 9
Reichbank (German bank), 223
Reinsurance Treaty (1887), 246, 248
Religion, imperialism and, 72–73. *See also* Christian churches; Protestantism; Roman Catholic Church
Renoir, Auguste, 61
Repeater rifles, introduced, 67
Rerum novarum (papal encyclical), 29
Reynolds, G. W. M., 52
Rhineland, 99, 121, 132, 133
Richelieu, Cardinal (Louis François Armand de Vignerot du Plessis), 127, 161
Rifled cannons in Austro-Prussian War, 135
Rifled guns, introduced, 67, 68
Rimsky-Korsakov, Nikolai, 65
Risorgimento, Il (Italian newspaper), 111

Roads, improved, 7, 8. *See also* Railroads
Rocroi, battle of (1643), 144
Roman Catholic Church, 27–31
  in Austria, 29, 120, 206, 208, 210
  in France, 29, 79–80, 193, 197–98
  in Germany, 29–30, 219–20
  Habsburgs and, 29, 102, 103, 108, 120, 206, 208, 210
  in Ireland, 29, 155
  in Italy, 28, 29, 198–200
Romanticism in music, 63–65
Roon, William Albrecht von, 124–25
Rosebery, 5th Earl (Archibald Philip Primrose), 72, 167
Rothschild (family), 106, 161
Rumania, x, 44, 72, 232, 237, 245
  formed, 83
Ruskin, John, 51
Russell, Lord John , 84, 151, 154
Russia, x, xiii, 44
  agriculturally competitive, 13
  Austria and, 82, 83, 110, 168, 179
    and Austro-Prussian War, 132, 136
    and Crimean War, 85, 88, 91
    and expansion of Russia, 181, 183
    and Habsburg customs union, 109
  bureaucracy of, 168, 169, 173–74, 180
  emigration, 18
  European opposition to, 81–83. *See also* Crimean War
  fear of, 81–82
  and Franco-Prussian War, 138, 140, 142
  and German alliance system, 244–50
  Germany, Balkan tensions and, 197
  Great Britain and, 149, 165
    Russia opposed by, 82–83
    Russian expansion and, 181, 183
    See also Crimean War
  imperial expansion of, 70, 71, 74, 75, 180–83
  Marxist doctrine in, 43, 177–78
  music in, 64–65
  nationalism in, 180–81
  oil discovery in, 5
  Orthodox Church in, 30
  parliament in, 174
  Poland and. *See* Poland
  potato in, 2
  Prussia and, 82, 83, 120. *See also* Poland
  reform in, 168–83
  repression in, 145
  rise of, 72
  Sardinia and, 112
  and Schleswig-Holstein question, 131
  serfs freed in, 18, 19, 170–76
  and stability of Eastern Europe, 229–33, 235–38, 244
  and stability of Western Europe, 239
  Turkey and. *See* Turkey, Russia and
Russian army, 173–74

Sadowa. *See* Königgrätz
Saint-Simon, Henri de, 92
Sale of Food and Drugs Act (1875; British), 161
Salisbury, 3rd Marquis (Robert Arthur Talbot Cecil-Gascoyne), 165–68, 232, 238
San Stefano, Treaty of (1878), 230–33
Sardinia, 98, 99, 104
  Austrian conflict with, 111–16
  Crimean War and, 91, 112, 113
  parliament of, 113
  and unification of Italy, 110–15, 117–19, 184

Scandinavia, 228
Schäffle, Albert, 207
Schmerling, Anton von, 203
Schnitzler, Arthur, 212
Schools. *See* Education
Schwarzenberg, Prince Felix zu, 77, 82, 108–10
Science
  faith in, 33–36
  impressionists and, 60, 61
  influence on artists, 54
  reaction to obsession with, 56
  realism in, 32
Scotland, 30, 153–54
Seamstress; or, The White Slave of England, The (Reynolds), 52
Second Empire. *See* Napoleon III
Second Republic. *See* France; Napoleon III
Second Mediterranean Agreement (1887), 248
Second World War (1939–1945), 183
Sedan, battle of (1870), 142, 243
Seeley, Sir John, 72
Serbia, 4, 44, 232, 236–38, 245
Serfs, emancipation of, 18, 19, 105–6, 170–76. *See also* Peasants
Seurat, Georges, 61–62
Sevastopol, siege of (1854), 86–88
Sewing machines, invented, 6–7
Shakespeare, William, 49
Ships
  building of, 10, 68, 109
  steamships, 9–10
    in Crimean War, 88
    French, 93
Shuvalov, Count Peter, 232
Sicily, 116–17, 184
Siemens, Werner von, 6
Sierra Leone, 70
Simon, Jules, 191
Sinop, battle of (1853), 83–84
Sino-Russian treaty (1881), 181
Social classes
  art and, 51
  industrialization and changes in, 25
  struggle of, 40–42
  See also Bourgeoisie; Middle class; Peasants; Working class
Socialism, 38–43
  development of, 25–26
  Roman Catholic Church and, 28, 29
  See also Marxism; State socialism
Socrates, 49
Solferino, battle of (1859), 114
South Africa, 18, 165
Southwest Africa, 243
Spain, ix, 70, 95, 99, 138–39
State, the
  as chief Russian entrepreneur, 175
  1873 depression and intervention of, in economic affairs, 13
  growing powers of, xii–xiii, 66–76
  and growth of imperialism, 70–76
  indoctrination used by, 45–46
  and new business enterprises, 12–13, 224
  new demands on, 66–69
  and social remedies to abuses of industrialization, 25
  support by, of spread of agricultural and technical schools, 3
  See also Bureaucracy; *and specific countries*
State socialism
  in Austria, 207
  in France, 92
  in Germany, 222–25

Steam engines, 4. *See also* Railroads
Steamboats. *See* Ships
Steel
  production of, in Germany, 223
  mass production of, 7
  in ship construction, 10, 68
Steel plows, 2
Stendhal (Henri Beyle), 54
Stolypin, Peter, 173
"Stonebreakers, The" (Courbet), 59
Stratford de Redcliffe, 1st Viscount (Sir Stratford Canning), 84
Strauss, Johann, 212
Streetcars, electric, 10
Studies on Homer and the Homeric Age (Gladstone), 155
Submarines, invented, 68
Sudan, 165
Suez Canal, 93, 161, 230, 231, 240–41
Sweden, 95, 131, 183
Switzerland, 95, 228
Sybil; or, The Two Nations (Disraeli), 160
Syllabus of Errors (addendum to papal encyclical), 28
Symbolism, 56–58

Taaffe, Count Eduard von, 208–10
Tahiti, 70
Talleyrand, Charles Maurice de, 32, 127
Tariff law (1879; German), 223
Telegraph, 88
  army movement coordinated by, 67
  in Austro-Prussian War, 135
  invented, 11
Tel el-Kebir, battle of (1882), 240
Temple, Henry John. *See* Palmerston, 3rd Viscount
Thiers, Adolphe, 100, 186–88
Thirty Years' War (1618–1648), 101
Three Emperors' League
  first (1873), 229–30
  second (1881), 233–36, 238, 244
Threshing machines (reapers), 2
Tisza, Kálmán, 214–15
Titian, 59
Togoland, 243
Tolstoi, Count Dmitri, 179
Torpedoes, invented, 68
Totleben, Count Eduard Ivanovich, 87
Trade. *See* International trade
Trade Union Act (1875; British), 160
Trade unions
  Catholic, 29
  development of, 25–26
  Hungarian, 214
  legalized in France, 96
Transportation, revolution in, 8–11. *See also* Railroads
Trasformismo, 200–202
Treatise on Instrumentation and Orchestration (Berlioz), 63
Triple Alliance (1882), 239–40, 245–46
Trochu, Gen. Louis, 184
Tunisia, 74, 232, 238–39
Turin, Treaty of (1860), 115
Turkey, x, 70, 74, 245, 248
  Balkan revolt against, 230–31
  British policy and, 161
  dispute over holy places in empire of, 83
  and German alliance system, 245
  Russia and, 82, 180–81, 183. *See also* Crimean War
  and stability of Eastern Europe, 232, 236
  trade with, 95

Typesetting machines, invented, 11
Typewriters, invented, 11

Unification. *See* Germany; Italy
Union, Act of (1801; British), 155, 163
United States, 75
    agriculturally competitive, 13
    emigration to, 19
    oil discovery in, 5
    rise of, 72
    Russian development compared with, 175
    spread of technical and agricultural schools
        in, 3
United States Civil War (1861-1865), 67, 95,
    100, 149–50, 158–59
University Tests Act (1871; British), 157
Urbanization
    city planning, 93–95
    migration and, 17
    railroads and, 9
    and transformation of society, 23–26

Van Gogh, Vincent, 62
Vatican. *See* Roman Catholic Church
Verdi, Giuseppe, 54, 64
Viaducts, 52–53
Victor Emmanuel II (King of Sardinia; later
    King of Italy), 91, 113, 117, 119
Victoria (Queen of England), 125, 145, 237,
    242
Victoria (Princess of Prussia; granddaughter
    of Queen Victoria), 237
Vienna, Treaty of (1864), 132
Villafranca, Peace of (1859), 114–16

Waddington, William Henry, 232
Wagner, Richard, 46, 57, 64

Wales, 30
Warships, 68, 88
Waterloo, battle of (1814), 87
Watt, James, 4
Weapons. *See* Armaments
William I (Emperor of Germany and King
    of Prussia), 124–25, 144, 216, 226, 242
William II (Emperor of Germany and King
    of Prussia), 121–22, 226–27
Will to Power, as basic ingredient of human
    creativity, 48–49
Women
    and British franchise, 153
    changing role of, 19–23
    and compulsory education, 23, 69
    nursing profession opened to, 87–88
    as servants, 20–21
Working class, 25–26
    Austrian, 105, 106, 207–8
    class struggle and, 40–42
    franchise for British, 153, 154
    German, 137, 224–25
    growth of, 25–26
    in Habsburg empire, 105–6
    in Hungary, 214
    misjudged, 43
    reforms for British, 160–61
    right to strike, in France, 96
    Russian, 175–76
    women as servants, 20–21
        in nursing profession, 87–88
    See also Trade unions
World War. *See* First World War; Second
    World War

Zola, Émile, 32, 54–56, 58
Zollverein (customs union), 109, 120, 122,
    123